Women in Twentieth-Century Africa

During a turbulent colonial and postcolonial century, African women struggled to control their own marital, sexual, and economic lives and to gain a significant voice in local and national politics. This book introduces many remarkable women, who organized religious and political movements, fought in anticolonial wars, ran away to escape arranged marriages, and during the 1990s began successful campaigns for gender parity in national legislatures. The book also explores the apparent paradox in the conflicting images of African women – not only as singularly oppressed and dominated by men, but also as strong, resourceful, and willing to challenge governments and local traditions to protect themselves and their families. Understanding the tension between women's power and their oppression, between their strength and their vulnerability, offers a new lens for understanding the relationship between the state and society in the twentieth century.

Iris Berger is Professor of History, Emerita at the University at Albany, State University of New York.

New Approaches to African History

New Approaches to African History is designed to introduce students to current findings and new ideas in African history. Although each book treats a particular case and is able to stand alone, the format allows the studies to be used as modules in general courses on African history and world history. The cases represent a wide range of topics. Each volume summarizes the state of knowledge on a particular subject for a student who is new to the field. However, the aim is not simply to present views of the literature; it is also to introduce debates on historiographical or substantive issues and may argue for a particular point of view. The aim of the series is to stimulate debate and to challenge students and general readers. The series is not committed to any particular school of thought.

Other books in the series:

1. *Africa since 1940* by Frederick Cooper
2. *Muslim Societies in African History* by David Robinson
3. *Reversing Sail: A History of the African Diaspora* by Michael Gomez
4. *The African City: A History* by William Freund
5. *Warfare in Independent Africa* by William Reno
6. *Warfare in African History* by Richard J. Reid
7. *Foreign Intervention in Africa* by Elizabeth Schmidt
8. *Slaving and Slavery in African History* by Sean Stilwell
9. *Democracy in Africa* by Nic Cheeseman

Women in Twentieth-Century Africa

Iris Berger

CAMBRIDGE
UNIVERSITY PRESS

University Printing House, Cambridge CB2 8BS, United Kingdom

One Liberty Plaza, 20th Floor, New York, NY 10006, USA

477 Williamstown Road, Port Melbourne, VIC 3207, Australia

314-321, 3rd Floor, Plot 3, Splendor Forum, Jasola District Centre, New Delhi - 110025, India

79 Anson Road, #06-04/06, Singapore 079906

Cambridge University Press is part of the University of Cambridge.

It furthers the University's mission by disseminating knowledge in the pursuit of education, learning and research at the highest international levels of excellence.

www.cambridge.org
Information on this title: www.cambridge.org/9780521741217

First published 2016
3rd printing 2017

A catalogue record for this publication is available from the British Library

Library of Congress Cataloging in Publication data
Names: Berger, Iris, author.
Title: Women in Twentieth-Century Africa / by Iris Berger.
Other titles: New approaches to African history; 10.
Description: New York: Cambridge University Press, 2016. |
Series: New approaches to African history; 10 |
Includes bibliographical references and index.
Identifiers: LCCN 2015046517 | ISBN 9780521517072 (hardback) |
ISBN 9780521741217 (pbk)
Subjects: LCSH: Women– Africa–History–20th century. |
Feminism–Africa. | Women–Africa–Social conditions. |
Women–Africa–Economic conditions.
Classification: LCC HQ1787.B473 2016 |
DDC 305.409609/04–dc23
LC record available at http://lccn.loc.gov/2015046517

ISBN 978-0-521-51707-2 Hardback
ISBN 978-0-521-74121-7 Paperback

In memory of my parents
Esther Skolnik Brown
and
Norman L. Brown
and
To my students at Machakos Girls High School

Contents

Illustrations

Maps

Preface

This book has its origins in the classrooms of the Machakos Girls High School in Kenya, where I taught history and English in the mid 1960s. Just out of college and scarcely older than some of the students in my classes, I began meeting periodically with a group of girls to talk about their personal lives and plans for the future. Perhaps prompted by the pregnancy of one student, who was allowed to remain in school, but had to live apart from her classmates in the small house designed for domestic science instruction, our discussions turned to marriage, sexuality, and childbearing. Over the years, all I recalled from these gatherings was the insistence of many students that they were eager to have children, but were skeptical about being married. I am deeply grateful to one of them, Maryam Murbe Solola, for her persistence in tracing me nearly four decades later. Our emotional meeting rekindled memories of the school and of a formative period in my own life.

My relationships with these lively and engaging young women contributed to my interest in African women's history. Although I was assigned to teach African history, the syllabus for the national examination at the time focused primarily on the activities of Europeans on the continent; women were never mentioned. As in the United States and Europe, research on the history of women in Africa developed only during the late 1960s as feminist scholars and activists began intensive efforts to "restore women to history." Over time, the field expanded from a concentration on economics and politics to include marriage, childbirth, sexualities, and the relationships between women and men, issues that this book will explore.

Rather than a chronological narrative that looks at African women's history region by region, I use case studies to analyze the interactions between personal and public life across the twentieth century, primarily in sub-Saharan Africa. North African countries shared the political challenges of European colonization, nationalist resistance, and the difficulties of creating a new postcolonial legal and political order. But by the early twentieth century higher levels of industrialization and commercialized agriculture, the erosion of small-scale peasant economies, and a shared history and culture made the lives of north African women different in significant respects from those of their neighbors to the south.

In addition to my students in Kenya, many other people have contributed more directly to this book. First, I am grateful to Martin Klein, editor of the series *New Approaches to African History*, for asking me to write a book on women and for his prompt and perceptive response to the completed manuscript. I also appreciate the suggestions of Sandra Greene and Margaret Jean Hay, who read the initial proposal. The invitation from Kathryn Kish Sklar and Thomas Dublin to write one of the scholarly essays for their online documentation project, *Women and Social Movements, International*, contributed to the sections on African women's participation in transnational women's movements. I also want to thank the editors of the *African Studies Review* for inviting me to deliver the *ASR* Distinguished Lecture at the Annual Meeting of the African Studies Association in 2013. Preparing for the talk gave me new insights into several of the book's main themes, as did comments from Teresa Barnes, Amina Mama, Ali Tripp, and other members of the audience. Peter Gelfan's astute questions and suggestions on an earlier draft greatly improved the final manuscript. The Department of History and the College of Arts and Sciences at the University at Albany contributed to funding for the photographs. Thanks also to Eloise Brière and Tricia Redeker Hepner for answering my queries about particular images and to Judith Tucker, who replied to my questions about women in north Africa. This book would not have been possible without the remarkable scholarship and literature on and by African women that has provided the basis for new insights into how women's lives changed during the course of an unsettled century.

Finally, Ron Berger's contributions to the book are immeasurable. As both a historian and a creative writer, he has read and critiqued numerous drafts of the manuscript, asked probing questions, and offered inspired suggestions for revisions. Most important, he never wavered in his encouragement and love.

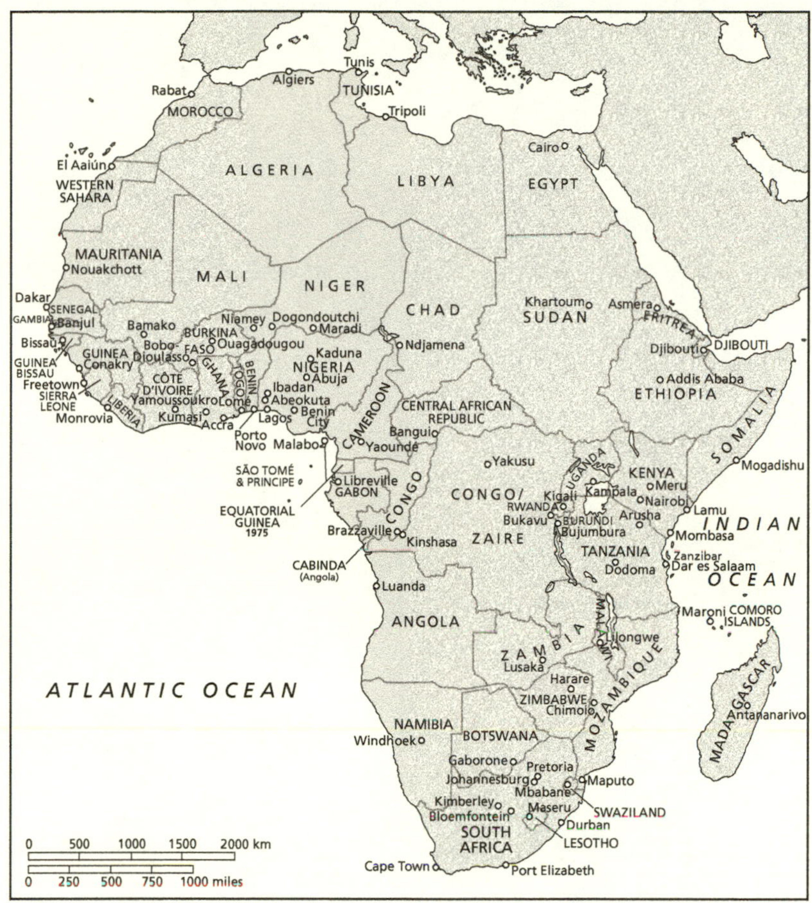

MAP 1 African countries and cities, *c.* 2000.
Source: Adapted from Frederick Cooper, *Africa since 1940: The Past of the Present* (Cambridge University Press, 2002).

Introduction

During the first decades of the twenty-first century, popular media portrayed Africa as a dangerous, disorderly continent that was particularly threatening for women. Reflecting such sentiments, Helene Cooper, a Liberian-born journalist for the *New York Times*, called Africa "the worst place there is to be a woman."[1] Writing of the city of Bukavu in the Democratic Republic of Congo, Cooper described "an old woman, in her 30s" walking up a hill away from town:

> She carried so many logs that her chest almost seemed to touch the ground, so stooped was her back. Still, she trudged on, up the hill toward her home. Her husband was walking just in front of her. He carried nothing. Nothing in his hand, nothing on his shoulder, nothing on his back. He kept looking back at her, telling her to hurry up.[2]

Yet Cooper's article communicated not despair, but hope for the women who, in her words, "somehow manage to carry that entire continent on their backs."[3] They were the women who in the Liberian election of 2005 ignored the threats from young men to resume war if their candidate were defeated and flocked to the polls to elect a Harvard-educated banker, Ellen Johnson Sirleaf, as president. With this election, Johnson Sirleaf, imprisoned under

[1] Helene Cooper, "Waiting for Their Moment in the Worst Place on Earth to Be a Woman," *New York Times*, November 16, 2005.

[2] Cooper, "Waiting for Their Moment."

[3] Cooper, "Waiting for Their Moment."

an earlier regime, became the first woman to be elected head of an African country. These events in another country led Cooper to conclude, "I want to go back to Bukavu to find that woman, and to tell her what happened in Liberia. I want to tell her this. Your time will come too."[4]

Despite the distressing conditions that Cooper depicted, the narrative of oppression oversimplifies the lives of African women by neglecting class, power, and regional and cultural differences among them. In both precolonial and current African societies, women's position was complex, depending on their age and marital status, the economic possibilities open to them, and whether they lived in matrilineal communities where kinship was determined through women or patrilineal societies where it was traced through men.

Cultures also differed in their understanding of female and male differences and similarities. Indeed, the study of African women's history reinforces this complex message, portraying some women as downtrodden and oppressed, yet many also in powerful positions: as queen mothers, wealthy merchants, spiritual leaders, participants in resistance and nationalist movements and revolutionary struggles, and as active modernized professionals in business, law, health care, teaching, arts, and literature. These women include the substantial numbers who hold seats in African parliaments, the three African women who have received the Nobel Peace Prize, and the large number of internationally recognized scholars and writers.

African women's history: historical and cultural contexts

These contrasting images of African women have historical roots in the continent's colonial past, a narrative of white domination that stretched in most places from the mid-nineteenth century into the 1960s and, in parts of southern Africa, from the mid-seventeenth century into the mid 1990s. Strong external influence predated direct European conquest, however. On the west coast, slavery and the slave trade, dating back to the 1490s, already had reshaped political and economic life, ravaging some communities while strengthening others.

[4] Cooper, "Waiting for Their Moment."

South Africa, colonized by Dutch settlers in the mid-seventeenth century, became a British colony in the early 1800s. Across north Africa and the southern borders of the Sahara and along the east African coast, Western influence was superimposed on Muslim societies, molded respectively by centuries of trade in gold and salt across the desert and maritime commerce across the Indian Ocean. This early period of foreign political, economic, and cultural contact transformed African life in innumerable ways, spreading Islam gradually through a combination of trade, warfare, and intermarriage between Muslim men and local women.

External influence notwithstanding, in both the interior and along the maritime and desert coasts indigenous political, economic, and religious systems were complex and varied, ranging from centralized kingdoms with strong rulers and clear patterns of social hierarchy to smaller-scale communities based around extended families and clans. Societies also differed economically, some depending more heavily on farming, others on herding, and still others on local and long-distance trade. Although most of Africa was rural, towns along the oceans and the "coasts" of the desert fringe developed distinctive patterns of indigenous urban culture, economics, and architecture. In most societies, men were politically and economically dominant, and men with sufficient wealth could marry more than one woman. Virtually everywhere, however, women were granted greater freedom and authority, both in their families and in public life, once they passed their childbearing years.

Although European traders strongly influenced many coastal areas of Africa beginning in the late fifteenth century, only in the nineteenth century did larger numbers of merchants, explorers, and missionaries begin to penetrate the interior in large numbers. In some regions, especially on the west coast and in South Africa, the presence of these outsiders began to create complex changes among small groups of Africans, encouraging them to convert to Christianity, send their children to mission schools, and (in west Africa) to replace traffic in people with the exchange of new commodities such as palm oil and groundnuts. By the mid 1880s, a combination of political and economic conflict within Europe and the tendency of explorers and missionaries from Britain, France, Germany, Portugal, and Italy to become enmeshed in struggles within and among African states and communities led to a "scramble for Africa" among the major European powers.

European governments staked out their competing claims to the continent at the Berlin Conference in 1884–5. Gradually over the following decades, often through military "pacification" campaigns, these outsiders established control over their new dominions – leaving virtually all of Africa under foreign rule. The exceptions were Ethiopia, whose long-established kings mobilized their military power to stave off occupation, and Liberia, founded by returning slaves from the United States. America's informal influence allowed this west coast country to escape formal colonization.

Twentieth-century transformations

By the early twentieth century, few areas of the continent escaped, even if indirectly, the effects of the new colonial occupation and its aftermath. This book will explore how women experienced, perceived, and influenced the transformations and cultural conflicts of their societies and how they struggled, both individually and collectively, to reshape their lives and communities. It will also examine the apparent paradox in the conflicting images of African women – not only as singularly oppressed and dominated by men, but also as strong, resourceful, and willing to challenge governments and local traditions to protect themselves and their families. I will suggest that women's critical position in society – producing, preparing, and selling food; giving birth to new generations; feeding, educating, and caring for their families; and sustaining traditions of healing and fertility – was precisely the reason that male family members and successive male-dominated governments sought to undermine their economic and political influence and to control their sexuality.

Understanding the tension between women's power and their oppression, between their strength and their vulnerability, offers a new lens for understanding the relationship between the state and society in the twentieth century. Through the transformations of this period – as the colonial state gave way to states controlled by African men, and as the nationalist movements of the 1940s and 1950s yielded to anti-colonial wars and to the democratization movements of the 1990s – women continued to struggle – with increasing success over time – to assert control over their lives and the lives of their families. Yet just as some women were poised to regain or even to surpass the power and authority they had lost during the colonial century, both local backlash and global economic forces threatened their achievements in new ways, helping to sustain the conditions and contradictions that Helene Cooper so poignantly described.

1

Colonizing African families

In her moving novel *The Joys of Motherhood*, Nigerian writer Buchi Emecheta portrays the dramatic changes in marriage, motherhood, and family life in early twentieth-century Africa, emphasizing her main character's struggles to survive in a confusing colonial city. Nnu Ego is forced to leave her home village for an arranged second marriage after an earlier union failed to produce children. Ironically, now unhappily wed to Nnaife, her fertility blossoms. After the tragic death of her four-week old son and her failed attempt to commit suicide, she becomes pregnant again and pictures her new son as an adult, unlike his father, a "perfect figure of a man."[1] When he grows up, she imagines, he will live next door to her in a rural compound bustling with goats and hens, and relatives and friends, where she will tell stories of her life in a crazy, demeaning town called Lagos.

The book goes on to explore the heartaches and challenges Nnu Ego faces trying to survive and raise her children in a "white man's world." As she struggles to feed her family by selling cigarettes, matches, paraffin, and chopped wood at a stall in the market, her husband Nnaife goes from job to job and squanders any extra money on alcohol and lavish ceremonies. Adding to the family's woes, after his brother's death, Nnaife takes the young widow Adaku as a second wife. Despite the stress of sharing their cramped quarters with a co-wife, Adaku's refusal to accept their husband's foibles provokes Nnu Ego to

[1] Buchi Emecheta, *The Joys of Motherhood* (New York: George Braziller, 1979), 78.

think more critically about her own life. When Adaku urges them to stop cooking for their husband until he provides sufficient housekeeping money, Nnaife responds violently, telling Nnu Ego that feeding the children is her responsibility. His response prompts her to reflect: "At home in Ibuza she would have had her own hut and would at least have been treated as befitting her position [as a senior wife], but here in Lagos, where she was faced with the harsh reality of making ends meet on a pittance, was it right for her husband to refer to her responsibility?"[2]

Nnu Ego's hardship intensifies when Nnaife is forcibly rounded up to fight for the British army during the Second World War, leaving Nnu Ego once again to ponder the circumstances of her life: "because she was the mother of three sons, she was supposed to be happy in her poverty … in her churning stomach, in her rags, in her cramped room."[3] When Nnaife finally returns, to great excitement, the costly celebrations continue for days. But in Nnu Ego's eyes, "There was one thing that did not change with Nnaife and that was his lack of judgement. Now that he had money, it had to be spent."[4] Again Nnu Ego consoles herself with the knowledge that when her sons grow up, they will support her and make her life more comfortable.

Nnaife's return also provokes additional challenges for Nnu Ego: her husband's new marriage to a sixteen-year-old girl, the arrival of a second set of twins – both girls – and then another girl, her ninth child, who dies at birth. Acknowledging men's disappointment at these female births, Nnu Ego wonders "who made the law that we should not hope in our daughters? We women subscribe to that law more than anyone. Until we change all this, it is still a man's world which women will always help to build."[5] Adaku, younger and more independent than Nnu Ego, is the only character in the novel to defy these expectations by educating her two daughters.

As time passes, Nnu Ego's first two sons leave for college and, to Nnu Ego's distress, Oshia, the eldest, accepts a scholarship to study in the United States rather than remaining at home to help the family. After one of the oldest twins refuses the marriage partner chosen by her father, preferring the son of a Yoruba butcher, Nnaife threatens

[2] Emecheta, *Joys of Motherhood*, 137.
[3] Emecheta, *Joys of Motherhood*, 167.
[4] Emecheta, *Joys of Motherhood*, 182.
[5] Emecheta, *Joys of Motherhood*, 187.

to kill the young man with a cutlass. The judge reduces his five-year prison sentence to three months with the stipulation that he return directly to Ibuza after his release.

Feeling old and defeated after her husband's sentencing, Nnu Ego leaves Lagos for Ibuza. But Nnaife's family rejects her as a "bad woman," forcing her to return to her home village, where her condition deteriorates quickly. What finally breaks her spirit, however, is not ill health, but "month after month" failing to hear from her eldest sons in North America. She dies quietly, "with no child to hold her hand and no friend to talk to her." The narrator continues: "She had never really made many friends, so busy had she been building up her joys as a mother."[6] When Nnu Ego's children learn of her sudden death, they all return to the village. Regretting that she had passed away before they were in a position to make her life easier, they organize "the noisiest and most costly" burial Ibuza had ever seen and have a shrine built in her name so that barren women might seek her assistance. In light of this sumptuous public display, everyone wondered why after her death she repeatedly failed to respond to their requests. "Nnu Ego had it all, yet still did not answer prayers for children."[7]

Colonial overview

The Joys of Motherhood was set in a single west African coastal city, yet the experiences of the book's characters reflected widespread trends after the British, French, German, Belgian, Portuguese, and Italian governments seized colonial territories across the African continent from the late 1800s through the first decade of the twentieth century. Sometimes through violent conquest, at others through more peaceful negotiation, these foreign rulers asserted their authority over African kings and chiefs and actively supported missionary efforts to convert Africans to Christianity. As part of their "civilizing mission," government officials and missionaries also founded schools to train a select group of African children, primarily boys, in European languages, history, and culture. Given the strong economic motives for conquest,

[6] Emecheta, *Joys of Motherhood*, 224.
[7] Emecheta, *Joys of Motherhood*, 224.

MAP 2 Colonial Africa in 1914.
Source: From Robert O. Collins and James M. Burns, *A History of Sub-Saharan Africa Second Edition* (Cambridge University Press, 2014).

colonial powers also began to exploit the land and mineral resources in new ways.

Beneath the surface of one family's struggles to survive under these new and disorienting conditions, *The Joys of Motherhood* also conveys a more profound message: that these rapid social changes not only disrupted individual lives, but threatened the health, well-being, and continued viability of African societies. By transforming relationships between spouses, and between parents and children, colonialism endangered the very survival of African families. The book's last line directly conveys this danger – in Nnu Ego's adamant refusal to respond to women's prayers for children.

In the early decades of colonial rule, still marked by both violent and covert protest and rebellion, colonial institutions were still in flux and the relationships between established local rulers and colonial officials remained contested. During this experimental social, economic, and political period, some girls and women began to exercise their rights in new ways. Challenging family control, many girls fled to mission stations to escape arranged marriages. In the absence of men, women also asserted a new autonomy in agriculture, experimenting with and adopting new crops.

By the 1920s, colonial powers and missionaries began to claim their hegemonic power more systematically. They reached more deeply into rural societies, codifying customary law and enhancing the power of the elders, who used these practices to control women and younger men. By recognizing or introducing new authority figures in rural areas (both new officials called "chiefs" and European appointees), colonial regimes ignored the power women had held in many societies, whether in their own right, as joint rulers with men, or through "dual sex" systems in which women and men each governed their respective activities. Whereas in some areas men's control over women had begun to loosen in the early twentieth century, the trend was now reversed, reflecting the shared beliefs of colonial rulers and older African men that women were inherently immoral and belonged under men's control.

In an effort to impose European values over cultures they saw as inferior and to control practices they judged "uncivilized," colonizers also began to intervene more aggressively in women's personal lives through efforts to transform and regulate coming-of-age ceremonies, marriage, and childbirth practices and to eliminate bridewealth gifts to the wife's family. In many areas, this "civilizing mission" coincided with efforts to staunch falling birth rates that disrupted the colonial labor supply. European rule also introduced more rigid ways of understanding the differences between women and men, undercutting the prior power of the exceptional women who were able to attain positions of wealth and authority generally associated with men.

"Here wives must work"

Unlike Western Europe in the late nineteenth and early twentieth centuries, women were fully engaged in the economic life of their

FIGURE 1 Senegalese women and child pounding millet with a mortar and pestle. African women not only grow most of the continent's subsistence crops but, using heavy wooden pestles, they spend many hours each day pounding grains such as millet, maize, sorghum, and teff into flour. Women often sing pounding songs to the rhythm of the pestle.
Source: Friedrich Stark/Alamy.

communities, whether primarily as farmers or as traders and farmers in much of west Africa. Often blind to their economic contributions, colonial rulers implemented policies that threatened women's ability to earn a livelihood, or burdened them with an increased workload, greater responsibility for raising their families, and more limited economic opportunities than men. When officials introduced lucrative cash crops such as cocoa and groundnuts, they assumed that men would be responsible for their cultivation, leaving women to grow the subsistence crops that fed their families, but had less economic value (Figure 1).

In southern, central, and east Africa, needing cash to pay taxes, large numbers of African men left their homes to find work in colonial cities, on European-owned farms and plantations, or mining the gold, diamonds, and copper that sustained the export economy. Burdened with the agricultural labor that women and men had shared, women became the backbone of subsistence farming. Although some women thrived in the absence of men, they also faced additional struggles and challenges. Luo women in western Kenya experimented creatively with new crops and agricultural techniques; in the northern Sudan, however, enslaved women remained confined as field laborers while male slaves successfully deserted their owners or gained manumission. In Zimbabwe (Southern Rhodesia), Shona households increased their production of grain, fresh produce, and other crops to sell to European settlers, farmers, and mine-owners. Using the surplus to pay newly imposed taxes, men were able to avoid working on European farms and mines; but women's work increased dramatically.

In areas of west Africa with a long tradition of women's trading, entrepreneurial women often experimented with varied products. Naa Kowa, who lived in the Ghanaian city of Accra, explained her wide-ranging and diverse activities in the early twentieth century:

> My education in trading was mostly given by my stepmother. I not only helped my father with selling drinks but also traded in many commodities with her. We sold cloth, beads, [red] pepper and groundnuts, and smoked and salted fish. At certain seasons ... I sent wax prints to distant markets for sale ... She taught me also how to polish beads and smoke and salt fish. My brother and I kept a rum shop for my father ... Some of the upcountry traders would buy as many as thirty caskfuls of rum at a time. We also had gin, schnapps, minerals and beer ... When I returned home from the shop I would polish beads, or smoke some fish if they were abundant.[8]

She later apprenticed as a seamstress, which enabled her to begin trading on her own.

A petition that Yoruba women traders in the Nigerian city of Ibadan submitted to the town's king and council in 1938 illustrates the contrast between British and Yoruba expectations about women's economic roles. Coming from the Union of Women Traders in Cotton Goods, they asked the authorities to restrict competition from men identified as "Syrians" who were using trucks to sell textiles at lower

[8] Claire C. Robertson, *Sharing the Same Bowl: A Socioeconomic History of Women and Class in Accra, Ghana* (Bloomington: Indiana University Press, 1984), 129.

prices than the women could offer. Their statement read: "Although we are women, we have responsibilities, same as our menfolk; we feed our children, send them to school, and support our old mothers and fathers; and pay taxes for our old or unemployed menfolk. It is not the practice in this country as it may be elsewhere, that husbands support wives; here wives must work, and maintain not only themselves but their children and other dependents."[9]

In west and central Africa, where the slave trade and its abolition had dominated European relationships with the continent since the late fifteenth century, women's labor was also affected by colonial efforts to abolish slavery within African societies. These new policies gave women greater safety and control over their lives; but women ex-slaves, like their counterparts in the Sudan, had greater difficulty eking out an existence than men. Furthermore, with limited understanding of African marriage practices, some colonial officials were confused about the difference between wives, female slaves, and concubines and they discouraged former slaves from leaving their masters. Abolition also left elite women who had owned slaves less able to recruit labor for farming than in the past.

Women as well as men were subjected to forced labor on European-owned plantations in Portuguese-ruled Mozambique. One woman's work song, expressing her distress about the rigors of her work, her husband's abuse growing sugar, and the forced separation of husbands and wives, repeated the refrain, "I suffer, my heart is weeping." Another song expressed anger and fear: "White man, pay me and let me leave, I want to stop and go home, pay me, I am afraid to flee."[10] These laments reflected not only exploitative conditions, but women's fears of sexual abuse and the maltreatment of their children. On one cotton concession a foreman took women's babies from them and locked them in a box until the owner judged that their mothers had worked long enough.

Although men greatly outnumbered women in the larger colonial cities, beginning in the 1920s increasing numbers of women began to migrate to urban centers such as Nairobi and Johannesburg, the towns of the Zambian (Northern Rhodesian) Copperbelt, and thriving

[9] Quoted in Majorie Keniston McIntosh, *Yoruba Women, Work, and Social Change* (Bloomington: Indiana University Press, 2009), 156–57.

[10] Quoted in Kathleen E. Sheldon, *Pounders of Grain: A History of Women, Work, and Politics in Mozambique* (Portsmouth, NH: Heinemann, 2002), 52.

west African trading centers such as Ibadan, Accra, and Dakar where women continued to follow established and sometimes lucrative traditions of market trading.

The formal jobs open to them remained extremely limited, but they survived through small-scale trade, marketing produce and prepared food, brewing beer, and selling various combinations of domestic and sexual services. In Kenya and Mozambique, women also worked as *ayahs* (children's nurses) and in parts of South Africa as household workers. Only very small numbers of women at this time qualified as teachers, nurses, or midwives. Nairobi sex workers, who cooked and did laundry for migrant men in addition to providing sexual services, sometimes earned enough to invest in urban houses. In South Africa, prohibitions on African liquor purchase made home-brewed beer a product in high demand, while the large white settler population opened up opportunities as launderers for white families.

During the 1920s and 1930s when colonial authorities, especially in areas of white settlement, were making new and concerted efforts to curb unrestrained urban development for reasons of health, crime, and social control, many problems were blamed on women's presence in towns. While Nairobi officials, in the name of health, drove African prostitutes from the streets, white South African legislators passed regulations in 1930 and 1937 that began the process of monitoring women's movement to the cities. The new legal codes adopted in some areas were intended in part to keep control over women's movement. In South Africa, the strongly patriarchal Natal Code, which established women as legal minors, was extended to all black women in 1927. In Zambia and Zimbabwe, by a more gradual process of codifying "customary" law, male chiefs and headmen helped to reshape "custom" in an effort to reclaim their authority over women and younger men.

Ambiguities of change

Women responded to these profound changes in varied ways. Some discontented women, particularly in the countryside where women's labor burdens had increased, initiated popular protests that expressed profound discontent with their lives under the new colonial order. Others continued to take advantage of the new regime and the presence of sympathetic European missionaries to flee arranged marriages and family restrictions. Women also flocked to, and sometimes founded, innovative religious movements that combined aspects of African religious beliefs and practice with Christianity or Islam. In Nairobi and areas near the Kenya coast where Islam had been established for centuries, other women converted to Islam because religious law allowed them to inherit and control their own property, including gifts they had received as bridewealth. Educational opportunities for girls varied greatly across the continent (and were generally scarce). But by the 1930s, conditions in a few urban centers, particularly in South Africa and in west African coastal cities, had created a small group of educated Christian young women. The class and cultural divide between women with and without exposure to Western schools would increase over time.

The results of girls' education were ambiguous, however. The same missionaries who sheltered runaways also preached conservative Western ideologies of appropriate behavior that contradicted African women's active economic engagement as farmers and traders. Mission schools envisioned women in the mold of late-Victorian wives and mothers. Trained for domestic life, they were to marry the new middle-class teachers, ministers, and evangelists. This colonial-sponsored cult of domesticity resonated with some African women, gaining them prestige and respect at a time when their families faced the threat of disintegration from both internal and external pressures. The European missionaries, nurses, and teachers who went to the colonies generally supported such limited ideas of women's place in the world, despite the fact that their own successful careers implicitly challenged these domestic ideologies.

The colonial impact on personal and family life also involved efforts to reshape sexuality and fertility control. As in the precolonial period, most African societies were sparsely populated and placed a high value on insuring women's fertility and controlling their reproductive lives. The Ghanaian trader Naa Kowa explained: "I had six children, but three died. I also had three miscarriages ... Because many children die one needs to bring forth many children so that after death has taken its toll the parents will still be left with some children."[11] The demographic crises of colonial conquest during the

[11] Robertson, *Sharing the Same Bowl*, 128.

1890s – including devastating outbreaks of rinderpest (a debilitating cattle disease), smallpox epidemics, military conquest, and the atrocities accompanying rubber extraction – strengthened the preference for large families. Colonial authorities, anxious to ensure a sufficient labor force to produce commodities for export, were as concerned as local elders with controlling women's sexuality.

Whereas young girls fell naturally under the watchful eye of their families, as girls drew closer to puberty the cultural rituals guiding their transition to womanhood intensified. This stage of transformation, with its preparation for sexual maturity and motherhood, was particularly fraught with challenges to missionary notions of purity and morality. But colonial officials and missionaries, as well as doctors, nurses, and midwives, also initiated changes in cultural practices related to marriage, childbirth, and motherhood in both intended and unintended ways. For women beyond childbearing age, freer of external restraints than in their younger years, colonialism created both greater space and greater vulnerability. Reflecting one of the continuities between the precolonial and the colonial periods, most societies depended on women's ritual and ceremonial expertise to ensure the health, healing, and fertility of both individual women and of their communities.

Gender, power, and marital struggles

Beginning in the early decades of the twentieth century, dramatic transformations in marital relations generally occurred as a result of other colonial policies. When colonial rulers abolished domestic slavery, introduced cash crops for export, or encouraged men to migrate to colonial cities or to mining compounds, their actions often affected marriage in unanticipated ways. In some of these urban centers, foreign men and men from different ethnic groups became eligible marriage partners for African women. Thus, as in *The Joys of Motherhood*, where the economic challenges of living in Lagos created constant tension between Nnu Ego and Nnaife, marriage became a critical arena in which women and men struggled to understand and to cope with the consequences of colonization.

Changes to marriage dated to the earliest years of European conquest. As soon as the railroad opened along the Lagos coast in Nigeria in 1900, women and girls began to bring trading goods to the construction camps, leading to court cases when married women and betrothed girls became mistresses of the clerks and artisans in these new communities. Responding to legal challenges to these relationships, some women ran away to the camps, attracted by the substantial cash earnings of railway workers, as compared with those of farmers. The railway also offered enslaved women a sanctuary from their masters and others a way to escape from lineage authorities, cruel husbands, or arranged marriages. After the town of Abeokuta was integrated into the colonial state in 1914, divorce and remarriage became more common as did marriage by mutual consent, formerly reserved for slaves and people without kin. This extension of British power enabled young women especially to challenge the authority of senior members of their lineage to initiate and regulate marriages, giving couples more freedom to choose marriage partners and weakening the social control of senior men and women over younger women. Yet, despite women's greater freedom to divorce, British policies also enhanced men's greater access to power and resources, leaving women unable to translate age or wealth into political authority as had been possible in precolonial times.

In the Maradi area of Niger, the abolition of slavery early in the twentieth century altered marriage patterns of the local Hausa community in significant ways. A French colony, Niger was predominantly Muslim and had little European settlement or Christian missionary activity. Women usually married at puberty, between the ages of thirteen and fifteen, and following common (though not universal) African practice, they moved to their husband's household, where they became outsiders in the community. Customary bridewealth gifts, transferred from the man's family to that of the woman, were generally low enough to be repaid easily in case of divorce, leaving women relatively free to end marriages. Although most women divorced at least once, they generally remarried, since they had no right to return permanently to their natal homes and marriage was considered women's normal state. Indeed, a recent study suggests that women's movement in and out of marriages became a kind of career through which they "progressively negotiate better material and social conditions."[12]

The colonial government in Niger tried to prevent girls from marrying young and also to require that both parties consent to the union;

[12] Barbara Cooper, *Marriage in Maradi: Gender and Culture in a Hausa Society in Niger, 1900–1989* (Portsmouth, NH: Heinemann, 1997), 63.

but it was the abolition of slavery rather than these unsuccessful efforts that most profoundly affected nuptial practices. Whereas in precolonial times, enslaved women in urban merchant families and rural aristocratic families performed most of the heavy chores, after abolition these onerous tasks became the domain of "wives" and particularly of junior wives and concubines acquired specifically to replace the labor of slave women. Although their entry into these households was framed as "marriage," they were treated more as the "captives" of the past than as "wives," with colonial rulers turning a blind eye to this continuation of slavery by another name. In another example of the fine line between marriage and servitude, both the legitimate wife and the concubine were seen as being "tied" to their husband.

As the hierarchy among women in the household became more indistinct, tensions among wives may have increased. A contemporary Hausa poem reflected on the disruptions these changes caused for the women who had owned slaves:

I have no slave, I am not able to practice purdah,
I have no slave girl who shall fetch water,
Who will go to the bush and fetch me a little wood.[13]

In the face of this new status ambiguity among wives, women began to stage more elaborate and public rituals, relying on extravagant marriage gifts from their husbands' families to highlight their free status and the prominence of their own kin.

In the Asante region of Ghana (then the Gold Coast), it was successful production of cocoa for export along with the end of slavery that profoundly reshaped family marital and economic patterns during the early decades of the twentieth century. As in Maradi, abolition put new pressures on women. In the matrilineal relationships of the past, a married woman retained her own family identity, which she transmitted to her children. Marriage was a fluid institution that took place in stages, often spread over a period of years, along with the gifts and payments made at each stage. With divorce relatively simple for either party, most people did not expect to have long-term marriages and couples were more concerned with their spouse's commitment to the marriage while it lasted than with the relationship's duration.

As cocoa became the dominant colonial cash crop, the practical issues involved in marriage and divorce were transformed along with

[13] Quoted in Cooper, *Marriage in Maradi*, 3.

the reciprocity that had defined earlier Asante marriage. In the past, when both men and women had farmed on matrilineal family land, there were no issues about either one exploiting the labor of the other or about the division of property in case of divorce. Women and men worked jointly on each other's land and, in case the marriage dissolved, both partners retained the land from their own matrilineage. Both women and men could also rely if necessary on the added labor of nonfree workers, both slaves and pawns – people given as collateral for a debt.

This relative equality changed during the early twentieth century. Men began to grow cocoa on newly opened land to which they were given exclusive rights. At the same time, colonial laws passed in 1908 abolished slavery and pawning, making women's labor on their husbands' cocoa farms essential, despite the fact that men now owned not only their farms, but the cocoa beans produced by the joint efforts of husbands and wives. This new economic regime made women's lives more difficult in a number of ways. These newly established cocoa fields were farther from their own family land and from their female family members; furthermore, the need for their labor left them little time for their own economic pursuits, both in farming and trading.

With women's independent economic power undermined, men became economically responsible for caring for their wives and for providing them with "chop money" to pay for food. As in Maradi and elsewhere on the continent, marriage gifts assumed a cash value, and were now spoken of as marriage expenses. The escalation of these cash payments created new conflicts when marriages ended, making divorce cases the subject of heated debate in colonial-era courts. As money became central to marriage rituals, the differences between free wives and pawns dissolved – but without the ceremonial distinctions that women in Maradi used to keep these designations separate.

By the 1920s, however, women began to react strongly to their economic disempowerment. They began to insist that their husbands set up farms for them, often divorcing men who refused to do so. They also turned to the customary courts to challenge matrilineal inheritance laws, demanding that they receive portions of the cocoa farm of a divorced or deceased husband. On this point, they often had the backing of missionaries, who believed in patrilineal systems of kinship. With marriage still seen as a process rather than as a single event, formal ties began to unravel, creating a chaotic period in which love affairs and informal relationships known to the wife's family proliferated.

Only after 1924, when the colonial state began to become more involved in marital disputes through the native courts, was marriage gradually transformed, especially in urban areas, from a fluid relationship that occurred in stages to an institution defined by a single payment to the wife's family and from a reciprocal connection to one in which the courts and the colonial state upheld a man's right to the labor of his wife and children, divorced from any responsibility to provide or care for them. Changes in marriage also altered childrearing in numerous ways, both as a result of the transformed basis of marriage and through interventions of missionaries and the colonial state.

Crossing racial lines

Just as the presence of the railroad camps offered new marriage opportunities for women in coastal Nigeria, in southern Mozambique the possibility of informal unions with Europeans and with South Asian merchants and shopkeepers provided an impetus for changes in marriage practices. Women interviewed later had positive memories of dancing, visiting, and negotiating sexual unions with these foreign men who brought new clothing styles, extended seeds or food on credit in time of drought, and provided transport for visiting and trading over longer distances. These interracial relationships became a "frontier" of colonial contact, where foreign men used kinship ties with local families to enhance their own political and commercial influence (as they had done for centuries in coastal areas and in the Zambezi Valley).

Sexual and domestic relationships between European men and African women were also common in colonial Gabon, particularly in the capital town of Libreville. The women involved, generally from ethnic Mpongwé communities, were often of mixed-race (*métis*) heritage. Although these partnerships were not considered legitimate under French law, they were quite common, particularly among *métisses* (racially mixed women). These unions were so well accepted by Africans that it was most commonly fathers and other male relatives of the women who initiated the marriage agreements, sometimes seeking the women's consent and sometimes not, just as would have occurred with an African man. In the words of one woman: "I had my first partner while I was at the house [of my uncle]. A white man, he was a soldier ... [A relative of mine] came to my house and said,

'You do not have a boy and I prefer to give you to this boy.' … Then we stayed together in his house and then he went to France. [A year later] I found a [French] policeman to take me to Port Gentil … It is my cousin who gave me this white man."[14]

Although not recognized under French law, Mpongwé communities considered these unions legitimate once bridewealth was exchanged. These cash payments as well as a monthly allowance allowed African families to tap into the resources from the local timber market, the major source of livelihood for Libreville's African residents. For Mpongwé women, the key source of respectability came from "living in a married way," with one man at a time, although these unions usually were temporary since most men eventually were sent back to France. Repeating the pattern of interracial relationships across generations, women who had been involved in interracial unions sometimes sought out French partners for their daughters.

These marriages had advantages for both the women involved and their families. With the departure of the European husband, the women often acquired the property where they had lived. One chief explained: "…in the beginning our men did not have sufficient means to construct a dwelling for his wife. So, women *preferred* to be courted by whites … because as recompense, if there was a child that was born the white gave her a house…"[15] An additional advantage came from the possibility for mixed-race women to attain French citizenship. Of the sixty-one *métis* granted French citizenship in 1936 and 1937, nearly 50 percent were women.

Coming of age in a new era

Only after the end of the First World War, when their sovereignty was more secure, did colonial powers take more deliberate steps to challenge local practices relating to birthing, rites of passage, and sexuality. These efforts earned the support of Christian missionaries, who often saw challenging polygynous marriage and bridewealth gifts as part of their "civilizing mission." Elite girls' boarding schools, aspiring

[14] Quoted in Rachel Jean-Baptiste, "'A Black Girl Should Not be With a White Man': Sex, Race, and African Women's Social and Legal Status in Colonial Gabon, c. 1900–1946," *Journal of Women's History* 22, 2 (Summer 2010): 65.

[15] From Jean-Baptiste, "Black Girl," 69.

to shape a generation of Christian African mothers, joined in these efforts. They assumed strong control over their pupils' puberty and marriage in an obsessive effort to keep their charges from the shame of premarital pregnancy. As younger women and men adopted the new values and the standing of rural authorities diminished, many women rejected precolonial forms of control over their sexuality by refusing to undergo virginity examinations and insisting on choosing their own lovers. At the same time that prolonged breastfeeding and sexual abstinence for one to two years after childbirth were becoming less common, especially in the cities, women's knowledge of and access to earlier methods of abortion declined.

In an interview in 1983, Wanjiku, a Kikuyu woman in central Kenya born in 1910, explained her traditional transition to womanhood, which began around the age of fourteen when her ears were pierced and the lower lobes cut so that wooden sticks could be inserted into the opening. The next stage, "buying maturity with pain,"[16] came with *irua*, circumcision, which took place before she began to menstruate. She explained:

> From *Irua* I learned what it meant to be grown-up, with more brains. This is because after circumcision, I began to listen to my mother's advice that moving about with men could easily make me become pregnant once I began menstruating. Also from *Irua*, I learned what it means to be pure Mũgĩkũyũ – to have earned the stage of maturity, when … one no longer moves about with those not circumcised.[17]

In a society based around age grades, the ritual gave Wanjiku a lifelong cohort of women with whom she had shared this challenging experience. Afterward, they were expected to monitor each other's sexuality before marriage and to help their age-mates farm and raise their families, organizing work parties and exchanging gifts after childbirth. During the course of the twentieth century, some of these rites of passage eroded gradually over time, while others such as female genital cutting came under direct attack, particularly from missionaries.

Although excision was not universally practiced, all African societies had rituals to mark and celebrate the transition from childhood to adulthood. Missionaries often opposed these coming-of-age

[16] Jean Davison, *Voices from Mutira: Changes in the Lives of Rural Kikuyu Women, 1910–1995* (Boulder, CO: Lynne Rienner, 1996), 40.

[17] Davison, *Voices from Mutira*, 42.

ceremonies along with practices of nonpenetrational sex that protected girls from pregnancy. In South Africa, for example, where rapid cultural and social change contributed to rising numbers of premarital births, missionary women organized lectures for mothers, encouraging them to discuss sexuality openly with their daughters. These outsiders were unaware, however, that in black South African societies, such discussions properly occurred only between girls and older women. Thus in the end, the misguided attack on customary practices led to an increase in out-of-wedlock births that became a new cause for alarm.

During the 1920s and 1930s, conflict over African rites of passage and sexual practices erupted with particular force in central Kenya where women's bodies became the focal point for the struggle between tradition and modernity. In 1929, after years of opposing excision with little success, the Church of Scotland Mission and the African Inland Mission forbade their converts to circumcise their daughters. This sudden and unexpected ultimatum stirred up instant resentment, perceived as an attack on Kikuyu marriage, procreation, and ethnic identity. To be excised meant becoming Karing'a, "pure," rather than an outsider, Kavirondo. Ninety percent of members withdrew abruptly from these churches and a woman missionary was murdered, apparently the victim of a botched circumcision attempt. Angry Christians who removed their children from mission schools launched independent schools that provided a Western and Christian education without forcing students to repudiate their own culture.

In neighboring Meru, "the politics of the womb"[18] took a different form and focused as much on abortion as on circumcision. Here female initiation was a prenuptial rite that occurred five years or more after puberty. Colonial officials during the 1920s and 1930s blamed this gap for high levels of premarital pregnancy and abortion and for a population decline that threatened the labor supply. Instead of seeking to abolish excision, however, these officials tried to lower the age at which the ceremony was performed and to transfer the power to regulate rites of passage from local women's groups to the officially recognized local councils. Emphasizing the transition involved in these ceremonies, Julia M'Mugambi, initiated in the early 1930s,

[18] This phrase comes from Lynn M. Thomas, *Politics of the Womb: Women, Reproduction and the State in Kenya* (Berkeley: University of California Press, 2003).

recalled a song that the council members sang as they brought initiates home: "Circumcised girl, come, we go home. You have come from uncircumcised girls and now return to women."[19]

Sexuality, morality, and demographic crisis

Notwithstanding the explosive conflicts over excision in Kenya, women's health was generally a low priority for colonial officials except when it impinged on other objectives, particularly the continuing quest for labor in societies that had been battered demographically by the brutal conquests and devastating population drop of the late nineteenth and early twentieth centuries. In the Belgian Congo, colonial anxieties about declining population prompted high-priority efforts to intervene in birthing practices that began in the 1920s. These initiatives led to the development of maternity clinics and hospitals and to training programs for African midwives. Nonetheless, nurses were generally male until after the Second World War and most women remained suspicious of maternity hospitals and clinics, continuing to rely on customary birthing practices.

The Yakusu region of the Congo, ravaged at the turn of the century by a violent regime of rubber extraction, illuminates the relationship between colonial fears of falling population and efforts to transform birthing practices. Although African families in the early 1900s occasionally turned to mission doctors in emergency cases, systematic efforts to medicalize childbirth began only during the 1920s when colonial officials (like their counterparts in Meru) began to fear that depopulation and a falling birthrate threatened the colony's economic vitality. The Protestant missionaries at Yakusu, who opened a new hospital in 1924, viewed hospital births and maternal hygiene primarily as a means of reaching women in order to enhance their more fundamental goals of evangelizing girls and promoting monogamous Christian families. At first, most hospital patients were men; a special women's ward opened only in 1930 – and even then women accounted for only one-third of patients. In addition to serving African women, Yakusu and other new hospitals opened after World War I also provided the infrastructure for Belgian women to join their husbands

[19] Thomas, *Politics of the Womb*, 32.

in the Congo once officials abandoned their fears that raising children in the colonies would contribute to racial "degeneration." Instead, as part of the effort to build popular pride in the empire, Belgian administrators encouraged European wives to join their husbands and to become models of good motherhood for African women.

Industrial development in the Congo after the First World War heightened the fears about a labor shortage, particularly in the burgeoning copper mining industry. Facing the need for more workers, the continent's largest copper company, Union Minière du Haut-Katanga, began to encourage African wives and children to live in mining compounds where they instituted a program of maternal and infant health care unique in colonial Africa. With population decline among the top concerns of this program, health officials discouraged the customary practice of breastfeeding and abstaining from sexual contact for two to three years after childbirth in order to increase the birthrate while also promoting monogamous marriage.

But importing new birthing practices impinged on complex and deeply engrained ideas about early infant care, marriage, and sexuality. At Yakusu, despite the concern to promote population growth, people believed that, rather than encouraging childbirth, the hospital's neglect of local practices posed a special danger to the fertility of girls and women – much as the efforts to change marriage practices had done earlier in the century when the church forbade polygyny among its members. But the high infant mortality rate – as high as 50 percent in the late 1920s – meant that this prohibition interfered with men's ability to have large families. People were also reluctant to train girls as midwives, believing that spirits might "use" them and cause death when girls were menstruating. Furthermore, single girls were not supposed to witness babies being born.

Faced with these obstacles, the new hospital became successful in attracting African patients only when missionary nurses began to work alongside African women who could bring local knowledge and understanding into the birthing process. When the clinic opened, missionary nurse Phyllis Lofts relied heavily on Bolau, a grown woman recognized in the area as a renowned healer and midwife. As a Christian, Bolau was able to cross the boundaries between the medicine of the forest and that of the hospital; during her first hospital delivery she confidently displayed her powers to translate local knowledge into a new idiom. Rather than rubbing the woman's abdomen with special pebbles and encouraging her to confess to adultery, the usual practice in cases of prolonged labor, Bolau reported an innovative message to the women assembled outside the hospital awaiting a progress report. She said, "I know what you're expecting me to do! I shall not do so, for I now know that we should pray to God, and ask His help – so shut your eyes and listen while I pray for this woman!"[20] Building on this success, eighteen babies were born in the mission hospital at Yakusu in 1930.

Bolau's successor, Malia Winnie, a Christian, received her midwife's diploma at the age of fifteen, and asserted her independence by leaving her husband when he married another woman. Although Western-trained, she too understood local metaphors and anxieties about childbirth as a struggle with death. Furthermore, her status as a mother enhanced her power both inside and outside of the hospital, giving her greater standing with women about to give birth than the missionary nurses, who were required to be unmarried. By the late 1930s, the hospital was becoming more accepted, drawing its obstetric patients from two groups – women who lived close enough to walk to the hospital, usually church members or wives of workers at the mission, and women from farther away experiencing difficult births, who often traveled to the hospital by canoe.

Although deeply concerned about population decline in the Congo, the Belgian government left the training of midwives to missionaries. In keeping with their preference for secular education, the colonial rulers of French West Africa were the first Europeans to promote government training of African midwives. When the first medical center was established in Dakar in 1918, it included a school of midwifery, L'École des sages-femmes. The colonial midwives trained here remained the most highly educated women in the region until two teachers' training schools for women were opened in 1938. Colonial administrators and educators modeled the school's curriculum on French medical procedures and made little effort to incorporate African birthing practices, which were viewed as regressive. Like students in all French medical institutions, midwives were also reminded of their personal debt to France and their obligation to become "loyal servants"[21] of the government committed to French culture. As in the

[20] Nancy Rose Hunt, *A Colonial Lexicon: Of Birth Ritual, Medicalization, and Mobility in the Congo* (Durham, NC: Duke University Press, 1999), 207.

[21] Jane Turrittin, "Colonial Midwives and Modernizing Childbirth in French West Africa," in *Women in Colonial African Histories*, eds. Jean Allman, Susan Geiger, and Nakanyike Musisi (Bloomington: Indiana University Press, 2002), 75.

Belgian Congo, however, maternal and child health were not priorities during the first decades of colonial rule, when the French were more concerned with controlling epidemic diseases. Only in the 1930s, when the administration became alarmed about high infant mortality rates, did these issues become priorities.

In British East African colonies, anxieties about population decline varied across regions. The Buganda area of Uganda, in British eyes the most "civilized" precolonial African state, was considered a showcase for successful Christian conversion. Missionary doctors there treated population decline as a crisis that required immediate action in order to support the kingdom's destiny as a great and prosperous nation. To these doctors, the crisis was in part a moral one brought on by the demise of earlier controls on women's sexuality that promoted sexually transmitted diseases. To confront these issues, it was necessary to intervene not only in birthing practices, but also in infant welfare and sexual morality.

Measures to carry out this campaign included enlisting the Buganda Lukiiko (parliament), made up of local Christian Western-educated chiefs who supported these efforts. An extensive Moral Purity Campaign to improve the morals of the lower classes was followed in the early 1920s by the development of maternity training schools designed to counter population decrease. Unlike the Congo, where panic over a declining population was prompted by the need to protect the labor supply, the Buganda campaign was designed to preserve the kingdom that the British regarded as the jewel in their East African crown, reacting to what they perceived as a moral as well as a demographic crisis.

Anxieties about women's morality also motivated the efforts of both German and British colonial rulers to counter the low birth rate among Manyema women in western Tanzania (then Tanganyika) that historians attribute to slavery, violence, and disease in the late nineteenth century. German colonial administrators, who ruled the country from the 1880s to 1918, blamed low birthrates on abortions, both induced and caused by syphilis. British colonial rulers, who took over after the First World War, continued to attribute low fertility rates to women's immoral conduct, prompting them to design programs to promote motherhood and improved family life modeled on those for working-class mothers in England.

Their measures also included establishing maternal and child health clinics. As in the Congo, it was difficult to find women who would agree to deliver their babies at the clinics, however, and even more challenging to find women to train as midwives. Under these circumstances, local midwives, herbalists, and spirit possession leaders continued to care for most pregnant women and their children. These efforts also reflected British beliefs, similar to those of the earlier German colonial rulers, that free urban women were dangerously promiscuous and responsible for the spread of venereal diseases. They especially blamed women's dance societies for encouraging drinking and illicit sexual debauchery. But despite these interventions, Manyema women continued to have multiple marriages and few children, a legacy of sexually transmitted infections and other diseases and a culture with high levels of divorce, remarriage, and alternate relationships.

In colonial Zimbabwe, where foreign rule loosened lineage constraints on women's choice of marital and sexual partners, officials were equally prone to view mobile, unattached women as a threat to white households. They also feared that the rapid spread of venereal disease was lowering the birth rate and sapping the productivity of African men working on the mines. Thus in 1922, the government decreed that all African men and women must be medically examined before being issued passes to seek work in the cities. These inspections had to be updated every three months. African women coming in and out of town were described as "stray" and "floating," words commonly used for domestic farm animals, and raids in effect criminalized unattached women, although they did not prevent them from traveling.

Throughout the 1920s and 1930s the position of urban Africans without formal employment continued to be precarious and, as late as the 1950s, these examinations for sexually transmitted diseases remained compulsory for all unmarried African women coming to the cities. Yet, unlike forced contract labor for men, which future generations publicly condemned, these hated exams remained private, rarely discussed, grievances. Although superintendents in black housing areas and medical officers insisted that women did not mind the exams, personal interviews belie this claim. To one Mozambican woman, Mrs Gosa, "It was the worst experience that had ever happened to me. Even my husband had never looked at my private parts like that. I just wished the earth would open up and swallow me … I had to close my eyes tight to stop myself from crying because of the shame that I felt."[22] No one had explained the purpose of the exam and she did not inquire. "Those were the days when you could never ask a white man anything for fear of being thrown into prison."[23]

Conclusion

The indignities, challenges, and opportunities of the new colonial order reshaped and at times upended the lives of women making difficult individual and family decisions about raising their daughters, choosing sexual partners, giving birth, and negotiating with their husbands over family resources. But women's more public, collective responses to the colonial encounter, which combined confrontation and defiance with acceptance and adaptation of new ideas, clothing, and institutions, had even greater power to alarm the new rulers and to challenge their ideas of African women as oppressed and docile. More profoundly perhaps, women responded collectively when the European presence seemed to pose dire threats to the health and continuity of their families and societies.

[22] Lynette Jackson, "'When in the White Man's Town': Zimbabwean Women Remember *Chibeura*," in Allman et al., 204.
[23] Jackson, "White Man's Town," 204.

2

Confrontation and adaptation

In 1938, a District Commissioner in the Kigezi district of southwestern Uganda wrote with alarm about a Christian revival movement that was sweeping his area. He reported, "The result has been particularly disturbing to the women, who have refused in some cases to cultivate at all, and have forsworn beer, tobacco, and beads, and made a habit of night services."[1] This flourishing religious movement, whose adherents called themselves *balokole*, the saved people, responded particularly to women's tensions over family life and sexuality. Through new "families" created among communities of converts, these women found refuge from the pressures of more "traditional" non-Christian relatives and support in confronting life crises such as infertility and unwanted marriages.

In addition to personal support, the movement offered women new and egalitarian social and religious roles, allowing them to take part in preaching teams and personal evangelical activities, which provided an avenue for becoming literate and for gaining equality with men in the community. As in many African churches, signs of conversion included charismatic experiences such as having visions, hearing voices, entering trance states, and experiencing uncontrolled shaking. The context for this religious innovation was both the new colonial regime and the declining power in the late nineteenth century of older

[1] Catherine Robbins, "Conversion, Life Crises, and Stability among Women in the East African Revival," in *The New Religions of Africa*, ed. Bennetta Jules-Rosette (Norwood, NJ: Ablex Publishing Corp., 1979), 200.

spirits that addressed women's life crises. The revival not only filled this spiritual vacuum, but created an entirely new alternative community that promised women equality and responded to their spiritual and practical concerns.

In the context of colonial transformations that displaced them economically, undermined their political authority, disrupted families, and threatened the life and well-being of their communities, women at times adapted to the new order, which they sought to shape to their own ends. But they also turned to more public and collective movements, both religious and political, in response to the social and political crises they were experiencing. Unlike European colonial officials and missionaries, who blamed African women and "traditional" practices for steep population decline, women sought to enhance their spiritual power in new ways to protest against colonial policies that endangered their tenuous control over their lives and families. They also took advantage of the new colonial order to test the boundaries of local and colonial authorities and to use clothing and fashion to adopt new individual and cultural identities.

Transforming religion

Like the followers of the *balokole* movement, many women reacted creatively to the challenges of foreign domination by transforming older ceremonial practices of both local religions and Islam. They also formed and joined new religious movements independent of European churches to escape the demand for conformity to foreign cultural codes. Since the nineteenth century, mission churches had sought not only to transform initiation ceremonies, but also to ban common African practices such as bridewealth gifts and polygyny.

The women who took the lead in creatively merging local traditions with Christianity were often prominent healers in their own cultures whose new calling was revealed in a dream. Their involvement in these innovative churches drew on widespread and longstanding beliefs that some women held special abilities to communicate with powerful spirits as mediums and priestesses, at times speaking in tongues and performing ecstatic dances to channel messages to the living. They also reflected deep traditions across the continent in which religious specialists were also healers, who focused not only on curing individuals of illness, disease, and especially for women, infertility, but also on mending broader relationships within the community and between the living and their ancestors. Reflecting this broad meaning, the terms for "healer" in many Bantu languages applied both to those who remedied the ills of individual bodies and those who sought to mend social and political tensions. These connections were clear in a popular religious movement that swept through one region of South African at the end of the First World War.

In the Eastern Cape, following the devastating influenza epidemic of 1918 that killed hundreds of thousands of people in the region, Nontetha Nkwenkwe, a widow with ten children, no formal education, and a local reputation as an herbalist and a seer, founded one of the numerous revival movements that sprang up as survivors sought to make sense of the disaster. After a series of dreams revealed her special mission to preach the Bible to uneducated people and to reform her society in the wake of this divine punishment, Nontetha drew on both Xhosa and Christian ideas to preach a message of renewal if people followed the Bible faithfully.

Unable to read, when she led services that lasted for two to three hours Nontetha stared at the palm of her right hand as if her words were inscribed there. As her movement spread, she went from appealing for African unity to attacking mission churches, evoking fears among whites already anxious about political unrest in the region. Late in 1922, in the wake of the Bulhoek massacre, when police slaughtered nearly 200 members of another independent church group a hundred miles north of Nontetha's area, she was arrested and confined to the Fort Beaufort Mental Hospital. To distance her from the devoted followers who visited her regularly, in 1924 she was sent a thousand miles away to Weskoppies Mental Hospital in Pretoria, where she remained until her death from cancer in 1935. Although authorities there treated her as insane, none of the Africans who knew her described her behavior as *ubugeza*, the Xhosa word for madness. Once in the hospital, she continued to preach, insisting that she was a prophet directly inspired by God. She also persisted in asking to communicate with Queen Victoria, for Africans a powerful symbol of British justice and legal equality.

Mobilized by specific colonial policies as well as by dramatic upheavals such as the flu epidemic, women also played prominent roles in religious groups founded by men, although a clear division of labor often persisted between male and female leaders. The Harrist movement, a religious revolution initiated by William Wade Harris in

1913, swept through Côte d'Ivoire, Liberia, and Ghana. Walking from village to village, within months he and his followers had baptized 100,000 to 120,000 people. Although not specifically addressed to women's issues, the Harrist church created a climate that nurtured a few women leaders. Among his followers was Grace Tani, like Nontetha a priestess known for her healing powers. While remaining a Harrist disciple, in 1918 Tani and Kwesi John Nackabah founded the Church of the Twelve Apostles that emphasized healing through faith in God and the use of sanctified water.

The appeal of independent churches to women should not obscure the profound importance of mission Christianity in many regions. For Ngwato women in colonial Botswana, Christian teachings offered a means of access to public political spaces, formerly reserved for men. By sharing with the BaNgwato kings a commitment to Christianity, learning, and literacy, women played a major part in constructing and embracing a new national identity centered on "the realm of the Word," an ideology that knit together the kingship, the Church, and the British colonial Protectorate. For these women preachers, as for those in other churches, infertility and problems giving birth were key topics, inspired in part by Christ's own miraculous birth. In the words of one woman evangelist describing what she might say to a group of non-Christian women:

> Women seemed better than men, because when they taught as women … they converted people. For instance, [we] taught about the birth of Jesus and thus touched our feelings, we women; when [we] talked about the womb. Now, all we women are joined together in certain troubles of faith which make us think we can speak – Yes – just as well or better than men [to one another].[2]

Despite the official influence that Christianity was acquiring in many areas, earlier religious traditions retained their vitality: a new spirit cult in Nyasaland (Malawi) led by female healers helped women to maintain visibility in their communities; in east-central Africa, girls' initiation ceremonies known as *chisungu* remained central to religious and cultural life; and in the Lovedu kingdom of South Africa, people continued to believe that their queens had the power to control

[2] Paul Stuart Landau, *The Realm of the Word: Language, Gender, and Christianity in a Southern African Kingdom* (Portsmouth, NH: Heinemann, 1995), 156.

rainmaking. Among Tumbuku women in Malawi and Zambia, spirit possession ceremonies became almost exclusively female, providing a therapeutic outlet for family tensions that resulted from the long absences of male migrant workers and the ongoing transition from a matrilineal to patrilineal kinship system. In the following song, empowered by the spirit that possesses her, a woman fearlessly condemns her father-in-law:

My father-in-law slanders me.
I shall do the same!
He is a mad fool!
My father-in-law insults me.
I shall insult him also![3]

In Muslim areas of the continent, which expanded during the colonial period as some communities opted for a universal religion not associated with European rule, women were excluded from formal political and religious roles. But neither Islam nor colonial rule dampened their exuberant religious expression through spirit possession groups known as *zar* in the Horn of Africa, *bori* among the Hausa of northern Nigeria and Niger, and *pepo* on the Swahili coast. Women also supported local rituals of saint veneration and pilgrimages to the tombs of local saints, although these parochial expressions of women's beliefs also undermined their standing in a religion that stresses unity and universality.

Islamic legal codes assured women of basic legal rights in marriage, divorce, and property holding, although they only inherited half of what men did. Practices that required women to wear veils or that mandated seclusion from public spaces varied by region, but were generally not strictly enforced in rural areas where women had to work outside the home. Even in towns women found ways around these restrictions. Maradi women in Niger remained productive farmers, while northern Nigerian women led active lives as traders, working from their homes and using children as their intermediaries in public spaces. Talking about her childhood, Baba, a Hausa woman born in 1890, explained:

> After the morning meal we went into the compound and if Mother had things to sell we went to the market and sold them for her. If she made

[3] Leroy Vail and Landeg White, *Power and the Praise Poem: Southern African Voices in History* (Charlottesville: University of Virginia Press, 1991), 254.

> you beanflour cakes you took them, if she made bean-cakes wrapped in leaves you took them, if she made cornflour cakes you took them, or little bean-cakes. We went to market and walked about selling our wares, and brought home the money.[4]

In the Kenyan coastal city of Mombasa, as in other African Islamic societies, women were barred from nearly all public positions of authority; mosques even lacked a screen to separate men and women, thus excluding women from any communal religious observances where men were present. Yet, despite this marginalization, women played major roles in popular versions of Islam. Women known as *wamiji*, people of the towns, led communal rituals such as weddings and funerals and older women exercised considerable authority in kinship and pre-Islamic ceremonies including ushering in the Swahili New Year. This period was designed to cleanse society of the old and insure its well-being in the coming year. From the late nineteenth century onward, women also helped to sustain alternative forms of Islam such as the Qadiriyya brotherhood in Tanzania and Habib Saleh in the Kenyan coastal town of Lamu. Both groups were Sufi orders dedicated to teaching Islamic mysticism and sacred knowledge that appealed particularly to women and to those of lower status. And, in Mombasa, as elsewhere, spirit possession ceremonies and associations offered women leverage and psychological compensation in their relations with men.

In northern Nigeria and Niger, pre-Islamic *bori* spirit possession ceremonies also thrived alongside Islam. Local Hausa spirits, which originally represented powers associated with trees, hills, and lakes, gradually became less tied to particular geographical features. By the early twentieth century the spirits might represent Muslim scholars, Arabs, Fulani pastoralists (the area's aristocratic Muslim rulers), or Europeans. Most *bori* leaders were women who appealed to these spirits for their healing powers, especially in matters of fertility. British colonial rulers in northern Nigeria, who sought to uphold the orthodox Islam that sustained the area's Fulani rulers, had no more success than earlier Muslim reformists in eroding the power of *bori*. Baba's story of a local Fulani administrator who issued an edict forbidding spirit possession ceremonies illustrates their inability to control these ecstatic

[4] Mary F. Smith, *Baba of Karo: A Woman of the Muslim Hausa* (New Haven: Yale University Press, 1954), 54.

practices. When a woman who was visiting the ruler's wives became possessed by a European spirit, she challenged the ruler: "Imprison me, bind me, call the police and lock me up! Isn't there an order forbidding *bori*? Very well, look at me, I have come. Lock me up then!"[5] In this case, because the spirit was European, the possessed woman could not be imprisoned because Europeans were subject to different laws than Africans. But in general these practices were impossible to stamp out because *bori* possession, perceived as beyond individual control, was believed to insure the health of the community.

In precolonial Maradi, the aristocratic woman heading the activities of *bori* spirits was responsible for judging and mediating conflicts by appealing to the spirits just as the king did by appealing to *sharia* (Islamic) law. As one woman explaining the system remarked, "It's women's work. It's none of the king's business."[6] Under French colonial administration the significance of these titled positions for women eroded as alternative forms of judicial, health, and administrative authority replaced them.

Women's wars

In the early years of colonial conquest, many women who combined traditional claims to spiritual or political authority with unique personal strengths supported violent opposition to colonial rule. They included Muhumusa, a medium of the spirit Nyabingi in northern Rwanda; Charwe, a powerful Zimbabwean spirit medium; and the Empress T'aitu Bitoul in Ethiopia. Metkatilili, a leader of the Giriama uprising in eastern Kenya, had no prior claim to authority, but combined personal charisma with an ability to articulate deeply felt grievances against the colonial administration. Fearful of losing land, women and their sons were among her strongest followers.

Women's collective responses focused especially on economic threats that interfered with their ability to feed and care for their families. In the Zaramo area of southern Tanzania following the Maji Maji Uprising of 1905–7 that the Germans brutally repressed, women

[5] Smith, *Baba of Karo*, 223–24.

[6] Barbara Cooper, "Gender and Religion in Hausaland: Variations in Islamic Practice in Niger and Nigeria," in *Women in Muslim Societies*, eds Herbert L. Bodman and Nayereh Tohidi (Boulder: Lynne Rienner, 1998), 30.

conducted a series of *ngoma* (ritual dances) to end a drought that endangered the year's maize crop. Dressed as men, they wielded muskets and appealed to local gods for rain. In their dramatic reaction to the danger of famine, women were deliberately challenging customary gender roles that German policies had disrupted by forcing men to migrate from rural areas to escape forced labor and to seek work. Left behind to sustain the subsistence economy in a time of drought, women had no choice but to assume men's place in guarding the land, leaving them responsible for staving off invasions of wild pigs and other predators. Women had reacted to these threats by increasing their work load and redefining land use patterns as well as by using medicines to protect their fields and to bring rain. As these women transformed the division of labor and renegotiated the gendered bases of household power, their dances expressed these changes through ritual and symbol.

Several years later, a dramatic protest in South Africa demonstrated the pressures that urban women faced in the southern and central African countries dominated by white settlers. In this region, thousands of men recruited to work in gold, diamond, and copper mines were forced to live in grim, single-sex barracks, with only occasional breaks to visit their families left behind in rural areas. Women who moved to cities and towns had limited means of earning money to feed, clothe, and house their families. In May 1913, residents of the conservative South African city of Bloemfontein were startled by the sight of 600 African and Coloured (mixed-race) women marching through the streets to protest a new provincial law that would compel women to carry passes, the identity documents required of all African men.

The town's black location (segregated neighborhood) was unusually comfortable, with "wide, straight roads with little square houses more or less European looking..."[7] Nonetheless, the eighty women arrested in the confrontation feared that mandatory pass checks would expose them to abuse and even rape at the hands of the police. Capturing their militant spirit, the local African Political Organization newspaper described the women wielding sticks at the skulls of police who tried

[7] Quoted in Julia C. Wells, *We Now Demand! The History of Women's Resistance to Pass Laws in South Africa* (Johannesburg: Witwatersrand University Press, 1993), 21–22.

to stop them. "We have done with pleading, we now demand," the women declared.[8]

Passes ignited their anger not only because of the potential for abuse and harassment, but also because of their effects on family life. By requiring a white employer's monthly signature, the system forced women out of their homes and into poorly paid jobs cleaning, cooking, and doing laundry and childcare for white families. Most women preferred instead to supplement men's meager wages by working at home, doing laundry, and brewing and selling beer, activities easier to combine with child care. Arrests and trials resulting from the demonstrations and political pressure on both local and national officials persisted until 1926, when a court ruling delivered welcome, but ambiguous news. Women would be exempted from having to carry passes because they were not considered "persons" in the eyes of the law.

In a pattern of leadership that would become more pronounced as the number of women with a Western education increased, a key organizer of these protests was Charlotte Manye Maxeke. She was one of a tiny group of African women at the beginning of the century that had the rare opportunity to travel abroad for higher education. In the late 1890s, while touring the United States with a celebrated African American group, Orpheus McAdoo's Jubilee Singers, she met a bishop of the African Methodist Episcopal Church. He arranged for her to attend Wilberforce University in Ohio, the country's oldest historically black private university. After graduation, she returned to South Africa and became a teacher and evangelist and a pioneer in doing social work with women and girls in Johannesburg. She was also the lone woman at the historic meeting in 1912 that gave birth to the African National Congress, a new political organization to protect African rights.

As colonial rule persisted, the grievances of some women provoked stronger and more forceful responses. On November 23, 1929 in eastern Nigeria, a senior Igbo woman named Mwanyeruwa, busy extracting palm oil in her village, was approached by an employee of the village warrant chief, Mark Emeruwa, a Christian and former school master. Prepared by rumors that the colonial administration planned to count women as a prelude to taxing them, Mwanyeruwa

[8] From Wells, *We Now Demand*, 42.

snapped at him: "Last year my son's wife who was pregnant died. I am still mourning the death of that woman. Was your mother counted?"[9]

This retort, implicitly blaming the census for the loss of two lives, expressed widespread fears that counting and taxing women was not only a new and unwelcome colonial economic intrusion, but one that would hamper women's fertility and reproductive capacity. The altercation that followed the interchange ignited a "war" by tens of thousands of women that engulfed both Igbo-speaking and neighboring communities. Angered at their treatment by corrupt warrant chiefs, women attacked and burned courts and other symbols of colonial rule, while chanting, dancing, and singing songs that ridiculed the hated officials. They also gathered around the compounds of African officials to demand that they relinquish their official red felt caps – symbols of their colonial positions.

The ensuing Women's War was characteristic of protests during the interwar period, when women's "political" and "religious" movements appeared to diverge more clearly from each other. But beneath the surface of political and economic grievances, these women also drew on customary idioms of public healing to respond to colonial conditions that appeared to undermine not only women's fertility, but the very life of their communities.

The Commission of Inquiry established to investigate this breech of the colonial order attributed women's fear of taxation to a decline in prices for the palm products that they traded, but failed to understand many other aspects of the protests, including the origins of their tactics, in earlier practices of "making war" or "sitting on a man." When a man had mistreated his wife, violated women's market rules, or engaged in some other offense, women would gather at his compound, expressing their anger by singing insulting songs, questioning his manhood, and damaging his hut. British observers also misunderstood that the women's dress – in short loincloths with faces smeared with charcoal and ashes and carrying sticks (the pestles used for pounding yams) wreathed with palm fronds – was a way of invoking their female ancestors.

Although threats of taxation sparked the protests, the "war" reflected far deeper discontent with the many ways that colonial rule had

[9] Marc Matera, Misty L. Bastian, and Susan Kingsley Kent, *The Women's War of 1929: Gender and Violence in Colonial Nigeria* (New York: Palgrave Macmillan, 2011), 137.

weakened women's position, disrupting a decentralized political system in which women and men had shared political power and undermining the importance of women's trading activities. More profoundly, however, the idea of counting and taxing women evoked deeper anxieties about the threat of colonialism to the people of southeastern Nigeria, fears rooted in beliefs about the close links between women's material interests and their cosmological position as mothers of the land.

When Mwanyeruwa lashed out at the census taker, she was expressing the widely shared opinion that counting human beings endangered women's fertility and by extension the fecundity of the land. Thus, counting women represented a general threat to human survival, part of a colonial male conspiracy to kill women and destroy their ability to reproduce life – the ultimate abomination in Igbo cosmology. The behavior of warrant chiefs and "native administrators," who routinely took wives without paying bridewealth or misappropriated the returned bridewealth in divorce cases, was equally threatening to the institution of marriage and thus to the continuity of life. Furthermore, growing male control of market spaces undermined not only women's economic position, but their general wealth, well-being, and reproductive capacities.

From this perspective, these women warriors were engaged in a ceremonial public healing, seeking to right the cosmological balance that threatened not only the position of women, but the continuity of land, human life, and the world of the ancestors and the spirits. One powerful voice to the Commission of Inquiry established to investigate the disturbances summed up the women's complaints. The speaker, Nwato of Okpuala, portrayed the women involved in these protests as seeking to heal the land and its people, to mend the relations among different groups, and to restore peace. She testified:

> Our grievances are that the land is changed – we are all dying ... We sang so that you might ask us what our grievances were ... It is a long time since the Chiefs and the people who know book ... have been oppressing us. We said that we thought that white men came to bring peace to the land. We were annoyed because men are born by women and they marry women ... We meet you here so that we might settle matters. We are telling you that we have been oppressed. If this oppression continues, how are we to praise you?[10]

[10] Matera, Bastian, and Kent, *Women's War*, 268.

The last line of this moving testimony reveals the speaker's deepest feeling about the protests. Their aim was not simply to air women's grievances, but to heal and bring peace to a battered society, restoring it so that those in power would once again earn people's trust and that women, the source of life, would be respected.

New boundaries, new challenges

In addition to the many collective campaigns through which women tested the boundaries of both colonial and local authority, some exceptional individuals were equally assertive. In one Igbo area of Nigeria, a woman named Ahebi Ugbabe, born in the late nineteenth century, challenged both "traditional" and colonial gender politics. When her family was plagued with misfortune, a diviner revealed that her father had offended the goddess Ohe and that Ahebi would have to be offered as a living sacrifice. Informed of this decision, she chose exile from her community rather than obedience to the goddess. Smart and resourceful, she at first became a prostitute, but also (like sex workers in other colonial areas) an "astute businesswoman." She learned several languages and invested her earnings in trade. Living in an area of eastern Nigeria that was subject to repeated British attacks in the early twentieth century, she put her language skills to good use by accompanying the British conquerors into her home town on the understanding that they would stamp out domestic slavery. Through her ties to both the British and the local political elite, she was honored with a rare appointment as a warrant chief, the only woman in all of Nigeria to hold that position, and as one of the four members of the Native Courts, empowered to decide local disputes.

After gaining this position, Ugbabe then mounted a campaign to become *Eze*, king, and was recognized in this hitherto masculine position during the 1920s. She acquired a reputation as a no-nonsense ruler, earning the title of "female leopard," reserved for kings and chieftains. Ugbabe's court also became a sanctuary for women whose husbands abused them. Drawing on widespread African practices that allowed powerful women to fill traditionally male roles, she used her wealth and power to "marry" some of these women, acting as a "female husband" for whom they bore children.

Although her domineering behavior unsettled the traditional political elite, the "final straw" came only when she sought to achieve full Igbo manhood by becoming a masked spirit, thus violating local norms in which masquerade secret societies clearly separated initiated biological men from uninitiated men and women – all of whom were supposed to flee at the sight of a mask. Not to do so was considered a crime. When she took part in the ceremony to present her masked spirit to Apeh Azegba, a powerful elder, Azegba retorted to her: "Do you not know our culture?"[11] Ahebi Ugbabe ordered Apeh Azebga and his council of male elders to court, but this time the British (now well established) supported community norms and forced her to relinquish her masquerade. Ugbabe remained powerful until her death in 1948, but her perceived abuse of power led the elders of Enugu-Ezike to vow that in the future no single individual, man, woman, or female man, would gain absolute power.

Fashioning change

Women expressed political attitudes and ideologies not only through popular movements, but also through dress and fashion. After the British abolished slavery on the east coast island of Zanzibar in 1897, formerly enslaved women and men quickly began to shed the simple dress that marked their servile status and to adopt new fashions. Among women, acutely responsive to changes in style, the brightly colored imported cloth known as *kanga* became popular. As a new hybrid, more mobile society developed, consumption of imported cloth and clothing that covered the body completely became markers of wealth, status, and a new "Swahili" identity. Innovative initiation ceremonies reflected this heightened concern with fashion, as gifts of *kangas* became markers of girls' transformation to well-dressed, fashionable women.

In one of the newly adopted dances associated with initiation, girls wore a costume formerly worn by the Arab aristocracy in the nineteenth century, now deemed *mtindo wa kiparisi* (the fashion of little Paris). From 1900 through the 1930s urban women symbolized their families' social transformation through these rituals and through ceremonial processions across town, laden with gold jewelry and carrying

[11] Nwando Achebe, *The Female King of Colonial Nigeria: Ahebi Ugbabe* (Bloomington: Indiana University Press, 2011), 183.

parasols, which nineteenth-century slaves were allowed to touch only to shield their master or mistress.

Similar transformations of dress and fashion accompanied colonial disruption all over the African continent with different patterns of change depending on local and regional historical and cultural trends. In the Yoruba area of western Nigeria, where many influential people had converted to Christianity during the nineteenth century, early in the twentieth century cultural nationalists expressed their critiques of colonization by rejecting the British garb of earlier converts – for women the tailored blouses that became widely popular – and adopting "traditional" Yoruba dress. The trend was particularly marked among men, the most prominent spokespersons for these expressions of cultural nationalism, but would take root among women in the years to come.

In western Kenya, by contrast, where earlier clothing was minimal, patterns of change took a different form. From 1895 until the First World War, debates over dress centered on whether appropriate modern dress should reflect coastal/Swahili influences or those of the West. Early Christian converts were known alternately as *jo-nanga*, "people of cloth," and *jo-somo*, "people who read." Between the two wars, as the labor market and Christianity expanded, and as women's earnings from trade increased, many women and men adopted Western-style clothing, although groups of traditionalists continued to favor the skins, beads, and sisal of earlier periods.

Controversies over clothing reflected men's widespread belief that they were losing control over their daughters and wives and that Western dress represented a provocative challenge to patriarchal authority. Expressing the general attitude that women in Western garb were sexually promiscuous, some husbands refused to provide the new clothing for their wives and destroyed the new dresses when women bought them. By the Second World War, however, most people in western Kenya had adopted the new fashions, and spouses now began to quarrel instead over the quality and amount of clothing that co-wives received.

In South Africa, with Christian influence, Western education, and labor migration dating back to the nineteenth century, Western dress was widely accepted in both rural and urban areas; the conflicts that developed elsewhere over appropriate attire had subsided in most areas by the dawn of the twentieth century. By the 1930s, however, many young women living in Johannesburg, the largest, most industrialized city of sub-Saharan Africa, were finding new ways to express their modernity and their identification with a transnational black cultural renaissance. Their concerns were reflected in *Bantu World*, the first newspaper for an African audience with a national distribution that targeted the large population of mission-educated African Christians who worked as clerks, teachers, domestic workers, nurses, and clergy.

The use of feminine beauty to attract readers exposed some of the tensions and contradictions in these efforts at a time when black male leaders across the continent were anxious to reassert patriarchal control over women, in face of their growing social and economic independence. Although photos submitted for the publication's beauty contests generally emphasized women modestly dressed in poses that conveyed modernity and respectability, the first-place winner of one contest, outfitted in a close-fitting hat, pearls, a low neckline, and ostrich feather stole, looked significantly more glamorous than the other contestants. Generally, however, *Bantu World* emphasized staid images of racial respectability. At one point the male "editress" of the women's section launched a campaign against black women trying to look "white" by wearing white powder and red lipstick. Yet, while reporters criticized commercial beauty products, the *Bantu World* featured regular advertisements for Apex, an African-American-owned cosmetics company that manufactured hair-straightening and other cosmetic products aimed at black women.

Conclusion

By the beginning of the Second World War, the world and the African continent were entering a new era. African men conscripted into the French and British forces were exposed to the anticolonial movements already simmering in Asia and north Africa. French Equatorial Africa was drawn directly into the conflict when the Free French forces, organized to resist official French collaboration with Nazi Germany, established their headquarters in Brazzaville, the capital of French Equatorial Africa. By the war's end, with all of the colonial powers weakened by yet another internecine European conflict and colonial legitimacy hanging precipitously in the balance, new opportunities and new challenges awaited African women.

3

Domesticity and modernization

In May 1940, a smartly dressed African American woman from Winston-Salem, North Carolina disembarked at Cape Town harbor. The war in Europe had postponed her trip to South Africa and her upcoming marriage to A.B. Xuma, a highly respected physician who was soon to become President of the African National Congress (ANC), the country's main nationalist organization. Well-educated and anxious to contribute her experience to the cause of black progress in her adopted country, Madie Hall Xuma revitalized the ANC Women's League and became its first President. But equally important, she founded a network of women's organizations, the Zenzele ("do it yourself") clubs. With a strongly domestic focus during the 1940s and a greater emphasis on social service after their affiliation with the international YWCA in the 1950s, these clubs formed the center of Xuma's life in South Africa, creating the legacy most commonly attached to her name.

In an interview in 1963, just before Hall left South Africa after her husband's death, she elaborated on how she perceived domestic skills:

> In the past twenty years there has been a wonderful change in African homes, despite the low income. The women can prepare meals and entertain with confidence and they often do so. High teas, morning teas, luncheons etc. are prepared by them and served beautifully. They have also learnt how to dress, with right colour combinations,

> and how to sit, stand and walk correctly. When buying furniture for their tiny homes, they choose carefully, giving attention to design and colour.[1]

Although the Zenzele clubs conveyed new domestic expertise and ideas about gracious living, Hall stressed the longer-term personal significance of these accomplishments. The clubs, she believed, gave women enhanced confidence and knowledge of how to run an organization and raise funds, and a new collective identity as sophisticated homemakers.

Women's accounts of their activities best convey the meaning of this experience. In 1947, R. Msweli, a founding member, wrote from the Johannesburg neighborhood of Sophiatown about her new level of self-assurance:

> The development the Club has roused in me could be the following:- (i) It has improved me socially and mentally (ii) It has removed inferiority complex in my person (iii) It has taught me to work cooperatively (iv) It has enable [sic] me to depend on myself regarding home management.[2]

While Zenzele groups emphasized domestic themes in the 1940s, Xuma denied that this concentration restricted women to the home. Perceiving these domestic accomplishments as the mark of modern womanhood, she argued that domesticity enhanced women's lives and those of their families and friends by adding new skills and expertise to the tasks they already performed. These skills, she argued, were markers of class, culture, and respectability that she shared with South African women, thereby "lifting" them to her own level of refinement.

Xuma's interpretation of the politics of domesticity and respectability helps to explain the gender ideologies that became increasingly important during the late 1940s and 1950s. By embracing a culture centered on home life and refinement, African women could earn admiration as modern and respectable, thereby striking back at the colonial discourses pervasive in the prewar period that branded them as purveyors of sin and immorality. These negative images persisted, particularly in the settler societies of southern Africa, in response to

[1] Quoted in Iris Berger, "An African American 'Mother of the Nation': Madie Hall Xuma in South Africa, 1940–1963, *Journal of Southern African Studies* 27, 3 (September 2001), 560.

[2] From Berger, "African American 'Mother of the Nation,'" 561.

a surge of women migrants to major cities during and after the War. Yet embracing a European domestic ideology as a means of empowerment also had adverse consequences, particularly when enshrined and reproduced in educational systems that offered gender-specific, second-class schooling to girls.

The Second World War accelerated political and social change throughout the African continent. With the former colonial powers devastated on their own soil, and nationalist movements and cold war rivalries putting colonial rulers on the defensive, new attitudes toward the colonial project came to the fore. In an era sometimes referred to as the "Second Colonial Occupation," European rulers made new efforts to invest in their colonies. This ideology of development and modernization brought more intensive and deliberate intervention in local economies, often in the form of programs to "modernize" agriculture that operated to the detriment of women. Assuming that men should be the primary farmers and ignoring women's central role in food production, instructors trained men in new forms of cultivation. Colonial states also began to take greater responsibility for welfare and educational programs once primarily the work of missionaries; these programs were popular with many women, but they also shared the emphasis of their religious predecessors on marriage, motherhood, and domestic capabilities.

As larger numbers of women moved to cities during the postwar period, the urban demographic imbalance began to shift to more equal proportions of women and men. To colonial authorities, particularly in the white settler colonies of southern Africa, this process triggered the alarming associations of urban women with prostitution, venereal disease, adultery, alcoholism, divorce, and high rates of illegitimate births that were established during the prewar years. Many officials included greater female independence and the growing number of women-headed families on their list of moral and social ills. Most firmly dedicated to keeping women out of the major cities, South African officials in the 1950s labeled urban women as "superfluous appendages" of male workers who had the legal right to work in urban areas. Yet, in a trend that went back to the 1920s, African women also took pains to construct their own systems of respectability and propriety, based on learning European cooking, hygiene, sewing and knitting, and leading exemplary lives. In Harare (then Salisbury), for example, being properly married – women for whom *lobolo* (bridewealth) had been paid – was also a primary marker of respectability.

In response to fears of urban women, some governments turned both to educational efforts to alter the moral and social conditions of women's lives and to legal restrictions on their residence in towns. The government of Zambia tried to insure that occupants of African housing had legally registered marriages, while South Africa in the 1950s took the first steps toward extending the pass laws to women, initiating the most stringent controls on their movement anywhere on the continent. According to 1945 legislation in the Congo, officials were required to refuse travel permits to wives and minor daughters who did not have a husband's or father's permission to move to the cities.

But women migrants also became more common in most cities. By the 1940s in Harare larger numbers of women became "migrant wives." These women lived with their husbands in town, but returned regularly to rural areas (which they identified as "home") to plant, weed, and harvest their crops. To some women, spending time living with their husbands in town became a defense against their husbands' developing *maputo* (temporary marriage) relationships with other women. Mrs Maria Chagaresango, who moved to Harare in 1945 explained:

> [After marriage I didn't stay in town.] I would just come and go back home [in the reserve]. I would come occasionally ... I would come when there was not work at home. During the plowing season I would be at home ... Later on with the coming of schools the women would stay [in town] with their children who were going to school here. But when it was time for work [in the reserves] I would just leave the children with their father.[3]

During these critical postwar decades, European intervention in African life and local responses to social transformation followed many patterns established earlier in the century. Both colonial officials and missionaries continued and sometimes intensified their efforts to transform rites of passage and marriage practices and to medicalize childbirth. Similarly, women still fled to towns and cities to avoid arranged marriages, adopted new cash crops and farming techniques, and sought out innovative forms of

[3] Quoted in Teresa A. Barnes, "*We Women Worked So Hard": Gender, Urbanization, and Social Reproduction in Colonial Harare, Zimbabwe, 1930–1956* (Portsmouth, NH: Heinemann, 1999), 115.

religious expression. They also took up new urban occupations – as petty traders, domestic workers, and sex workers. But with the expansion of Western schools in most colonies, the number of educated young women climbed (though unevenly) throughout the continent. Expanded educational programs intensified the cultural and economic divisions among women and contributed to spreading a modernized women's culture to cities and towns. In this new context, many "traditional" practices such as bridewealth and polygyny became topics of heated debate not simply between Europeans and Africans, but among Africans with different attitudes toward local customs.

Education and domesticity

As part of the effort to promote the "advancement" of African women and to supply a growing male elite with suitably trained wives, colonial states began to take a more active role in promoting girls' education, although one that varied greatly from one colony to the next. The number of girls attending school increased rapidly in some areas; but boys continued to outnumber them by a substantial margin. As in the past, these efforts at female education combined academic subjects with a heavy emphasis on domestic science. Formal instruction was matched by a vast network of official and voluntary programs designed to promote women's "domestication" on a European model. In both urban and rural areas, instructors in these projects taught basic literacy and math, along with cooking, sewing, health, hygiene, and childcare. Whether initiated and promoted by women's clubs in Tanzania and South Africa, the Maendeleo ya Wanawake (Women's Progress) movement throughout Kenya, "improvement associations" in the coastal city of Mombasa, *foyers sociaux* (housekeeping schools) in Bujumbura (Burundi), mining companies in Zambia, or the Women's Corona Society in British Cameroon all conveyed a morally charged message emphasizing women's primary place in the home and family. (See Figure 2.)

The Belgian Congo illustrates the ambiguous impact of colonial education on women. As in many other parts of the continent, education was the sphere of missionaries, especially of the Catholic Church. Boys received instruction in French, girls (smaller in number

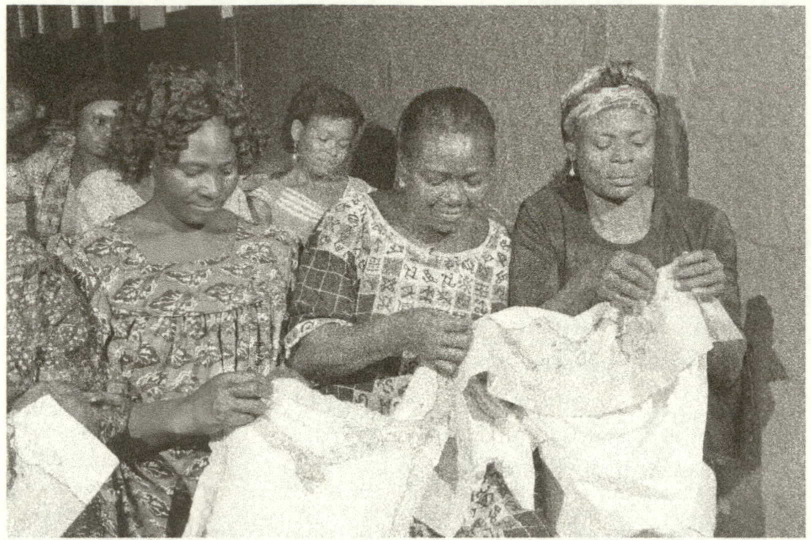

FIGURE 2 Women doing needlework in Kumba, the largest town in south-west Cameroon. Needlework was very popular among the domestic science subjects taught to African girls and women, along with household sewing and dressmaking, cookery, housekeeping, and maternal hygiene. Despite the limitations of this curriculum, women often learned valuable skills that provided them with independent sources of income.
Source: imageBROKER/Alamy.

as students) in indigenous languages with a focus on homemaking skills. During the interwar period, these men became the first group of *évolués* (meaning "evolved" or "developed," applied to those who emulated European values and behavior) in the colony. After the war, through the influential publication *La Voix du Congolais* (*The Voice of the Congolese*), the members of this all-male group, who aspired to be as much like whites as possible, also expressed influential views about the position of women, in the process articulating a new model of gender relations.

At first, according to both colonizers and missionaries, the purpose of school was to turn boys into artisans and girls into Western, Christian mothers and wives. A set of reforms introduced in 1948 lengthened the period of study for both boys and girls and was intended to prepare a small number of boys for professional positions and postsecondary study. Girls, trained only by nuns, would receive a practical, moral education, still aimed at making them better wives and household managers, but also prompting a few to become teachers, nurses, nursing assistants, and midwives. Girls' instruction in French (the colonial language) was minimized, except at the secondary level and courses focused on housekeeping, flower arranging, laundering, ironing, sewing, fieldwork, and cooking – as well as on home furnishing and window decoration. One Congolese nun expressed the view that educating a woman pulls "her out of her semi-servile state, permits her to respond to women's eternal calling in veritably every human society, which is not only to give birth to, but also to raise, men."[4]

The *évolués* justified their claims to superiority over other Congolese by pointing to their monogamous families and to women's domesticated position, using *La Voix du Congolais* to articulate their views on gender relationships. One article explained that, although men clamored for French instruction for their daughters, they were not advocating women's emancipation or gender equity. Another argued that they did not want their wives to acquire knowledge that would place them "at a level which is not naturally reserved to them," but wished only that their wives "be brought closer to our degree of evolution and understand us."[5] Still another explained the importance of teaching girls household skills. "If domestic work isn't accomplished with orderliness and cleanliness, a man won't stay at home."[6] The belief of these men that women should not work outside the home was reinforced by legislation that placed women under male guardianship and required a husband's authorization to allow a wife to work.

In the Congo and elsewhere, cultural questions related to marriage and family life were hotly debated during the 1940s and 1950s. But in the Congo, the *évolué* position on marriage was unequivocal – that polygamy and matrilineal succession in kin relationships were un-Christian, exploited black women, and should be abolished. According to one writer, "A married woman must not be under her brother's [authority]. She must belong to her husband, author of the home that he founded with his wife."[7] This group did not favor eliminating bridewealth, however, but did support drastically reducing

[4] Gertrude Mianda, "Colonialism, Education, and Gender Relations in the Belgian Congo: The Évolué Case," in *Women in Colonial African Histories*, eds Jean Allman, Susan Geiger, and Nakanyike Musisi (Bloomington: Indiana University Press, 2002), 147.

[5] Mianda, "Colonialism," 149.

[6] Mianda, "Colonialism," 150.

[7] Mianda, "Colonialism," 154.

its cost – part of the strategy of rejecting customs they regarded as "primitive," while retaining those that safeguarded men's authority over women.

Homemaking schools and social centers run by Catholic missionaries reinforced instruction in domesticity, promoting practices that were considered the signs of "civilized" status, teaching women appropriate dress, cooking skills, and interior decoration, and training them to serve family meals at the dining table. Because of the association of Western ideas of domestic life with modernity and respectability, some women were pleased with the skills they learned. According to one woman:

> I learned many new things at the social center, but what interested me was the way to raise and educate children, to put a cloth on the table, and to eat at the table with my husband and all our children ... I was enchanted with that. Because a woman who maintains her home well and accomplishes all the duties of a homemaker honors her position.[8]

Not all women believed that men were living up to the expectations of "civilization," however. In the first article by a woman in *La Voix du Congolais*, Louise Efolio wrote:

> We can say that many of our men have not yet acquired anything of true civilization, as meant by the Europeans. We will admit that a man is civilized when he gives proof of a true evolution, when he abstains from the irregular maintenance of two or three women, and when he no longer frivolously dissipates money which is indispensable for the maintenance of his household. If men want to imitate whites, they'd better do a good job of it.[9]

In Portuguese-ruled Mozambique, where few girls received a Western education and even fewer postprimary schooling, some girls greatly valued the benefits they received. Even when girls were officially enrolled in school, however, they attended for fewer hours than boys and were often required to stay home to work in their families' fields or to care for younger children. Unlike South Africa in the 1920s and 1930s, where there was ambiguity about whether girls were being trained in domestic skills to use in their own homes or

[8] Mianda, "Colonialism," 156.
[9] Mianda, "Colonialism," 157.

as household workers, the majority of domestic workers in colonial Mozambique were men. In keeping with the tiny number of women who advanced beyond primary school, only a very small number of African women became nurses or teachers. According to the 1960 census, for example, of 115 African primary school teachers, only four were women. Given this emphasis (and the dearth of formal jobs for women during the 1940s and 1950s), it was rare for women to work for a wage. The scarcity of schooling is apparent in the literacy figures. According to the 1970 census, the last before independence in 1975, 93 percent of Mozambican women and 86 percent of men were illiterate in Portuguese.

Muslim areas did not escape the postwar eagerness to educate African girls. Before British colonizers introduced secular education, most young girls on the Swahili coast of east Africa received some religious instruction from a trusted male relative or family friend or from an educated woman, learning the proper way to pray, recite the Quran, and to perform other religious obligations. When controversy erupted over the question of girls' education during the 1930s, prominent Muslim clerics defended the practice of girls' schooling, provided it was not a trap to convert them to Christianity. In 1931, Sheikh al-Amin argued:

> The Prophet himself says that women and men both should be educated. In fact educating one woman is worth educating ten men, because she passes on her good character to her children ... Also, a man should take pleasure in his wife's betterment. The Prophet says that better than worldly comfort is a good wife. If she is a fool, she will not know how to make a happy house for him, or know the rights of her husband.[10]

When the Government Arab Girls' School opened in Mombasa in 1938, more than a decade after a similar school for boys, the curriculum included domestic science, Arabic, and Swahili alongside other subjects. Only in the 1950s, however, did girls' education take off, in part to address fears, also expressed elsewhere, that educated men would want wives with comparable learning. The British head of the school, Sylvia Gray, took pains to communicate with parents, to include religious and Quranic studies in the curriculum, and to respond to family

[10] Margaret Strobel, *Muslim Women in Mombasa, 1890–1975* (New Haven: Yale University Press, 1979), 105–06.

concerns, although her efforts at diplomacy did not prevent heated controversy when the hula hoop was introduced to vary the physical education curriculum. Despite quadrupling of the school's population between 1952 and 1962, from 220 students to 880, nearly 70 percent of Swahili girls still received no secular education in the year prior to Kenya's independence. Nonetheless, continuing seclusion provided an additional rationale for women's education – to fill the demand for female doctors, teachers, and midwives.

In British-ruled Zanzibar, an island off the coast of Tanzania then ruled separately from the mainland, girls' education was equally controversial. As in Mombasa, parents in Zanzibar demanded that schools uphold the laws of *purdah* (female seclusion) and into the 1940s gave priority to domestic science, fearing that teaching girls to write would ruin their reputations. Reading and oral performance were less suspect, however, since memorizing and reciting the Quran in Arabic was the basis of Islamic education for girls as well as for boys. Muna, who came of age in the 1950s, explained that her father agreed to let her attend the government school only after she had demonstrated her ability to recite the Quran – a skill that established a young woman's proper religious upbringing. Similarly, following the practice of religious recitation, the secular classroom also emphasized singing and storytelling. As Muna explained, "Whatever we read in the book we dramatized."[11]

Despite fears that teaching girls to write would ruin their reputations, former students found learning to read, speak, and write in Swahili, English, and Arabic as the most critical aspect of their education. During the 1930s and 1940s literacy underpinned their self-perception as "modern girls," and by the 1950s and early 1960s, "the time of politics," as participants in the social and political transformation of the island. Thus, while debates about girls' education centered on the issue of *heshima* ("honor"), schoolgirls reshaped the definitions of the concept to suit their own "modern" forms of respectability.

If elders accepted reading and speaking as integral to girls' schooling, writing was suspect for fear that, if girls learned to write, they would send love letters to boys. Jamila, who enrolled at a rural school

[11] Quoted in Corrie Decker, "Reading, Writing, and Respectability: How Schoolgirls Developed Modern Literacies in Colonial Zanzibar," *International Journal of African Historical Studies* 43, 1 (2010), 100.

on the island of Pemba in the 1940s, characterized her defiance of her parents in the act of writing. Although her family did not wish to send her to school, she enrolled on her own, recalling, "I sent myself, I wrote my name and I stayed [at school] … by myself."[12] At the heart of these anxieties was the link between literacy and puberty – the time when girls ended their Quranic education and were separated from boys. Before the Second World War, many parents removed their daughters from government schools to prepare them for marriage. But by the 1940s, following a new mandate from the British Colonial Office, education officials began to embrace more widespread education for girls as well as for boys. By the time of the revolution in 1964, when the Sultan of Zanzibar was overthrown and the island united with Tanganyika (becoming the new country of Tanzania), girls were expected to reject *purdah* and universal education was embraced as a key aspect of the socialist development agenda.

Cultural collisions: education and its reverberations

As Western education became more widespread, its implications resonated throughout African societies, affecting all stages of women's lives, with consequences for both women and men. Although in most situations African women welcomed the opportunity to become more "modern" and "respectable," the meaning of these concepts was hotly debated and the question of whether being "modern" meant forgoing established cultural practices would continue to provoke controversy throughout the century. By contrast with the early colonial period, however, the lines now were less likely to be drawn between outsiders and African communities than between Africans with different interests, perspectives, and cultural backgrounds. But the challenge of Western ideas to longstanding beliefs about marriage, courtship, and coming-of-age ceremonies was no less fraught in the postwar period than in the early years of the twentieth century.

One dramatic illustration of these tensions occurred in the mid-1950s in the Meru area of central Kenya. After local African officials (all of them male) banned genital cutting in 1956, adolescent girls sought to initiate their own transformation into womanhood

[12] From Decker, "Reading, Writing," 102.

by attempting to excise each other. Using razor blades in place of special-purpose knives, and abandoning the public celebrations normally associated with this rite of passage, these girls exerted peer pressure throughout the district to encourage others to join them, sometimes with the collusion of their mothers and grandmothers. Occurring at the time of the violent "Mau Mau" insurgency against the British government, the girls involved saw their observance of traditional ceremonies as a means of expressing their solidarity with the freedom fighters who were being tortured and killed in the anti-colonial struggle.

More widespread education for girls also had important intergenerational implications, particularly where educated young women might command higher bridewealth gifts when they married. In the Maragoli area of western Kenya, widows were able to take advantage of this prospect, though sometimes with unanticipated consequences. During the Second World War, the region's high population had led colonial officials to recruit large numbers of Maragoli men as forced laborers and soldiers. Not surprisingly, their death rates were high and the number of widows increased. In order to survive, these widows began to place greater value on educating their daughters, encouraging them not only to learn to read and write, but to study home economics so that they might become respectable wives for the newly emerging generation of educated men. Elima Visru, widowed in the 1940s, explained:

> I sent my younger daughter to school because the missionaries taught her good manners. Because my daughter was clever and a good houseworker, I knew she would make a good wife and would draw on the teachings of the missionary education to fear and respect her husband. Education turned young girls into *omugosi* [docile] young women. And respectable men like to marry and pay high dowries for such women.[13]

The investment was a wise one. Bridewealth payments, now generally in cash rather than in livestock, more than tripled during the 1940s, despite the strenuous efforts of colonial administrators to limit them. These official efforts failed because well-paid young soldiers

[13] Kenda Mutongi, "Widowed Mothers, Daughters & Masculinities in Maragoli, Western Kenya, 1940–60," in *Readings in Gender in Africa*, ed. Andrea Cornwall (Bloomington: Indiana University Press, 2005), 73.

could at the same time impress prospective brides with their cash and fulfill the ideals of Maragoli masculinity by helping widows to meet their economic and social needs.

What seemed like an ideal solution for both widows and conscripted men also had its downside, however. When men returned to their duties, some of their young wives began to have love affairs with other men. Although widowed mothers felt responsible for controlling their daughters' conduct, they lacked the authority to do so without a man to enforce discipline. Janet Kaveya, widowed in 1942, described her difficulties in controlling her daughter:

> It was hard when your husband died because you were left alone and, sometimes, people and, even, your own children took you for granted. But during the Italian War [World War II], even the married daughters became very hard to discipline, for they had loose manners with men. If your husband was alive ... your daughters obeyed your rules and behaved themselves around men because they knew that if they did not, their father would discipline them.[14]

Indeed, young women's free sexual behavior became so pronounced that complaints about women running away dominated district annual reports in 1942. When men returned, knowledge of their wives' independence and infidelity strained their marriages and contributed to incidences of wife-beating. In such cases, widowed mothers were sometimes compelled to go to the African courts, an unfamiliar and threatening public space, to defend their daughters from abusive husbands.

Cases of domestic violence came to court more frequently after the mid 1940s, when colonial reforms made the courts accessible to women for the first time. The young women and widows who initiated these cases intended only to force the men to stop beating their wives, counting on the public humiliation of a trial to encourage the men to recommit themselves to the marriage. (Divorce would have benefitted neither the widows nor their daughters.) In cases of extreme brutality, however, mothers were willing to sacrifice honor and respectability to save their daughters' lives. Unlike the situation in many parts of southern Africa, where the colonial judicial system generally reflected the interests of elder men, these Maragoli women were able to use the

[14] Mutongi, "Widowed Mothers," 75.

courts both to control their daughters and to regulate the behavior of younger men.

Despite its widespread popularity in the postwar period, Western education also may have caused deep social and psychological distress to many girls and women. In her moving novel Zimbabwean writer Tsitsi Dangarembga explores the "nervous conditions" of the two main characters. Tambudzai is desperate for the European education she is able to receive only after her brother dies, yet she grapples with the resulting alienation she feels from her poor, more traditional rural family. Her cousin Nyasha is anorexic and in intense conflict with her headmaster father who embodies both a deeply traditional patriarchal authority and the "Englishness" at the root of the girls' struggle. When Tambudzai receives a scholarship to attend a prestigious secondary school, her rural mother confronts her:

> Tell me, my daughter, what will I, your mother say to you when you come home a stranger full of white ways and ideas? It will be English, English all the time. He-e, Mummy this, he-e, Mummy that. Like that cousin of yours … I've had enough, I tell you, I've had enough of that man dividing me from my children … If I were a witch I would enfeeble his mind … and then we would see how his education and his money helped him.[15]

The life of "Lily Moya," a pseudonym for a young South African woman, reflected similar conflicts over colonial education, sexuality, and estrangement from her family. In the late 1940s, Lily escaped from the prospect of an arranged marriage to an older man, traveling alone to the east coast city of Durban in a desperate struggle to continue her education. She showed great spunk and determination in enlisting the support of a liberal white benefactor, Mabel Palmer, who helped her get into Natal's top secondary school. But her isolation from her family, her alienation from the other students as the only girl in her class, and Palmer's inability to be the "mother" Lily needed soon overwhelmed her. In her final letter to Mabel Palmer, Lily wrote of her distress:

> For congenial reasons I had to leave Adams, [the school she had attended] due to the fact that I was never meant to be a stone but a human being with feelings, not either an experimental doll.

[15] Tsitsi Dangarembga, *Nervous Conditions: A Novel* (Seattle: Seal Press), 1988, 184.

> ...
>
> About Adams. I think in December 1950, if your memory is still good, I told you that I didn't want staying ... You refused ... and I stayed there in Adams ... not according to my will. I didn't want staying there. You arranged that at my back ... I have no news. I'm very ill.[16]

When historian Shula Marks tracked down Lily and her family in the 1980s, she had spent twenty-five years in mental hospitals after visits to local healers failed to cure her distress. She was confined first at Sterkfontein, one of the few institutions for Africans, and then at Randfontein, a hospital for chronically ill psychiatric patients. Then about fifty, and heavily medicated, Lily was barely able to speak English, and had survived the appalling conditions for black patients in these hospitals: lack of bedding, inadequate clothing, overcrowded wards, filthy sanitary facilities – often with bucket toilets, and inedible food. An article in the South African newspaper, the *Sunday Times* described these institutions: "The number of these human warehouses where care is reduced to a minimum and cure a forgotten word is growing year by year – as are the profits of the company which now has such a monopoly on madness that as one authority told me, 'it can virtually dictate mental health care in South Africa.'"[17]

Debates about "tradition"

South African publications aimed at "modernized" urban communities were deeply involved in creating new gendered images of respectability and in debating issues relating to women's position and family life. Their advertising and advice columns shaped new forms of black consumerism, conveying powerful messages that equated "progress" and modernism with stylish Western clothing, hair-straightening and skin-lightening creams, soaps and detergents, deodorants, sanitary napkins, blood-strengthening pills, correspondence schools, and cereals. The combination of advertising and the women's pages of these

[16] Shula Marks, ed., *Not Either an Experimental Doll: The Separate Worlds of Three South African Women* (London: The Women's Press, 1987), 185–86.

[17] From Tiffany Fawn Jones, *Psychiatry, Mental Institutions, and the Mad in Apartheid South Africa* (New York: Routledge, 2012), 149.

publications served to define "female interest" in terms of what to wear and on how to furnish a home, put on make-up, cook proper meals, and raise well-nourished families. In the long term and less obviously, they constructed new images of social status, defining and justifying women's domestic role and presenting stereotyped black women who aspired to the values of white suburban housewives. It was hardly coincidental that the prevalence of these images emphasizing domesticity, respectability, and motherhood coincided with growing concern about black women's independence. Such advertisements also underscored the growing number of middle-class black women living in South Africa's segregated urban townships.

Men's ambivalence about women's equality was reflected in heated controversy over customary marriage practices in magazines directed at urbanized Africans literate in English. In the early 1950s, the South African magazine *Zonk* generated discussion among readers with articles on bridewealth: "Lobola: Is it Right, or Is It Wrong?" and "Lobola: For and Against." Opinions varied – and not necessarily with the gender of the writer. While some readers believed it to be one of the "beautiful traditions" of African culture or a "sacred and respected" transaction, others felt it symbolized a woman's possession and subservience, making her akin to her husband's cattle. The writer concluded, "To the fire with Lobolo!" Another deemed it "a social menace."[18] *Bantu World*, on the other hand, published a letter condemning the *tsotsis* (thugs) who criticized *lobola* as part of their desire to get everything for nothing. "Lobola to them is disastrous, because they cannot afford ONE beast." Yet, since anything obtained for nothing is valueless, "I hope you ladies will heed this grave warning."[19]

Debates on polygamy, *Drum* magazine's discussion topic for December 1955, generated similarly intense disagreement. The winner of the question "Should Polygamy Be Allowed?" argued that although Adam had twenty-four ribs, God made one wife for him – thus proving that having multiple wives was a "social evil." The second-prize winner dissented with a more practical argument – that polygamy gave barren wives company when their husbands were away and help in times of illness; given the number of illegitimate children, perhaps it was ordained by nature. Interestingly, William Ngakane, a pioneering black social worker, then a field worker for the South

[18] *Zonk*, May, June, and July, 1952.

[19] *Bantu World*, August 20, 1995.

African Institute of Race Relations, argued forcefully, "Man is a polygamous animal and any attempt to change him is against nature." Mr G.D. Pewa, a librarian and teacher, took a decidedly more feminist perspective, arguing that polygamy was associated with a marked inferiority in women's status.[20]

Religion and healing

During the late colonial period African-initiated churches remained important avenues for women's spiritual expression and leadership. In an era that stressed marriage and home life as the source of respectability and modernity, the churches assumed particular importance for women whose ambiguous social position – as single, childless, older, or widowed – made them vulnerable. Although some leaders and active members still emerged from among women with spiritual power rooted in earlier religious and healing practices, this was also a period of transition. Mirroring their growing political prominence, educated young men were beginning to usurp women's position, setting a trend that would become more pronounced after independence.

In the Roho Church in western Kenya, which broke from the Anglican Church and expanded aggressively between 1935 and the mid 1950s, charismatic fervor tended to transcend restrictions of age and gender and women maintained their prominent position. In these years, they were free to hold leadership positions and to take long and arduous journeys, often traveling for seven or eight months, to proselytize. Small numbers of women never married, opting instead to devote themselves fully to the church and to live in Christian communes that welcomed single, divorced, and widowed converts. Esta Songa, who worked as a Roho missionary for ten years before agreeing to marry, explained her decision: "People really laughed at me. But I said that I must do as I had promised ... The spirit had found me when I was young and I could have married earlier. But if [the Spirit] gets you, then you must do what it arranges."[21] Both women and men became teachers, healers, catechists, and pastors; pastors' wives

[20] *Drum*, December 1955.

[21] Cynthia Hoehler-Fatton, *Women of Fire & Spirit: History, Faith, and Gender in Roho Religion in Western Kenya* (New York: Oxford University Press, 1996), 104.

were empowered to perform all his duties when their husband was away and to assume full religious responsibility after his death. When women became grandmothers, their renown as healers increased, a reflection of Luo assumptions, shared in most African societies, about the mystical powers of older women.

Oral traditions of the movement portrayed the founding women as strong-willed and defiant, challenging colonial characterizations of them as ignorant, hysterical, "lusty wenches." Elderly women recalled their attraction to a religion that allowed them freedom to preach, forbidden in mission churches at the time. They also remembered suffering beatings from their menfolk for attending Roho meetings. Hymns such as "We Are Women of War" kept alive the memory of women's important role in founding the church, celebrating their courage as *askeche* (soldiers) in the violent encounter in which the Roho founder and others were burned to death in their house. One hymn reflected this militancy:

(We are women of war, we are women of fire;)
...
(We are women of victory, we are women of spears;)
...
(We will be happy, we will be happy in heaven!)[22]

On the west coast women initiated important Christian-inspired religious movements devoted to healing women, eradicating witchcraft, and sometimes to challenging local practices burdensome to women. In Côte d'Ivoire, Marie Lalou, a childless woman, was viewed with great suspicion after the deaths of her husband and his brother – whom she had refused to marry following local custom. Returning to the village of her birth, she began to preach that God wanted people to stop harming their neighbors through poisoning and witchcraft, but she had to flee once again when she was blamed for deaths in the village. Finally, in 1942 Lalou established the Deima Church that focused on healing people with holy water, attracting the suspicion of the colonial administration as the church became more popular.

In 1951, shortly after the movement began to grow dramatically, Lalou became ill. Before dying she commanded her followers to use only her holy water for healing and not to force widows into another

[22] Hoehler-Fatton, *Women of Fire & Spirit*, 103.

marriage against their will. One of her successors, Blé Nahi, after receiving a vision from God became known as Jesus Onoï, "woman in the service of God on earth." Both women were considered misfits because they did not have children and were accused of using witchcraft for making their husbands ill or killing them; and both women had visions suggesting that their inability to fill customary women's roles was a sign that God had chosen them for a more exalted position. Blé Nahi was one of a series of important prophetesses who continued Lalou's focus on healing; by the 1970s, however, men held the official positions, directing worship services and controlling administration.

Founded by Grace Tani, the Church of the Twelve Apostles in southwestern Ghana focused its ideology on "bringing into the open" spiritual influences linked to sources of illness – especially women's reproductive capacities, misfortunes in trade, the work of witches, mental "disorders," and general family issues. With rituals very similar to those of earlier religious traditions, but still being practiced at least up to the 1970s, patients – mainly women – began with prayers and chanting, then entered a possession state to speak to the prophetess or her female assistant. The first goal was to identify the spirit and then to reveal why it had been troubling a person or working with witches, and to determine the offering or sacrifice that would restore the patient to good health. Rituals ended with a communal sharing of "Madame Tani's holy water." On Fridays, the day of healing, women directed and presided over ritual activity. In a pattern common to many churches, on Sundays educated younger men directed more conventional Western-style prayer services, though these services ended with Fante lyrics and chants, dancing processions, and testimonials about healing work.

Religion and nationalism

Among the most controversial and successful postwar religious figures, at least initially, was Alice Lenshina Mulenga, who began the Lumpa Church in Zambia in 1953 after undergoing a near-death experience in which she claimed to have met Jesus Christ. Her assumed name, Lenshina, came from the Bemba form of "Regina," or Queen. Unlike many other local churches, women and men were completely equal in handling church matters. With Lenshina as their model, women moved from earlier positions as local religious leaders to a religion with universal appeal. Followers came from all over Zambia and neighboring countries to be baptized, leading to a movement estimated at 60,000 to 100,000 at its peak – a following that exceeded the combined membership of the Catholic and Protestant missions.

As in many other independent churches, women were attracted by policies that allowed widows freedom either to remarry men of their choice, or not to remarry at all. The movement also developed new forms of social morality that supported mothers and motherhood, with commandments that prohibited polygamy and banned drinking and smoking. Both were perceived as male habits that squandered women's resources. Lenshina's aim was to create heaven on earth by eradicating the sin of witchcraft. When people came to her temple, she or her agents dispensed medicines to insure health, fertility, and bountiful harvests. While clearly Christian in its belief in Jesus Christ, Lumpa followers also borrowed deeply from the symbols and images of earlier Bemba initiation ceremonies, restoring women's roles as religious intermediaries. By the late 1950s, their rejection of conventional initiation rituals led to increasing numbers of unmarried mothers in the church.

Although women had their own reasons for joining the new church, some young men found it a useful vehicle for political agitation against the colonial government. As more explicitly political outlets developed in the late 1950s, a cleavage emerged between the supporters of the main nationalist movement, the United National Independence Party (UNIP), many of them men, and more devoted Lenshina followers, disproportionately women. Through the late 1950s, the Lumpa relationship with political authorities deteriorated, first with the colonial administration and then, increasingly, with the UNIP and the chiefs, who were threatened by Lenshina's popularity and spiritual authority. In July 1964, just prior to independence – in the interim period when the UNIP controlled the government, but British officials still managed the security forces – open conflict erupted when Lumpa followers refused to abandon the independent villages they had founded to protect themselves from UNIP violence. Over the next two months, at least 1,000 people died in military attacks and starvation as Lumpa followers fled into the bush. Tension also stemmed from widespread resentment at a woman having more support than the messianic nationalist leader, Kenneth Kaunda. One man interviewed many years later reported:

> All of these people were annoyed and could not understand why people were following a woman ... So it was a tug-of-war ... UNIP wanted everybody to support them so they could win the elections ... But she had her own principles. "I can't worship God and work for the party," she said. That brought a lot of trouble because she refused to be part of UNIP. She only taught the gospel.[23]

In the wake of the violence, Lenshina surrendered on August 11, 1964 in exchange for guarantees of her personal safety. She suffered the next eleven years in detention.

Conclusion

The distressing history of the Lumpa Church highlights the ambiguities of nationalism for some women. Yet, not all women shared the position of Lenshina's followers, nor did the prevalent ideologies of domesticity deter them from political action. Indeed, as Africans became more vocal and assertive in protesting colonial policies and demanding self-government, many women justified their involvement in anticolonial struggles as a way of caring for their families. Challenging privatized European views of home life, they often cited their responsibilities as mothers to justify their political engagement. These women contributed to nationalist movements in important ways, transforming the widely accepted narrative that independence movements were the product of an elite group of Western-educated men.

[23] David M. Gordon, *Invisible Agents: Spirits in a Central African History* (Athens, OH: Ohio University Press, 2012) 137.

4

Mothers of nationalism

The year 1955 was a turning point for women in Tanzania. John Hatch, the British representative of the Labour government, visited Dar es Salaam in June to meet with members of the fledging nationalist movement, the Tanganyika African National Union (TANU), and to encourage them to press for independence without violence. After witnessing a speech that the group's leader Julius Nyerere gave to a crowd of 25,000 people, Hatch posed a question to the officials he met: "I see there were a lot of people at Nyerere's meeting today ... but do you have a women's section ... I want to meet their leader."[1] They promised a meeting the following day. But, in the words of Bibi Titi Mohamed, who would become the women's leader:

> The truth is, they didn't have a woman then! ... Everyone had locked their wives away [in the house]. Everyone refused. "Then what shall we do?" they asked themselves. Then Sheneda [one of the men] said, "I will go and collect Titi." ... her husband is my friend. I'll talk to him and she will come.[2]

The following day she was taken to the TANU office and introduced to John Hatch as "leader of the women's section." From then on, after TANU officials contacted her husband asking his written

[1] Susan Geiger, *TANU Women: Gender and Culture in the Making of Tanganyikan Nationalism, 1955–1965* (Portsmouth, NH: Heinemann, 1997), 57.

[2] Geiger, *TANU Women*, 57.

permission, Bibi Titi Mohamed became the head of the party's women's section. Adopting a pattern unique to Tanzania, she mobilized her followers through *ngoma*, women's dance groups, which united Swahili-speaking women from all over the country. As was common across the continent during the 1950s, in many of her speeches, she appealed to women as mothers, emphasizing the ability to give birth as the source of their power:

> "I am telling you that we want independence. And we can't get independence if you don't want to join the party. We have given birth to all these men. Women are the power in this world. I am telling you that we have to join the party first." So they went and joined the party.[3]

Bibi Titi Mohamed was a young Muslim woman born in the coastal city of Dar es Salaam in 1926. In an interview with historian Susan Geiger, she explained that her father was a businessman and her mother a farmer and housewife. She learned to read the Quran as a child and attended Uhuru [Government] Girls School up to Standard Four; upon reaching puberty she was compelled to stay indoors to avoid seeing strangers without her parents' permission. She compared the experience to captivity: "You stay in as if it were a prison ... You can't even peep through the window. It is strictly forbidden."[4] She later recalled accepting this confinement because it was mandated by religion and custom.

When Bibi Titi turned fourteen, she was married to Mzee bin Haji, a forty-year-old mechanic for the Public Works Department whom she had never met. In those days, she explained, parents chose their children's spouses: "... if you were ever to bring a husband to them you would be looked upon as a spoiled child."[5] He divorced her after they had one child. She told Geiger that she then remarried Buku bin Athmani, the chief clerk at the Water Supply Department, whom she knew and loved, but who died a number of years after their marriage. She elaborated, "This marriage was not like my first ... We loved each other. But he died."[6] In other interviews, however, Bibi Titi spoke of three marriages, not including this second husband.

[3] Geiger, *TANU Women*, 58.
[4] Geiger, *TANU Women*, 47.
[5] Geiger, *TANU Women*, 48.
[6] Geiger, *TANU Women*, 48.

Like most Swahili women, Bibi Titi was active in one of the city's numerous *ngoma*, popular dancing and musical groups, each with its own name and hierarchy of officials modeled on British titles: the "chief secretary" who did the organizing and planning, followed by the "kingi" and the "governor." The members of her group, Roho Ni Mgeni (Heart is a Stranger), not only performed at weddings and festivals, but cooperated in organizing burial ceremonies and taking part in the annual community event that celebrated the birthday of the Prophet Muhammed. Before her impromptu recruitment as the leader of TANU women, Bibi Titi had heard about the nationalist organization from her brother-in-law. The group was headed by Julius Nyerere, a young secondary school teacher with a teaching diploma from Makerere University in Uganda and an M.A. in history and economics from the University of Edinburgh. Typical of nationalist leaders at the time, he was a widely revered figure who became the embodiment of the country's aspirations for independence.

In the months that followed John Hatch's visit, Bibi Titi began speaking to leaders of *ngoma* groups and going from house to house to persuade women to join the freedom struggle. But women still were not expected to speak in public. Finally, male leaders persuaded Bibi Titi that she needed to address her supporters. She later described her shock and discomfort as she began her inaugural speech: "I stood up, as if God had caused me to rise. I didn't look at the people." But, she recollected, "I spoke well, and all the people listened attentively." She reported her words, which again emphasized motherhood as the source of women's power:

> What authority is God giving us? He has given us authority! We shouldn't feel inferior because of our womanhood ... We have given birth ... Those whom you see with their coats and caps, they are from here [pointing to her stomach]! They didn't come to our backs and direct from their fathers. Yalaa! God has given us this power ... he knew that he did it so that you can bring children into the world. Without our cooperation, we won't achieve our country's freedom. So we must join. I say that it is necessary for us to join.[7]

Bibi Titi's success in using dance societies to mobilize relatively uneducated Muslim women challenges accepted ideas that nationalist

[7] Geiger, *TANU Women*, 61.

movements succeeded through the efforts of Western-educated young Christian men who rallied popular support through new political parties. More important than TANU, dance societies engaged women in "performing nationalism" by bringing together women from different ethnic groups in a common activity that was central to their daily lives.

Tanzania was not alone in pressing for independence from colonial rule. In the standard account of African nationalist politics, during the late 1940s and 1950s, educated young men, some of whom had expanded their horizons as soldiers during the Second World War, became more assertive in challenging both their elders and European rulers in new ways. Their boycotts, demonstrations, grassroots campaigns, new political parties, and in some cases violence, eventually led most colonial rulers to negotiate an exit from imperial control and to hand over power to this new male elite.

As numerous historians have demonstrated, however, this male-oriented story of top-down decolonization is only partial, ignoring the campaigns of women across the continent whose protests against colonial policies also galvanized political organizing. It also omits the exceptional women who used their leadership skills and their ties to grassroots women's groups to mobilize broad-based constituencies. At times these women leaders drew on their connections to existing women's organizations (such as women's dance societies) while in other cases they formed new politicized women's groups that lent support to established nationalist parties. As auxiliaries to political parties, women were sometimes less concerned with gender equality than with the goals they shared with men – of putting an end to colonial domination. Even when acting in concert with men, however, women (again like Bibi Titi) often drew on their role as mothers as a basis of their political authority and empowerment and occasionally clashed with male nationalists who were unconcerned with gender equity.

The women who devoted their talents and energy to nationalist movements were able to mobilize new constituencies and sometimes to infuse women's agendas into the narratives of nationalism – shaping and supporting, but also challenging and transforming male-led political groups. Many popular actions of the postwar years were sparked initially less by anticolonial sentiments than by resistance to particular colonial policies such as new taxes and land use regulations; over time, however, these grievances often meshed with those of nationalist parties. Women targeted not only unwelcome policies, but also the chiefs responsible for implementing and enforcing them. Though different in many respects, most of these revolts (like those earlier in the century) were intense, spontaneous, and relatively short-lived, the responses of peasants or poor urban women to perceived threats to their livelihoods and to a disruption of customary relationships with local officials. In other cases, however, women generated political unrest that lasted up to independence.

Grassroots actions

Protests in Tanzania and Cameroon typified these grassroots actions, although they ranged widely in their methods and the numbers of women involved. In 1945, 500 women in the Pare District of northern Tanzania marched to the district headquarters to support their husbands' opposition to new taxes that they believed would disrupt their family and agricultural life. The demonstrators battled with local police officers and issued the outrageous demand that the British district officer impregnate them all, since his policies undermined the position of their husbands. Significantly, although this campaign contributed to persuading British colonists to enact limited reforms of local government, women were excluded from the decision-making process.

More than a decade later, between 1958 and 1961 Kom women in Cameroon staged a much larger, more disruptive series of actions, also provoked by threats to their economic position. The Cameroonian protestors were angered by rumors that the British planned to sell their land to Igbos from Nigeria and by a new law that called for farming along the contours of the ridges in order to prevent soil erosion. They also resented the failure of chiefs to protect their crops from the cattle of neighboring Fulani herders. Relying on *anlu*, a traditional practice for protecting their interests, as many as 7,000 women organized a series of mass demonstrations that disrupted political life until the country's independence in 1961. During their dramatic actions, similar to those of Nigerian women three decades earlier, large groups of women issued shrill warning cries, dancing and singing, and taunting men who had offended them. Dressed in rags and leaves and dirty men's trousers, with sticks perched like rifles on their shoulders, they gathered at men's compounds, sometimes urinating and defecating to drive people from their homes in order to shame men into meeting their demands.

Similar grievances against taxes and colonial policies also prompted urban women to engage in massive, often volatile expressions of discontent, sometimes independently and spontaneously, sometimes in conjunction with larger nationalist protests. In Lagos, organizing during and after the war drew on the Lagos Market Women's Association, active since the 1920s. Led by Alimotu Pelewura, an uneducated Muslim political activist, thousands of women traders banded together to protest the taxation of women and to oppose a price-control scheme implemented during the Second World War. As an explicitly anticolonial group, these women also joined a general strike called in 1945 that lasted for thirty-seven days and helped to launch militant mass movements calling for self-government in the near future. Similarly, in Sierra Leone, 10,000 women gathered in 1951 to protest the rising cost of food in Freetown. Led by Mabel Dove Danquah and Hannah Benka-Coker, they sought to regain their monopoly of the trade in palm oil and rice that had been appropriated by Lebanese traders and large foreign companies.

Other complaints galvanized women in South Africa and Burundi. In 1959, women in Durban, responding to restrictions on their involvement in domestic beer-brewing and to government support for competing municipal beer halls that threatened their independent livelihoods, invaded and burned beer halls. Beginning in the segregated township of Cato Manor, an estimated 2,000 women picketed, clashed with police, and set fire to municipal buildings. Also in the late 1950s, Muslim women in Bujumbura organized an effective revolt against a special tax on single women. Protestors, who refused to pay this exaction for several years, were incensed at the implication that all widowed, divorced, and polygynous women were *malaya* (prostitutes).

As movements for independence from colonial rule ignited in the years after the Second World War, women leaders across the continent both responded to and helped to mobilize such grassroots constituencies, making resistance to foreign domination as much "women's work" as the work of the men usually credited with its spread. Among the most prominent of these women were Funmilayo Ransome-Kuti in Nigeria, Frances Baard in South Africa, and Wambui Waiyaki Otieno in Kenya.

But other countries had equally robust women's involvement in nationalist organizations. In Sudan, for example, a high level of women's participation was generated first through the local Communist Party and later through the larger nationalist movement. Although it began among urban educated women, the Women's League (and its successor, the Women's Movement), expanded to workers and peasants in the northern part of the country. In Cameroon, several different political parties worked specifically to mobilize women. But, most uniquely, women nationalists submitted an astonishing 1,000 of the 6,000 recorded petitions sent to the UN Trusteeship Council calling for independence, withdrawal of foreign troops, the reunification of the British and French territories, and lifting economic restrictions on local businesses. With an equal focus on women's rights, the Sierra Leone Women's Movement played a major role in nationalist politics, aiming specifically to improve women's status, protect the rights of market women, and insure women's representation in key government bodies. One of the group's leaders, Mabel Dov, became the first west African woman elected to the national legislature. She was followed by Constance Cummings-John, who a decade later became the mayor of the country's capital, Freetown. As independence neared in Uganda, the Ugandan Council of Women began to prepare women for leadership roles by running voter education and leadership training courses as well as promoting literacy and formal education for women. As in Sierra Leone, these efforts helped to promote women's political representation. By the time of independence in 1962, nine women (seven of them African) had served on the Legislative Council.

Nigeria: mobilizing market women

Funmilayo Ransome-Kuti, the Nigerian activist, differed from Bibi Titi in many ways. Well-educated, she was active in promoting girls' and women's education in the 1920s and 1930s. Her British education made Ransome-Kuti unusual for an African woman of her time. Using her exceptional organizational abilities, she and her husband, Rev. Israel Oludotun Ransome-Kuti, ran a boarding school together. In the mid 1940s she was the key figure in transforming the Abeokuta Ladies' Club (ALC), a group of middle-class, Western-educated Christian women, to include poor market women for whom they set up literacy and tutoring classes. But, involving market women became a recipe for political action when the women decided to use the club to rally against British colonial officials who were confiscating their rice without compensation, a continuation of policies intended to balance wartime food shortages and to provide for soldiers.

This move led to other complaints about officials seizing women's goods or paying less than the market value for them. Involvement with these popular protests launched Ransome-Kuti on a personal journey when she realized how removed educated women were from the lives of ordinary people. From this time on, in a symbolic effort to bridge this gap, she shed her Western clothing and began to dress only in Yoruba garb. Her new attire included a loose blouse and distinctive cloth wrapped elegantly around the head and body "to make women feel that I was one with them."[8]

As protests continued, the ALC expanded the scope of its actions to press for the establishment of health clinics, school playgrounds, improved sanitation, and safer water; the group also demanded an end to government control of trading and a pledge not to increase women's taxation. As its objectives widened and its membership swelled, the ALC grew more militant. Reflecting its avowedly pro-independence and activist goals, the group also adopted a new name – the Abeokuta Women's Union (AWU). The new group was inclusive in its membership, attracting women of all educational levels as well as Christians, Muslims, and followers of Yoruba religions. Famed Nigerian writer Wole Soyinka later described these "wrapper wearers," distinguished by their traditional Yoruba dress from middle-class Christian women, as they filed into a meeting. He wrote: "Women of every occupation – the cloth dyers, weavers, basket makers and the usual petty traders of the markets – they arrived in ones, twos, in groups, they came from near and distant compounds, town sectors and far villages whose names I had never heard."[9]

The AWU was also larger and much more tightly organized than many other African women's groups at this time. With about 20,000 dues-paying members and another 100,000 active supporters, they were able to coordinate massive demonstrations. Ransome-Kuti was a vigorous and dynamic leader. According to her biographers, "Her high cheek bones and piercing gaze could be quite intimidating. She

[8] Quoted in Cheryl Johnson-Odim and Nina Emma Mba, *For Women and the Nation: Funmilayo Ransome-Kuti of Nigeria* (Urbana-Champaign: University of Illinois Press, 1997), 66.

[9] Johnson-Odim and Mba, *For Women and the Nation*, 72–73.

had a hearty laugh and a strong, clear voice that … could be heard well even by a large crowd."[10] The first target of the AWU attacks was a local one – the Alake (King) of Abeokuta, the official responsible for implementing the hated colonial policy of taxing women. In the course of the successful campaign against the Alake and the system of government that gave substantial power to "traditional" authorities recognized by the British (a campaign that, in 1949, forced the Alake out of power), Funmilayo Ransome-Kuti became a nationally and internationally recognized figure.

That same year (1949), relying on a strong, local base in Abeokuta, the AWU members formed a national organization, the Nigerian Women's Union (NWU), to increase support for its long-term goals of enfranchising all women in the country and promoting their equality in the political process. As a feminist and socialist whose politics were well-formed prior to the nationalist era, Ransome-Kuti was less closely tied to a single political party or movement than leading women in some other parts of the continent. By 1953, branches of this nonpartisan group had expanded throughout the country, working together to achieve women's franchise, direct popular elections, and proportional representation for women.

As President of the national organization as well as its Abeokuta branch, Ransome-Kuti expressed strong feminist ideas on women's subordination. In a speech to the Federation of Nigerian Women's Societies, she observed, "As women we still feel that we are inferior to men, we inherited this from our mothers whose spirits had been subdued with slavery and we have to join hands together to shake off this feeling so that the forthcoming Independence may be of reality to us."[11] She also opposed customary marriage practices such as polygyny, which she saw as disrespectful to women, and objected to bridal gifts. In her eyes, these gifts reinforced male domination and discouraged women from leaving unhappy relationships. Taking up another issue that crossed party lines, Ransome-Kuti also led an unsuccessful campaign to extend the franchise to women in conservative, Muslim-dominated northern Nigeria.

Although Ransome-Kuti's campaigns on gender issues appealed to women across the country, she also presided over the Women's Wing of one of the regional parties – the National Council of Nigeria and

[10] Johnson-Odim and Mba, *For Women and the Nation*, 76.
[11] Johnson-Odim and Mba, *For Women and the Nation*, 102.

the Cameroons. Thus, just as women's dance societies formed the basis for TANU women's groups, in western Nigeria a group centered on women traders became the core of a national organization whose goals and militancy widened along with its membership.

South Africa: fighting apartheid

In South Africa, the most highly industrialized country on the continent, women's organizers during the 1940s and 1950s were closely tied to nationalist organizations such as the African National Congress that were fighting for democratic rights for the country's African majority. These groups especially attracted women living in segregated urban shantytowns, threatened by the white minority government's campaign to force them to carry identity documents known as passes. Of those with formal employment, many earned their living in low-paying jobs stitching clothing, weaving textiles, or preparing and canning food. Unlike Tanzania and Nigeria, South Africa had a minority population of permanent white settlers who monopolized political power. They entered the postwar period determined to reinforce racism and white domination rather than moving to end colonial rule. Under this new system, known as apartheid, African women and children living in the cities were designated as "superfluous appendages" of male workers, and at times terrorized with threats of deportation to squalid, underdeveloped rural communities. Frances Baard, who found a job in a canning factory during the war, eventually became an active trade union organizer who mobilized her constituency in the struggle against passes for women and an end to white domination.

Coming from a much more modest background than Ransome-Kuti, Baard, born in the diamond mining town of Kimberley, attended a Methodist primary school through Standard Six (eighth grade) and briefly attended a teacher's training school. After a short stint as a teacher, she took a job as a domestic worker, one of the few formal jobs open to women in South Africa. Once married, Baard, who lived in the segregated African township of New Brighton outside Port Elizabeth, found work in a food and canning factory – an industry that flourished during the war. Conditions in the factories at the time were harsh. Workers who peeled and canned the fruit had no plastic aprons or gloves and often worked sixteen-hour shifts.

When Ray Alexander, a white communist, organized a union at Baard's factory in 1948, Baard was elected Organizing Secretary for the African Food and Canning Workers' Union. From then on, she worked in the trade union office, learning organizing skills, giving speeches, listening to workers' complaints, negotiating with management, and confronting the difficulties of keeping seasonal workers involved in the union. In doing so she honed the political expertise that would equip her for a lifetime of political engagement. After new laws were enacted in 1950 that intensified urban racial segregation, Baard faced additional problems. Because the unions legally defined as "African" and "Coloured" shared an office and refused to separate, she was constantly harassed by the police.

In addition to her trade union activities, Baard was drawn to attend a meeting of the main nationalist organization, the African National Congress (ANC), after her shock at seeing people forced to sleep outside on a cold, rainy night for lack of accommodation, in a climate where winter temperatures could fall into the mid-forties. She soon became involved in the ANC Women's League as well, at first going from house to house to talk with women about their problems – lack of money, high rents, difficulty feeding their families, and men's harassment under the pass laws. According to these regulations, men were required to carry an identity document that gave them permission to work only in the city where they resided; they could be stopped, searched, and imprisoned or deported to rural areas at any time if their passes were not "in order." Baard also learned of the special hardships that widows faced – the threat of losing houses that could be registered only in men's names. When her husband died suddenly in 1952 and she assumed sole responsibility for raising their two young children, her reputation as an activist protected her from being forced out of their house.

Baard's leadership role in both union and women's struggles resulted, in part, from the close ties between the Food and Canning Workers' Union, its African affiliate, and the broader political movements against apartheid during the 1950s. These protests were organized by the African National Congress (ANC), whose leaders included Nelson Mandela. Thus, she was active in the Defiance Campaign, the first major nationwide program of civil disobedience aimed at challenging the apartheid regime. In support of the tightly organized groups that deliberately violated laws mandating segregated facilities and residential areas, crowds of exuberant supporters gathered in mass meetings and demonstrations, carrying banners and chanting protest slogans. In her home area of Port Elizabeth, among the most militant communities in the country, thirty people marched through the European-only entrance to the railway station singing freedom songs. Accompanied by cheering friends and family, they chanted "Mayibuye Afrika!" ("Let Africa come back!"). Those defying the law in support of democratic reform voluntarily courted arrest and prison sentences (usually two to three months) rather than pay fines. In doing so they were following the tradition of nonviolent resistance pioneered by South Africa's Indian community a half century earlier under the leadership of Mohandas Gandhi.

In keeping with her wide-ranging involvement in organizations challenging the apartheid state, Baard became a member of the National Executive Committee of SACTU (the South African Congress of Trade Unions), the new multiracial federation formed in 1955 in defiance of apartheid laws. During the late 1950s, SACTU campaigned aggressively to raise the minimum wage and organized a potato boycott that won some improvements in the brutal conditions of farm workers. She was also a founding member of the Federation of South African Women (now known as FEDSAW). Launched in 1954, this multiracial organization led women's struggles against the new requirement that African women as well as men carry passes. Alongside Baard, leaders included Lilian Ngoyi and Ray Alexander (both with strong trade union ties), and Helen Joseph, a British social worker and political activist, then working for the Garment Workers' Union. Emphasizing women's common bond as mothers, FEDSAW leaders castigated apartheid policies for separating migrant workers from their families. Lilian Ngoyi thundered in a speech, "My womb is shaken when they speak of Bantu education,"[12] the system of inferior schooling that was being imposed on African children.

As a leader of FEDSAW, Baard was in the forefront of the historic protest on August 9, 1956. Resisting official efforts at intimidation, 20,000 women assembled at the Union Building in Pretoria (the government's administrative center) to rally against the apartheid government's plans to extend the pass laws to women. They carried thousands of petitions to the Prime Minister, Johannes Strijdom.

[12] Quoted in Tom Lodge, *Black Politics in South Africa since 1945* (London: Longman, 1983), 151.

When he refused to see the women's representatives, they stacked the petitions outside his office door and marched back to the expansive plaza overlooking the city. The demonstrators, many with babies on their backs, stood silently for thirty minutes and then burst into the song that became emblematic of their movement: "Strijdom, you have tampered with the women, You have struck a rock."[13] Following on the success of the demonstration the Federation planned a massive campaign of civil disobedience in which women would refuse to take out passes, going to prison if necessary to make their point. Although the ANC leadership weighed in against this plan, women's unrest continued to spread. In both the cities and in rural areas, women rallied, sometimes violently, against both passes and schemes to "improve" rural economies (Figure 3).

Prior to the Pretoria demonstration, in 1955, as the South African government intensified its campaign against resistance movements, Baard and women's movement leaders Lilian Ngoyi, Ida Fiyo Mntwana, Bertha Mashaba, and Helen Joseph were among 156 people arrested in the famous Treason Trial, along with Mandela and other antiapartheid campaigners. Although all the defendants were acquitted in 1961, the lengthy ordeal drained the time and energy of the ANC and exhausted the group's resources. Nonetheless, it also strengthened the commitment and solidarity of the defendants. In the words of Helen Joseph, "We led a life within a life and became ever more firmly bound to our organizations and to our common struggle. The effort to turn us from our path had resulted only in a stronger determination to follow it, as almost the whole of the Congress leadership … sat together, discussed together, planned together for the future."[14]

Once exonerated, Baard continued her trade union and women's organizing until she was rearrested and banned in 1963, at the height of the apartheid government's crackdown on the struggle for democratic rights. Although the Women's Federation was never formally outlawed, most of its leaders were detained, banned, or forced into exile. Under banning orders, individuals were restricted to a particular district, had to report regularly to the police, and were prevented

[13] Cherryl Walker, *Women and Resistance in South Africa* (London: Onyx Press, 1982), 195.

[14] Helen Joseph, *Side by Side: The Autobiography of Helen Joseph* (New York: William Morrow and Co., 1986), 63.

FIGURE 3 Leaders of the Federation of South African Women delivering petitions to government officials at the Union Building in Pretoria on October 27, 1955. Carried by representatives from each of the officially designated racial groups, the petitions outlined women's grievances under apartheid, and particularly their opposition to the extension of the pass laws to African women. This march of 2,000 women was a prelude to the historic march of 20,000 women the following year on August 9, 1956. Pictured from left to right: Rahima Moosa, Lilian Ngoyi, Helen Joseph, and Sophia Williams-De Bruyn.
Source: Jurgen Schadenberg/Getty Images.

from associating with more than one person at a time. They could not be quoted in the press or in any other publication and were prohibited from taking part in political groups or unions. Such orders effectively silenced entire organizations.

Following her arrest, Baard spent a punishing year in solitary confinement, where she was allowed nothing to read and a light was kept on at all times, day and night. When finally taken to court she adamantly denied the lengthy list of charges against her, insisting, "I contravened all this? Rubbish!"[15] At this point, she was returned to prison for another five years. Recalling the ordeal, she was convinced that her interrogators were trying to kill her – but that her strong spirit enabled her to survive.

[15] Quoted in Iris Berger, *Threads of Solidarity: Women in South African Industry, 1900–1980* (Bloomington: Indiana University Press, 1992), 257.

Kenya: Mau Mau women

Kenyan nationalist leader, Wambui Waiyaki Otieno, was equally tough and resourceful. A rebel from childhood, she described her independent spirit from an early age: "As a Kikuyu and a Christian, I was brought up to be a part of both cultures, yet I rejected many of the restrictions imposed by each."[16] Living in a colony where a tiny minority of British settlers clung to power, the nationalist movement faced colonial intransigence similar to that in South Africa. This unwillingness to yield power made Kenya one of the few European colonies in Africa, apart from French-ruled Algeria and French Cameroun, where sustained violence accompanied the decolonization process during the 1950s.

Like Ransome-Kuti, Otieno was born into an observant Christian family. Her father was the first African chief inspector of police in Kenya during the 1930s. Raised in a rural area, she was expected, as most girls were, to cultivate her own crops, to herd sheep and goats, to milk cows, and to carry water from a nearby stream while attending school. Living in a community where strong divisions remained between Christian converts and traditionalists – a legacy of the battles over female circumcision during the 1930s – Otieno was constantly teased by her classmates for being uncircumcised. In her life history, she quotes the lyrics of a song that proclaimed the uncircumcised girl as evil and cursed by the ancestors. During the periods when other families celebrated the life stages of their daughters, the children in her family were locked indoors to protect them from these "heathen" songs and dances. A strong student, she completed secondary school and, after several years as a political activist, went on to Tengera College in Arusha, Tanzania where she received a diploma in community development, political science, and leadership.

Despite her Christian upbringing, Otieno chafed at school over the European version of Kenya's history and the school's insistence that she adopt a British name. When the British government declared a State of Emergency in October, 1952 to quell a simmering rebellion against colonial rule, she was a sixteen-year-old school girl who felt: "All the contradictions of my Christian upbringing and the cultural bias I experienced in school led me, inevitably, toward the

[16] Wambui Waiyaki Otieno, *Mau Mau's Daughter: A Life History*, ed. Cora Ann Presley (Boulder, CO: Lynne Rienner, 1998), 25.

rebellion."[17] Too young to join her sister and brothers who were studying abroad because of the Emergency, Otieno became more and more drawn into "freedom fighting activities," which she perceived as "getting rid of colonialists and their black collaborators."[18] Her commitment involved taking a successive series of oaths that expressed her loyalty to the secret underground segment of the freedom movement. Known as Mau Mau, these combatants were retreating into nearby forests and arming themselves.

By late 1954, so involved in the movement that she could no longer pretend to be leading an ordinary life, Otieno ran away to Nairobi and became a full-time Mau Mau fighter. She enrolled house servants into the freedom struggle, smuggled firearms and information to the forest fighters, and acted as a scout in areas targeted for attack. She observed: "A typical scout was a young, smartly dressed woman … her working tools included paraphernalia such as wigs, various uniforms, *buibui* (the caftan-like dress and head cover worn by Muslim women), and make-up."[19] This was an essential job for women in the movement, who had to report on the precise details of each location, including the number of attackers required, the best weapons to use, and where to flee in case of trouble and to regroup. Stressing the danger of these activities, she emphasized, "Scouts lived from day to day, as one wrong move could mean death."[20] Almost as an aside, she noted the difficulties of raising the three children she had before 1960, with assistance and funding from her fiancé, a nanny, and her mother.

In addition to her underground activities, Otieno became involved in the Nairobi People's Convention Party (NPCP), which worked closely with Mau Mau by fighting against racial segregation and campaigning for the release of detained leaders, especially the leading nationalist figure, Jomo Kenyatta. She worked with the group's Women's Wing that, like the Federation of South African Women, was dedicated to the broader struggle for freedom. Unlike women activists in South Africa, their demands did not specifically include equality for women. They did, however, organize massive demonstrations, sometimes involving as many as 200,000 to 300,000 people from all ethnic groups, demanding land, freedom, and Kenyatta's release.

[17] Otieno, *Mau Mau's Daughter*, 32.
[18] Otieno, *Mau Mau's Daughter*, 34.
[19] Otieno, *Mau Mau's Daughter*, 38.
[20] Otieno, *Mau Mau's Daughter*, 43.

Like the Defiance Campaign in South Africa, members of the NPCP also held what Otieno described as "sit-ins" to desegregate European-only hotels, restaurants, and toilets in Nairobi. She was served with a restriction order for her activities, which limited her movement and obligated her to report daily to the district officer between 8 A.M. and 10 A.M. each day. Under repeated questioning, she refused to disclose information about the struggle. She was also detained in the coastal town of Lamu, where she was raped several times by an officer who was interrogating her. Reporting his words after these multiple assaults, she said, "He then told me that he had given me a baby girl. He ... said that impregnating me was a decision of the British government. They hoped that Mau Mau would either kill me or hate me for having a white man's child."[21] When the State of Emergency was ended in late 1959, the NPCP was folded into the new political party, the Kenya African National Union (KANU) and Otieno became head of its Women's Wing.

Armed struggle and its consequences also opened up space for challenges to accepted ideas about men's and women's social roles. For those who took up arms against the colonial government as forest fighters, relations between women and men became critical to how they organized daily life in an isolated environment. Steeped in Western Christian ideologies of family life, the more literate group, who called themselves the Kenya Parliament, enforced monogamous marriage and a traditional gender division of labor, under which women cooked and gathered firewood regardless of their rank. Less educated and less hierarchical, the Kenya Riigi men and women fought side by side, spurning marriage along with a customary division of labor. Their debates about military strategy – particularly about whether African women and children who opposed Mau Mau should be killed – also challenged them to hone their ideas about the differences between women and men, particularly in relation to women's maternal roles. For fighters who were captured and detained in sex-segregated prison camps, some men were forced into doing "women's work" such as cooking, while some women were pressed into building roads and quarrying rocks.

Otieno's harsh treatment was part of a history of brutal suppression of the uprising by British forces and their African allies in the Home Guards. By the time the State of Emergency was lifted in 1960,

[21] Otieno, *Mau Mau's Daughter*, 83.

between 80,000 and 100,000 Kikuyu had been imprisoned in concentration camps, more than a million civilians had been forcibly moved to "protected villages" to separate them from the forest fighters, and about 11,500 suspected Mau Mau were killed, 1,000 of them hanged. For the women left behind, life was very difficult. Muthoni Likimani, a Kenyan writer whose fictionalized account was based on extensive interviews with women, explained:

> The British gave an order to demolish the homes and to build huts in one camp so that they could guard the Kenyans every movement. The women in the camps were being beaten up, raped, harassed, and overworked at the forced communal labour. Yet, they made sure that all the gardens were weeded and growing food ... One really remarkable thing that Mau Mau women did was to continue to educate their children. Women would collect money and do all they could to smuggle the brightest children out of Kenya to study overseas. They would smuggle them through Sudan, Ethiopia and Egypt. The women did so with the hope that their children would come home to be the future leaders of their government. And sure enough, they did.[22]

According to Otieno's life history, which she related to historian Cora Ann Presley, many women took part in the oathing ceremonies that created bonds to the Mau Mau freedom fighters. Smaller numbers joined the armed guerrilla forces in the forests surrounding the Kikuyu reserves – the areas of land allocated to African communities under British rule. But women sympathizers were critical to maintaining the supply lines that funneled food, information, medicine, and weapons from the towns and reserves into the forests. These tasks were vital to sustaining the guerrilla movement.

Guinea: challenging men to "wear the pants"

In French West Africa, the dominant nationalist party, the *Rassemblement Démocratique Africain* (RDA) [African Democratic Rally] had separate branches in each of the eight countries that comprised the Federation of French West Africa. Although women were not involved in the

[22] Muthoni Likimani, speaking with Teresa E. Turner and Teena Jo Neal, New York, May 22, 1993, in Teresa Turner, Foreward, *Mau Mau Women*, www.uoguelph.ca/-terisatu/MauMau.

party's founding in 1946, in Guinea they played a crucial role in sustaining a seventy-day general strike in 1953. This action led the male RDA leaders to enlist them in the nationalist movement and encourage them to use their own networks and organizations to mobilize new members.

Like their counterparts in Tanzania, most of the grassroots women activists in Guinea were Muslim, earning their livelihoods as market traders, cloth dyers, and seamstresses. Political organizing was taxing, often requiring women to act in ways that violated accepted behavior by speaking in public and leaving their families to travel unescorted in the countryside. Yet they became engaged in the struggle for independence because colonial policies interfered with their ability to sustain their families. Unlike many African political parties of the period, the RDA in Guinea encouraged women's involvement, putting forth practical demands that might improve women's lives in tangible ways. These ideas included adding rations of rice to workers' wages, encouraging the use of charcoal for cooking fires to reduce the burden of collecting firewood, and advocating for the construction of public water taps in the capital city of Conakry. The party also called for paid maternity leave, increased educational opportunities for girls as well as boys, and expanded medical facilities, including maternity clinics.

As in Tanzania (and unlike Nigeria) women's initial involvement came from the party leaders; but they soon mobilized themselves independently to support both their own grassroots interests and the nationalist project. Unlike Tanzania, however, Guinean women's associations in the 1940s tended to be ethnically exclusive, although their ethos of mutual support helped them to transcend these boundaries.

With long-established social and cultural networks as the basis of their mobilization, women activists in Guinea also were able to promote their organizational efforts by circulating information quickly at markets and public water taps. Just as Kenyan women became valuable couriers for the Mau Mau insurgents (as did women in Algeria), Guinean women used their networks to sell RDA membership cards, which they hid in their headscarves and under their armpits, covered with long, flowing clothing. They also sold party newspapers, distributed tracts, posted announcements of meetings, and gathered intelligence as they went about their daily lives. In addition, a few women formed violent "shock troops" in the large cities that fought against opposition members.

Since few women were literate, songs became an essential tool for mobilizing them and others who were unable to read party material or newspapers. After the colonial authorities rigged the elections in 1954, women sang at the markets that the other party had stolen the votes; by the time the results were announced, everyone knew the election had been manipulated. Like the Igbo women in 1929, their songs were often sexually suggestive, mocking and shaming the opposition and ridiculing men who refused to join the RDA. Women composed these songs spontaneously and then sang them in the market in teams. Men who refused to join them were considered to be "behaving like women."[23] Women also taunted such men by comparing them unfavorably to nationalist leader Sékou Touré, challenging them to wear their pants. After the falsified elections, women paraded across the capital city of Conakry chanting the praises of Touré and singing songs that characterized his rival as a "dog" and uncircumcised, the worst insult to an adult man. Unlike Ransome-Kuti in Nigeria, these women firmly believed that men should "wear the pants," with women showing courage and initiative only if men refused to do so.

As in most nationalist movements, women's active participation could lead to domestic tension and open clashes. While some husbands supported their wives' political activities, others strongly opposed this challenge to their control over their wives. These disputes led to increases in wife-beating and divorce; men taking additional, more subservient, wives; and misrepresentations of the RDA as a refuge for prostitutes, divorced women, and loose women. But these accusations did not deter most women, some of whom threatened to refuse to have sexual relationships with husbands who would not join the party.

Yet, as historian Elizabeth Schmidt concludes, women took on traditionally male roles during the independence struggle because of unusual circumstances that thwarted their ability to fulfill their obligations to their families. In the end, however, they sought to recreate a society that allowed them to resume their accepted positions as mothers, traders, and caretakers, not to challenge social practices that accepted women's inferiority and inequality.

[23] Elizabeth Schmidt, "'Emancipate Your Husbands!' Women and Nationalism in Guinea, 1953–1958," in *Women in Colonial African Histories*, eds Jean Allman, Susan Geiger, and Nakanyike Musisi (Bloomington: Indiana University Press, 2002), 288.

Cameroon: petitioning for freedom

In Cameroon, like Tanzania a former German colony ruled as a United Nations mandate, the main nationalist group, the UPC, Union des populations du Cameroun (Union of the Peoples of Cameroon) was a leftist party with a revolutionary ideology. Inclusive in its membership, the UPC spanned class, ethnic, and regional boundaries and embraced women as equal partners in the struggle for independence. It also sought to merge the British- and French-ruled parts of the country. With ties to international anti-imperialist organizations, Cameroonian women followed the path of Funmilayo Ransome-Kuti and came under the influence of WIDF, the Women's International Democratic Federation. In 1951, after accepting an invitation to travel to Vienna to take part in planning a conference on the rights of children, women founded their own organization, the Union démocratique des femmes camerounaises (Democratic Union of Cameroonian Women, the UDEFEC). They also joined with the UPC to launch the Écoles des Cadres, a school to train a new generation of administrators and civil servants.

In the course of the independence struggle, which turned violent in 1955, women leaders remained on an equal footing with men, aggressively voicing their concerns internationally through the thousands of petitions they sent to the United Nations Trusteeship Council. Many of their grievances concerned the ways that colonial policies had restricted women's economic independence and, by encouraging male migration, disrupted fertility patterns. Rural women, seeking to restore control over the fertility of the land, sought the right to grow coffee and to be given agricultural machinery. In the Grassfields region, where women were the primary farmers, they relied on established village associations known as *fombuen* or *anlu* to take more militant action. By digging up roads and planting them with crops women activists could block French troops and military vehicles, while also by-passing traditional constraints on where to plant their fields.

As the movement expanded in the countryside and larger numbers of men disappeared (whether exiled, in hiding, or in prison), fears about women's fertility transformed into more general alarm about Western biomedicine and rumors of campaigns to defeat nationalism by harming babies and expectant mothers. Although earlier in the struggle women's leaders had pressed for the expansion of prenatal care and birthing clinics, they now began to refuse treatment at European medical facilities, to distrust injections, and to perceive doctors as sources of infection. As violence escalated in French-ruled parts of the country and stories of rape and torture of women escalated, so did heightened fears about a colonial project to exterminate nationalist supporters. Gradually, UDEFEC members came to see both European administrations and missions as sources of ill health, infertility, and death. In this view, independence would restore abundance and well-being to society.

In Cameroon, as elsewhere, women identified as mothers and wives in ways that empowered them to play a full role in ending colonial rule. More than in many other nationalist struggles, however, they were both active and independent in relating to their male counterparts. This difference resulted, in part, from the revolutionary ideology of the UPC that envisaged dramatic social and political change as a result of independence. In the course of the struggle women also politicized issues of agricultural and reproductive fertility and began to reclaim motherhood and birthing practices as acts of resistance to colonial rule. In the opinion of historian Meredith Terretta, for the neocolonial government that took office in 1960, excluding women from government was integral to staunching the radical social and economic change that the UPC and the UDEFEC had envisaged.

Conclusion

The involvement of some educated women in nationalist struggles followed the standard narrative of independence movements – that elite Africans facing the strictures of colonial society and government (such as Ransome-Kuti or Waiyaki Otieno) rebelled in order to create political systems in which they could move into privileged positions in place of Europeans. But taking women into account expands and counters this top-down view of decolonization to include peasant women, traders, domestic and factory workers, and members of dance societies and village associations. Their mobilization and leadership challenges narrow male-oriented narratives of African nationalism in the 1940 and 1950s as a call for self-government by a small elite class. Rather, the movements that engaged women were popular protests, often risky, that supported nationalist struggles to express women's hopes of a better life for themselves and their families. Though women's equality was rarely the primary concern of women activists, in

Nigeria, the conservatism of northern politicians prompted a call for women's suffrage and one of the country's most prominent nationalist leaders, Ransome-Kuti, identified herself as a feminist. Cameroonian nationalists embraced a revolutionary ideology that treated women as equals. In South Africa, a broad-based multiracial women's organization issued a wide-ranging Women's Charter calling for gender equality, although since all blacks were disenfranchised, African women were most concerned with ending apartheid pass laws that were destroying family life.

By the mid 1960s, the nationalist phase of Africa's history had concluded for most of the continent and a majority of countries began a new period of self-government, with more or less interference by former colonial powers. Yet just as some European historians have posed the question "Did Women Have a Renaissance?" historians of Africa may justifiably ask whether and how "independence" applied to African women. To what extent did women attain greater power over their own lives in these newly independent countries; how did norms and expectations change to reflect women's contributions to the struggles for independence; and how did the pervasive ideologies of motherhood and domesticity affect their political participation in a new era? Adding another dimension to women's politics, the events of this period included not only newly installed African governments, but also continuing struggles for liberation in white settler societies and Portuguese colonies and the emergence of a strong transnational women's movement.

5

The struggle continues

In 1960, three years before Kenyan nationalists declared victory in their struggle for independence, a young Kikuyu woman, Wangari Maathai, was among a small group of students selected to study at American universities. The committee had chosen well. After earning her BA at Mount St Scholastica College in Atchison, Kansas Maathai went on to earn a master's degree in biology at the University of Pittsburgh. In 1971, she became the first east or central African woman to receive a PhD – a degree in anatomy from the University of Nairobi (then the University College of Nairobi). Her education launched her on a stellar career as a university professor; the founder of a pioneering environmental group, the Green Belt Movement; and, in 2004, the first African woman to win the Nobel Peace Prize.

But the struggles Maathai faced when she returned to Kenya in 1966 reflected the experience of many women in the postindependence decades. In her autobiography, she wrote of her six years in America:

> The United States prepared me to be confident … to critique what was happening at home, including what women were experiencing. My years in the United States overlapped with the beginnings of the women's movement and even though many women were still bound to traditional ideas about themselves at that time, I came to see that as an African woman I was perhaps even more constrained in what I could do or think, or even hope for. This was to come into sharper

perspective when I returned to Kenya in 1966, thinking the sky was the limit for me.[1]

Instead of limitless opportunities, Maathai confronted innumerable professional and personal challenges. As a faculty member in the School of Veterinary Medicine at the University of Nairobi, she discovered that married women were denied the full housing, health insurance, and pension benefits of their male colleagues. She also realized the cultural disadvantages of her education, the "unspoken problem" as she put it, "that I and not my husband had a Ph.D. and taught in the university."[2] When her husband, a Member of Parliament, suddenly left her and sued for divorce, he justified his actions during the contentious, highly publicized trial by describing Maathai as "too educated, too strong, too successful, too stubborn, and too hard to control."[3] Following an interview for *Viva* magazine in which Maathai argued that, with flimsy grounds for granting her husband a divorce, the judge must be either incompetent or corrupt, she was sentenced to six months in jail for contempt of court, a penalty later reduced to three days. When she decided to stand for a seat in Parliament in a by-election in 1982, at a time when there were only two women elected MPs, Maathai was forced to resign her position at the university. Political officials found a technicality to keep her off the ballot; but the university refused to rehire her, alleging within twelve hours of her resignation that she had been replaced. She was devastated, with no job, no salary, little savings, and on the verge of eviction from her house. "I was forty-one years old," she wrote, "and for the first time in decades I had nothing to do. I was down to zero."[4] Shortly thereafter, the successes of her new environmental movement began to transform her life once again, but also led her into new, more contentious, clashes with the government.

Struggles for independence had drawn many women into new forms of political activity, heightening their expectations for a better life. But, as Maathai discovered, African self-rule no more solved women's problems than it did other pressing dilemmas of poverty, economic dependency, or competition for scarce resources. Neither the Western political

[1] Wangari Muta Maathai, *Unbowed: A Memoir* (New York: Anchor Books, 2007), 96.
[2] Maathai, *Unbowed*, 139.
[3] Maathai, *Unbowed*, 146.
[4] Maathai, *Unbowed*, 163.

models that shaped early independence governments nor the one-party states that emerged shortly thereafter were concerned with women's public roles. Focused especially on national unity, leaders assumed that their goals of modernization and improved social services would benefit women and men alike. Furthermore, the emphasis on domesticity that had enhanced women's status during the postwar period now locked them into a network of apolitical organizations and strategies. Nonetheless, the early decades of independence coincided with the continuing struggles for liberation in southern Africa and the Portuguese colonies and the emergence of an energized international women's movement under the auspices of the United Nations. Both sets of events contributed to reshaping gender politics in new and challenging ways.

During the 1960s, despite increasing female literacy and improved educational standards, few women rose to party leadership or to positions as elected officials. In the 1970s and into the 1980s, with falling prices for African commodities and widespread political instability across the continent, women's marginalization deepened. Their economic situation was particularly dire in areas of southern Africa still under white domination. Economic and political crises sharpened tensions between men and women, as did state assaults on women's rights. Conflicts intensified during the 1980s when military coups, economic collapse, and structural adjustment programs imposed by the World Bank and the International Monetary Fund forced African states to cut their employment rolls, eliminate agricultural subsidies, and trim spending on medical care, housing, and education. Women bore the brunt of these reforms, in part because their roles as mothers made them more dependent than men on social programs. When household income dropped, they tended to absorb the shock, cutting their own consumption and increasing their workload to make up for the losses. As infant malnutrition and mortality rose, more women died in childbirth and poverty became increasingly feminized. In this increasingly difficult climate, many women grew more critical of government policies and officially sanctioned women's organizations.

"Development" for women?

In the brief postindependence euphoria of the 1960s, the "development" programs designed to transform and modernize African economies tended to view women's subsistence farming as "backward"

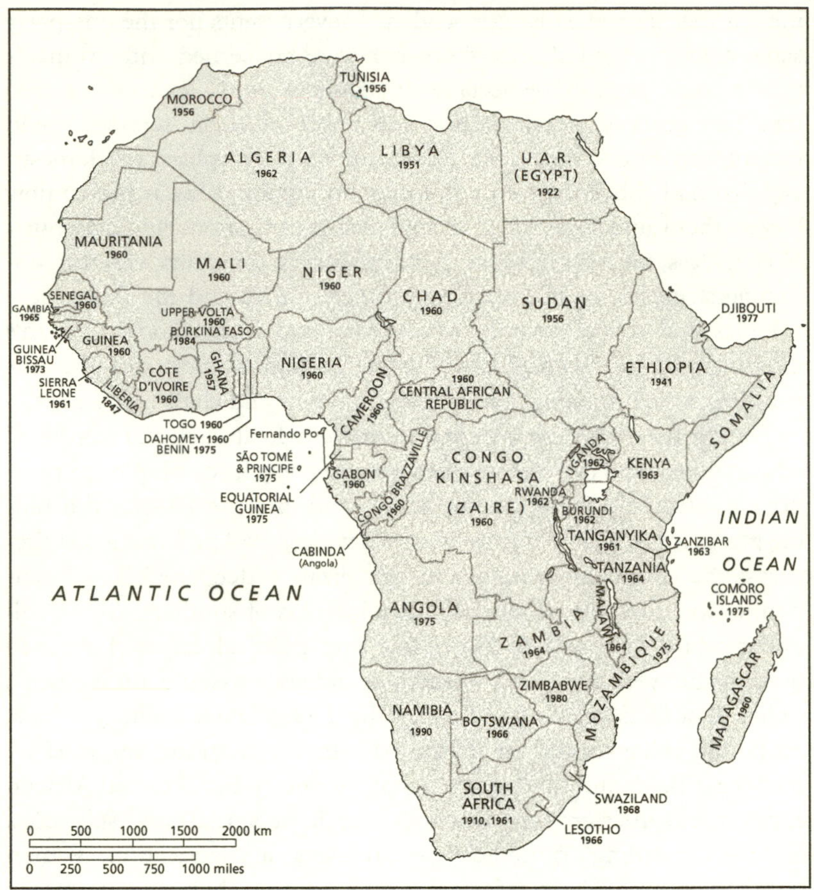

MAP 3 Independent Africa.
Source: From Robert W. July, *History of the African People Fourth Edition* (Waveland Press, 1992).

and to aim at increasing the production of cash crops at the expense of food production. These plans generally took for granted the division of labor between women and men established under colonial rule. Even from the1970s onward, when the UN Decade for Women and the widespread food crisis generated greater sensitivity to the plight of women, most projects continued to ignore women's central role in farming just as colonial interventions had done decades earlier.

Programs to rationalize and privatize individual holdings by registering and consolidating land were particularly detrimental to women;

in several cases documented for Kenya, such projects deprived all but a small percentage of women of any independent access to land. In the Luo area of western Kenya, for example, by the late 1970s women held only 5 percent of individual land titles, and the government planned no provisions to establish access rights for other women. Similarly, in the initial postindependence Tanzanian settlement schemes, land and all its proceeds went to the husband, and calculations of labor time took no account of women's domestic responsibilities. Although officials who established the later collective (*ujamaa*) villages responded to criticism and provided for women's rights to land, they remained disadvantaged in access to labor and decision-making power. In west Africa, where small-holder farmers increased their production for both local and international markets after independence, many rural women struggled to feed their families on increasingly marginal land with little help from male relatives. Forced to expand their trading activities in order to survive, they increased their workload without escaping from poverty.

The negative consequences of these attitudes and policies were striking. Women continued to have more limited access to land than men and their small parcels were less fertile and produced lower crop yields. Furthermore, legal barriers to women's land ownership persisted as did their lack of access to credit and to agricultural extension services. New technology, rather than improving women's lives, often increased their workload without producing tangible benefits.

One study that compared three development projects in the west African nation of Gambia found that all three assumed that male household heads controlled land, labor, and crops and would redistribute any increased income gained from technological changes in rice production. By focusing exclusively on men and on investments in expensive, capital-intensive irrigation, these projects discounted women's valuable expertise and increased their economic dependence. Improving women's rain-fed and swamp rice, the alternative to large-scale irrigation, would have been far cheaper. Informal discussions with women revealed their great disappointment when they learned that the Taiwanese technicians planning the study intended only to deal with men. By-passing women in these schemes left them with two equally unattractive options, either badgering male relatives to lend them irrigated land to grow rice during the dry season or working for wages on men's plots.

Responses to environmental crises in Mali document the ways that unanticipated events influenced the lives and choices of rural women in complex, though more ambiguous, ways. As in other countries on the southern fringe of the Sahara Desert, severe drought in 1972–4 coincided with rising energy prices and internationally mandated cuts in government funding for social services. Another drought in 1983–4 exacerbated the emergency, causing 30,000–50,000 refugees to flee southward; they joined the 22,500 people relocated from 1979 onward to accommodate two major dam-building projects. Although men in Mali did the majority of the grain and commercial farming, women required land to grow vegetables, peanuts, and spices. Resettled women, with less access to land than in their former homes, compensated by gathering wild plants from the forest and preparing them for sale, or by trading in fish and grain. But, with forest areas shrinking, in part because of resettlement, many poor women were forced into more casual labor, selling firewood, doing seasonal work on tea plantations, or washing clothes or grinding grain for more prosperous families. Throughout all these crises, male politicians responded by encouraging men to grow more lucrative crops. As resettled households came to rely more on nuclear families than on the wider kinship networks in their former homes, husbands and wives needed to collaborate more closely than in the past, making women increasingly dependent on men.

In Zambia, with a long history of women's unequal access to agricultural training and resources, women's projects after independence were left to the understaffed Home Economics Section of the Department of Agriculture; excluded from important training programs, women had difficulty accessing land and credit. In addition, widespread illiteracy among rural women persisted, marriages under customary law continued to define women as legal minors, and women married under British civil law had no rights to their husbands' property. Only after the UN Decade for Women was launched in 1975 did the government begin to acknowledge the severe problems that confronted rural women; but by then the state had neither the capacity nor the commitment to respond effectively.

Hoping to improve their lives and escape from the heavy labor involved in farming, increasing numbers of women migrated to cities in the years following independence. By 1980, 30–35 percent of all Africans (including north Africans) resided in urban centers, as compared to 13 percent in 1950. The lives of most urban women changed little, however, either economically or in terms of negative attitudes that blamed women for the "corruption" of family life and viewed them solely as mothers and wives whose sexuality should be controlled within the family. Often single heads of household, they persisted in independent, casual labor (especially market trading), and performed a variety of activities to feed their families. They also continued rural patterns of growing food crops on any patches of available land. Families that remained in the countryside often sent young girls to relatives' homes in town, with assurances (often unfulfilled) that they would be sent to school in exchange for assisting with domestic work and childcare. Despite the low earnings of most women, their income was often critical to family survival. One study in Sudan found that 80 percent of market vendors were the sole or major support of their families.

By comparison with men, only a small number of women found wage-paying employment, a few in professional positions as nurses, teachers, or office workers, but many others in low-paying positions in domestic service. Especially in apartheid South Africa, household workers faced extreme vulnerability and powerlessness, an absence of bargaining power, and time demands that created tremendous tension between their roles as mothers and as wage earners. As the most vulnerable members of urban communities, poor women were often easy targets for overzealous campaigns against prostitution, vagrancy, unlicensed trading, and beer-brewing. Women and children also continued to be among the main victims of South African laws to clear the cities of those whose labor was not needed by whites.

Women faced the most extreme deprivation in the rural areas of southern Africa (some still under white rule), where male migrant workers were absent for months or even years at a time, and in other regions (such as Ethiopia) during periodic famines – when starving women and children crowded into relief camps. Extreme poverty and malnutrition, few opportunities to earn income, and high rates of infant mortality devastated the impoverished South African homelands. One such community gained notoriety through a widely distributed film, *Last Grave at Dimbaza*, that showed half the children dying before the age of five. In neighboring Lesotho, where 95 percent of wage earners worked in South Africa and 70 percent of rural households were, in effect, managed by women, their agricultural activities yielded little cash and insufficient food for subsistence. Women here survived thanks to occasional remittances from men employed in the mines and factories of South Africa, bridewealth payments, beer-brewing, petty trade, and informal sexual relationships. This system created both material and emotional misery and placed women in a situation more similar to that of poor urban women than to that of more prosperous rural women.

Though industrialization was relatively limited outside South Africa, increasing numbers of women in a few other countries also began to work in factories. Their jobs were low-paying and semiskilled (as in the rural areas of South Africa); they usually worked with textiles, clothing, or food, and were likely to be replaced by men when mechanization occurred. In Swaziland, in the shadow of South Africa, small cottage industries spinning cotton and producing textiles and garments opened in rural areas and on the urban periphery. Though deriving some income from the low-wage, nonunionized jobs, virtually all the women surveyed in the 1980s also grew cash and food crops on extended family land to supplement their pay.

Other countries in southern Africa also began to develop large-scale textile factories during the 1980s. By the early 1990s, the clothing and textile industries in Lesotho were becoming increasingly important to the economy, partly as a way for international investors to by-pass sanctions against apartheid South Africa, which for decades had monopolized the region's production of clothing and fabric. Also, as in the rural areas of South Africa, Taiwanese and other Asian investors became increasingly critical to developing textile and other manufacturing, relying primarily on the cheap labor of women. By 1990, 92 percent of all employees in these factories were women, a result of their low wages combined with stereotypical myths of women's manual dexterity and docility as workers and, in Lesotho, a female literacy rate of 70 percent, among the highest in Africa. As demand for men's labor in the South African mines decreased during the 1980s, large numbers of women urgently needed employment to support their families.

The experience of one young Hausa woman who lived just outside the northern Nigerian city of Kaduna illustrates both the continuing constraints and the new possibilities of urban life. After independence Kaduna expanded into a major political, commercial, and industrial center, attracting six large textile factories, a Peugeot assembly plant, and factories producing fertilizer and refining oil and gas. By 1985, with a population of 600,000, the city was growing at an annual rate of 9–11 percent. This rapid economic expansion attracted a heterogeneous population of migrants from all over the country.

Binta, born in the late colonial period, lived in the predominantly Hausa-Fulani community of Unguwan Kanawa just outside of Kaduna. As a young girl, she attended Quranic school and hawked food on the streets for her mother. Her first marriage, when she was twelve or thirteen, lasted only five years; following Hausa custom, her former husband retained custody of their two children. During this time, she was secluded. After the divorce, she met and married a railway worker. By the mid 1980s, Binta had borne three more children, was pregnant with a fourth, and remained his only wife. No longer secluded, she earned her living selling clothing, jewelry, and food in the market and also working for a senior female patron from whom she received gifts. She earned additional income as a commission agent, buying and selling goods on behalf of her patron's husband.

Regretting that she never attended secular school, living in a diverse city allowed Binta the possibility to continue her education and to move freely through the city and the surrounding area. In 1983, she began to spend two hours daily attending a new Islamic school, where she learned to read in Hausa and Arabic, and also studied English. Although many of her friends remained in purdah, the urban environment allowed her the space to live more freely, thereby pushing the boundaries of women's roles. During the severe recession that followed the international oil crisis of 1982, Binta's earnings became increasingly critical in helping to support her family.

Education

One postindependence change that would eventually underpin great improvement in women's lives was the expansion of Western education. In the 1960s, the numbers of girls with access to schooling varied greatly across the continent. In independent English-speaking countries large numbers of girls attended secondary school by the 1960s and 1970s. The numbers were smaller in francophone regions, both as a result of lingering colonial policy and, in many places (as in formerly British northern Nigeria), a large Muslim population opposed to educating girls. While South Africa led other parts of the continent in female literacy before the Second World War, it fell behind under apartheid. Less gender specific in their policies, the Portuguese colonies resisted the education of all Africans.

Although the widespread growth of Western education was among the most positive developments of the early independence years, across the continent girls were still less likely than boys to go to school or to remain in school beyond the primary level. In 1988, girls made up 44 percent of primary school enrollment in sub-Saharan Africa, 34 percent of enrollment in secondary school, and 21 percent at the tertiary level. With school fees a major expense for most families, girls could be more valuable working on family farms or in the market, whereas investing in boys' education was more likely to lead to wage-paying jobs. There were also negative consequences of schooling. In west Africa, where many urban women tried to educate their daughters in order to increase their own economic security in old age, educated girls missed out on potential apprenticeships with women traders and other self-employed women, denying these traders valuable assistance, and depriving educated women of economic skills they might need even with their formal learning.

Despite extensive inequities, expanded schooling for girls, combined with the Africanization of positions in government and industry, led to increasing numbers of women in wage-earning work. Yet one study of five countries from the mid 1980s showed women in only 14 percent of positions outside of agriculture. Many of women's professional jobs were in stereotypically female fields such as teaching, nursing and midwifery, secretarial work, and social work, although during the colonial period, men had monopolized clerical work and held more teaching positions than women. In Kenya, where women made up roughly 30 percent of university students in the 1980s, like male graduates, most women found work in the public sector and earned only slightly less than men in comparable positions. Nonetheless, few women attained the highest-paid positions and, once women married, like Wangari Maathai they lost the housing allowance granted to other state employees.

Politics: a male preserve?

Politically, the first decades after national independence also were disappointing for women, many of whom had high hopes that their lives would improve under newly Africanized governments. Pumla

Kisosonkole, a South African then living in Uganda (and in 1956, the first woman on the Legislative Council) articulated these hopes in a 1962 speech:

> These days the cry of the "role of women" is being heard in Africa from East to West, and from North to South. What is the answer for East Africa? It is this: times have changed and are changing very fast, and the woman must change with them in order that she does not become the "forgotten factor" ... and [she] will be ready and willing to play the fullest part in shaping the destinies of her country.[5]

Many new states sought to meet these expectations by expanding education and health care and investing in economic development. Yet, few national constitutions specifically outlawed gender discrimination, many exempted family and customary law from constitutional regulation, and few male politicians made a serious effort to increase women's political participation in government. Nowhere did women regain the authority they had held in the precolonial political systems in which women's and men's councils each managed their own spheres of influence. As one-party states and military regimes proliferated throughout the continent, they often channeled women's votes and energy through official women's organizations headed by the wife (or other relatives) of the head of state and party leaders.

In most countries, women's participation in the political process was restricted to the local level, and many male politicians found women to be convenient scapegoats for their own shortcomings. At various times women were blamed for divorce, illegitimacy, and the "loss of African customs," leaving young urban women particularly open to verbal and physical abuse for wearing mini-skirts, makeup, or foreign styles. Women attained a political voice most often where men were absent, as in Lesotho, where most men between eighteen and forty-five spent twelve to eighteen months at a time working in the South African mines. Rural Basotho women had strong female village networks and were represented disproportionately in village development committees, theoretically vehicles for people to communicate with the government. Yet since families relied primarily on

[5] Quoted in Margaret C. Snyder and Mary Tadesse, *African Women in Development: A History* (London: Zed Books, 1995), 28–29.

men's income to improve their lives, most women felt that their roles as wives promised a better chance of access to valued resources than public participation.

Even where national politicians tried to increase women's involvement in nation-building and development, they generally conceptualized women in terms of domestic rather than economic activities and channeled state funding through community development and social welfare agencies. This "women in development" approach was intended to create and sustain depoliticized and conservative women's organizations that supported ruling party initiatives rather than advocating for women's rights. In Tanzania, for example, women's interests remained marginal in debates over public policy. The Third Five Year Development Plan, adopted in 1976, included no projects focused on women, despite its primary goal of creating self-sufficiency in food production.

Furthermore, the female activists so critical to the success of TANU in the 1950s nearly all disappeared from the political scene. With limited formal education, most were unsuited to assume positions in the new government and returned to the casual pursuits of other urban women of their class – selling fruits, vegetables, and prepared foods or making clothing, brewing local beer, running small restaurants, and renting property. Just as the dependence of Umoja wa Wanawake wa Tanzania (the Union of Women of Tanzania) on TANU muted women's voices in Tanzania, after the 1974 revolution in Ethiopia, rural women's organizations were subordinated to larger peasant associations. These groups, designated by the ruling military committees to promote development and manage land reform, had little interest in women's perspectives. Similarly, in Kenya, the ruling party gradually coopted Maendeleo ya Wanawake (Women's Progress), the dominant women's organization. Although made up of 20,000 member groups, by 1987 it was fully under the control of the ruling political party, KANU (the Kenya African National Union), and the organization was confined to such nonpolitical activities as handicrafts and agricultural techniques, improving childcare, promoting literacy, and engaging in sports.

The Kenyan example graphically illustrates women's difficulties in breaking into political life. When Ruth Habwe, the first woman to stand for a seat in Parliament, failed to receive KANU support in 1966, she was suspended from the party for running as an independent. MPs told her to "go back to the kitchen and cook for Mr. Habwe's children."[6] From then on few women were elected to Parliament, and those who succeeded were marginalized in decision making. In 1975, one Kenyan minister closed an International Women's Year Seminar by telling his all-woman audience, "I am forced to believe that the woman is lazy in her mind ... You women think and believe that you are inferior to men ... It is a psychological problem and 99.9% of women suffer from it."[7] Only in the 1980s did a few women earn high-level judicial and administrative appointments, although these appointees did not necessarily support or implement policies to end discrimination against women. The queue voting method, used in the 1988 general elections, was particularly detrimental to women standing for office since a husband might instruct his wife and other family members not to line up behind a female candidate.

The authoritarian governments that seized power through frequent military coups, mainly (but not exclusively) in west and central Africa, had a decidedly mixed record on women's rights. Uganda's military ruler Idi Amin banned all independent women's organizations and in 1978 established the National Council of Women to serve as an umbrella organization to oversee his control of existing women's groups. In Nigeria, however, a military government was able to defy longstanding local objections and in 1976 granted women in the Islamic north the right to vote.

More generally, these governments tended to manipulate gender norms in ways that were detrimental to women, often by setting them up as scapegoats in times of economic and political crisis. In the 1970s, Mobutu Sese Seko, the military ruler of the Democratic Republic of Congo (then Zaire), sought to legitimize his repressive regime by formulating an ideology of *authenticité* that he touted as a return to authentic, "traditional" African values. These values included a male-dominated state under the complete control of its ruler in which "authentic" women were to be mothers and housekeepers who obeyed the authority of their husbands, male family members, and, ultimately, the President. Women were responsible for the system of morality, however, and had to be reformed and policed if

[6] *Drum*, November 1966, quoted in Jim Bailey, *Kenya: The National Epic*, compiled and edited by Carole Cooper (Nairobi: Westlands Publications, 1993), 176.

[7] From Maria N. Nzomo, "Kenyan Women in Politics and Public Decision Making," in *African Feminism: The Politics of Survival in Sub-Saharan Africa*, ed. Gwendolyn Mikell (Philadelphia: University of Pennsylvania Press, 1997), 236.

they deviated from their designated subordinate roles. Furthermore, Mobutu decreed that women had achieved full emancipation under his rule and took any criticism as a direct challenge to his authority. In a 1982 speech, he emphasized his government's commitment to improving the status of women and granting them equal rights, but warned that "there will always be one head in each household. And until proof to the contrary, the head, in our country, is he who wears the pants. Our women citizens also ought to understand this, to accept it with a smile and revolutionary submission."[8]

Similarly, the Federal Military Government that seized power in Nigeria in 1984–5 at a time of declining oil revenues, attributed the crisis to "indisciplined" groups in society, including working wives and mothers (charged with neglecting their children), single women (considered prostitutes), and petty traders (accused of hoarding goods). Acting on these charges, and inspired by an ideology that assumed that women's proper place was at home, the government sent soldiers to the markets to beat female traders in an effort to force them to lower their prices. Paradoxically, however, in both Congo and Nigeria, governments that claimed to be sustaining "tradition" by holding women responsible for morality also characterized small-scale subsistence farming as a "backward" sector of the economy that should be replaced by cash crop farming and industrialization.

A similar situation prevailed in Cameroon where the Women's Cameroon National Union (WCNU) was an extension of the ruling party, the Cameroon National Union Party. In the 1960s, using the pretext of building national unity and destroying "tribalism," the government banned all independent women's organizations and prohibited the WCNU from developing an independent agenda. Their constitution confined them to discussing social issues such as family planning, juvenile delinquency, prostitution, housekeeping, being a good mother, and individual and household hygiene. These women also provided entertainment at party-organized parades and rallies and catered political events and celebrations.

This widespread cooptation of women's groups effectively crippled their leadership and channeled women into mobilizing around a

[8] Catherine Newbury and Brooke Grundfest Schoepf, "State, Peasantry, and Agrarian Crisis in Zaire," in *Women and the State in Africa*, eds Jane L. Parpart and Kathleen A. Staudt (Boulder, CO: Lynne Reinner, 1990), 102.

narrow set of issues. The focus was on top-down strategies that benefited only a small group of privileged urban women at the expense of rural and poor urban women. While built by drawing on a wide base of support from grassroots women, these patronage-based women's organizations, with close personal connections to the national leaders, were often out-of-touch with rural women, and acted patronizingly toward them. A key example was the Better Life for Rural Women Programme (BLP) launched by Nigeria's military regime under Ibrahim Babangida and headed by his wife Maryam Babangida, assisted by the wives of other prominent political figures. The group's \$18 million funds between 1987 and 1992 went mainly for offices, vehicles, salaries, and overseas travel. These party-affiliated and funded organizations became gatekeepers of women's admission into politics, restricting women's political activities and their ability to define and mobilize around their own issues.

The situation in Zambia illustrates these themes once again as another country where women's political voice was muted after independence. With the change in 1973 from a multiparty to a single-party political system, women's issues gained greater attention, however. In efforts that coincided with the UN Decade for Women, the Women's League was granted formal representation on the Central Committee of UNIP (United National Independence Party) and drew up an ambitious Ten-Year Programme of Action that emphasized equality and development and began a process of granting women and women's issues greater representation on the Central Committee. With a chapter on Women in Development incorporated into the national development plan, UNIP became increasingly active in efforts (not always successful) to improve rural women's access to healthcare, education, and improved housing and water supplies.

During this period, however, many factors hampered progress in confronting women's inequality, including high rates of female illiteracy, limited educational and employment opportunities, and the widespread belief that women should confine themselves to being wives and mothers. As in Nigeria, class and cultural divisions among women also inhibited meaningful change. The party-affiliated Women's League was dominated by less-educated urban women, mainly petty traders, who gained much of their prestige from being wives of UNIP men. They showed little sympathy for educated, single urban women whom party leaders sought to control by labeling them prostitutes and barring them from public places without male escorts.

Rather than uniting on the basis of gender, the Women's League joined party officials in blaming urban women for economic decline, moral decay, and undermining traditional values. By the late 1980s, however, new forces were at work, with more educated women forming innovative advocacy organizations, international NGOs bringing new pressures on local governments, and a few experts in Women and Development in key ministries encouraging greater sensitivity to women's issues.

Thus, by the end of the 1980s, while women's opportunities had improved somewhat since independence, they still trailed men substantially in their access to resources; in addition, discriminatory laws governing marriage and inheritance remained common, and laws that protected women were rarely enforced. Significant change was impeded both by the small numbers of women in policy-making positions and by both women and men accepting male dominance of public life. Nonetheless, economic crisis; pressure from articulate, educated women; and the international women's movement continued to create conditions conducive to change.

One exception to these patterns was a short-lived experiment in the revolutionary government of Thomas Sankara, a young military officer in Burkina Faso. An outspoken Marxist and pan-Africanist, Sankara seized power in 1983 along with a group of other officers and civilian activists. They ruled until Sankara was assassinated in a French-backed coup in 1987. From the start, women's emancipation was among the high priorities of the new government. Their interests were specifically included in social and economic programs promoting literacy, health care, and marketing cooperatives. Creating more controversy, the new family code sought to curb bridewealth, establish a minimum age for marriage, and allow divorce by mutual consent. It also recognized the rights of widows to inherit land and attempted to end the practice by which a widow was forced to marry one of her husbands' brothers. Other government-sponsored campaigns aimed to end female genital cutting, forced marriage, and polygyny. Although many of these efforts faced strong opposition, sometimes from both women and men, Sankara's government also took innovative, less controversial steps to empower women politically, appointing them to cabinet positions and to other high political offices and as judges, provincial commissioners, and directors of state enterprises.

Women, war, and liberation

Equally significant in contesting the status quo were the armed struggles for liberation that coincided with the early decades of independence. Challenging the respectable domesticity that infused many women's groups, their widespread imagery of women combatants holding a baby in one arm and a machine gun in the other announced a militant conception of mothers as freedom fighters. The violence of daily life and the recruitment of women as fighters also tested older conventions of gender relations in deeper ways than earlier, more peaceful, nationalist movements and led many women combatants to pose new questions about the pervasiveness of male domination.

Throughout southern Africa, where large numbers of white settlers had attained power under colonial governments, and in the Portuguese colonies of Mozambique, Angola, and Guinea-Bissau, independence (and in South Africa democratic elections) came later than elsewhere and only through armed conflict. During the same period, Eritrea, a former Italian colony federated with Ethiopia since 1952 and annexed a decade later, also was engaged in an armed struggle for independence. In all these cases, to varying degrees, women were incorporated into armed units, and their specific concerns entered public political discourse, although they generally remained underrepresented in leadership positions. Alongside the armed underground struggle, grassroots women's groups in South Africa provided the impetus for a succession of political organizations, including the Black Women's Federation, formed and banned in the mid 1970s; regional women's groups during the 1980s; and the Women's Section of the outlawed African National Congress (ANC). Women in the Eritrean People's Liberation Front (EPLF), struggling for autonomy from Ethiopia, were particularly successful in promoting gender-balanced land reform, education for Muslim girls and women, and more egalitarian marriage relationships in the areas under the movement's control (Figure 4).

In the national liberation movements that brought independence to Mozambique and Zimbabwe, Frelimo (the Front for the Liberation of Mozambique) and ZANU (the Zimbabwe African National Union) voiced support for liberating women from what they characterized as the degrading and inhibiting aspects of both "customary" practices (such as polygyny and bridewealth) and the colonial heritage of

FIGURE 4 A Muslim woman fighter in the Eritrean People's Liberation Front carrying a Russian-made Kalashnikov AK-47 rifle. The EPLF, which fought for independence from Ethiopia from the mid 1970s until 1991, was committed to women's equality and their participation in the armed struggle. Toward the end of the war, women made up 35–40 percent of EPLF members and 25 percent of frontline troops.
Source: Getty Images/Alex Bowie.

women's subordination. In both movements, women (mainly young and educated at least through primary school) took part in the military struggle and engaged in fighting and other support activities in significant numbers. "Without the women," in the words of one recent study of Zimbabwe, "the war could not have been won."[9]

Yet recent research suggests that conditions on the ground did not live up to the rhetoric of gender equity, which was often tailored to

[9] Irene Staunton, *Mothers of the Revolution: The War Experiences of Thirty Zimbabwean Women* (Bloomington: Indiana University Press, 1990), xii.

international supporters, and that struggles over pregnancy and sexuality became predominant preoccupations for both female and male freedom fighters. Furthermore, following the struggle, party leaders returned to older perceptions of women's place, seeing the goal of government programs as assisting them to be better mothers within the existing family structure. When a rural woman in 1994 suggested that land permits in resettled areas be registered jointly in the names of both spouses, President Robert Mugabe retorted, "If women want property, then they should not get married."[10] Many women remained politicized, however, and continued to be involved in the lower ranks of ZANU and in spontaneous political activity such as rent strikes, strikes over food prices, and demonstrations over licenses for petty traders.

In Mozambique, more attuned after independence to the continuing struggle for gender equality, many women remained active in party affairs and in political and economic projects at the village level; yet because the division of household labor remained unchanged, the new situation burdened them with a triple weight of work in food production, home, and politics. Nonetheless, sustained pressure from Frelimo and from the Organization of Mozambican Women created a favorable environment for change until the war and famine of the 1980s and early 1990s made continuing social transformation impossible.

The life story of Teckla Shikola illustrates how women were drawn into these armed struggles. Born in Namibia (South West Africa), then under the illegal rule of apartheid South Africa, Shikola found the liberation war impossible to escape. The lengthy conflict lasted from 1966 until the country won formal independence in 1991. Women were active in all aspects of SWAPO (the South West Africa People's Organization), including as combatants in PLAN, the People's Liberation Army of Namibia. In 1977, when she was sixteen years old, Shikola fled Namibia, in part to escape the South African soldiers who came to her school and beat the students, pressuring them to join the South African military. Instead, she and several friends escaped across the border into Angola to join SWAPO. Too young to be allowed to fight, she was sent to Zambia for four years of schooling at the United

[10] A.P. Cheater and R.B. Gaidzanwa, "Citizenship in Neo-patrilineal States: Gender and Mobility in Southern Africa," *Journal of Southern African Studies* 22, 2 (1996), 200.

Nations Institute for Namibia. When she returned to Angola, Shikola underwent six months of arduous military instruction. After earning the title of commissar, she devoted part of her time to training others. Within three months, she was sent to the front and served in the army for eight years, four of them fighting in Angola and northern Namibia alongside 300-400 other women. In retrospect, she reflected: "The commanders and chiefs came to respect me. They thought they were going to ... make love to me and make me pregnant, but I was strong and now they respect me."[11] As a member of the SWAPO Women's Council, her responsibilities included checking on the women, seeing that the bases had soap and sanitary supplies, and teaching family planning. She was also sent for refresher courses, once to Bulgaria for a year of leadership training, or as she later described it, as "brain-washing in communism."[12]

As in other military camps, the sexual exploitation of women was rampant. Shikola argued that many women became pregnant because conditions were so terrible that pregnancy became an excuse to leave. Men were generally against family planning and mocked her for not having any children. The only available supplies were contraceptive pills; condoms were not available until late in the war and SWAPO opposed Depo-Provera because of rumors that the injections were being used to kill black babies. She also observed that the culture of obedience in the military fostered an acceptance of rape. Describing the training of new recruits, she explained:

> Whenever someone in charge calls you, you shouldn't refuse, you don't say no, you have to go. You feel scared of saying no, you cannot talk directly to a commander. Sometimes the chiefs would call out these poor young girls fresh from home. The chiefs made love to them, and the women became pregnant without knowing the person who impregnated them, sometimes they didn't even know his name. Some commanders had fifteen or eighteen kids. It is not really rape in a direct way as such but just the way the chiefs were.[13]

Because SWAPO cared for both the women and their children, and there was prestige in bearing the commander's child, Shikola claims

[11] Teckla Shikola, "We Left Our Shoes Behind," in *What Women Do in Wartime: Gender and Conflict in Africa*, eds Meredith Turshen and Clotilde Twagiramariya (London: Zed Press, 1998), 141.

[12] Shikola, "We Left Our Shoes Behind," 142.

[13] Shikola, "We Left Our Shoes Behind," 143.

that most women did not find the situation difficult until after the war. What she described as "real rape" occurred mainly inside Namibia where women in the villages were attacked by black forces fighting alongside the South African troops. Thus, in these wartime conditions, the line between forcible and consensual sex was often blurred and, in the midst of a lengthy period of war and violence, shifts occurred in people's perceptions of morally acceptable behavior. Contrary to her expectations, Shikola's return home was difficult in part because women's contributions to the liberation struggle were ignored. She reflected, "That's true all over the world. You never find an appreciation of what women did. Men appreciate women who cook for them, and they respect women who fought in the war with them, but after independence, they didn't really consider women as part of the liberation movement."[14]

In the liberation war in Zimbabwe, which lasted from 1972 until independence in 1980, the Zimbabwe African National Union (ZANU) did not consciously set out to transform relations between women and men. Once the new African government assumed power, however, leaders were anxious to proclaim that women had played an active role in the struggle. As elsewhere, in the early years of armed conflict women were deliberately recruited to serve as cooks, nurses, and porters. Although many of these women were sexually exploited, the party sought to elaborate and enforce puritanical rules about sexual relations and marriage that drew on ostensible "customary law" and on the teachings of Christian missionaries. As the war was ending in 1979, leaders began to voice politically progressive slogans about women's liberation and the transformation of gender relationships that bore little connection to their wartime experience, proclaiming that women had emerged from the war emancipated. Although the liberation war marked the first time in the country's history that women had fought as soldiers, as in Namibia, the majority of women fighters received little recognition for their efforts. On returning home they were classified as "refugees" rather than as "veterans," thus excluding them from veterans' benefits.

Women's participation in the liberation struggle changed over time, however. In the war's early years, they were conceptualized as

[14] Shikola, "We Left Our Shoes Behind," 148.

"mothers" who were insuring that their "sons," the guerrilla fighters, had enough to eat. Hence the slogan of the period was: "Forward with the cooking stick!" Both sides focused their propaganda campaigns around their role in protecting women from the abuses of the other side. For women themselves, most of whom had no formal education, the primary goal of the struggle was to liberate the country, not to transform gender relations.

The situation of women changed in the mid 1970s, and especially after 1975 when Mozambique's independence allowed Zimbabwe's liberation army to move from Zambia to Mozambique. This relocation made it easier for larger numbers of recruits to join the war effort, and brought Zimbabwe's leaders into closer contact with FRELIMO's Marxist ideology, which included a commitment to women's equality. Women conscripts now included greater numbers of high school leavers, nurses, and teachers whose education made them more prone to question the military hierarchy. In 1977, as part of an effort to respond to women's demand that the rhetoric of equity be matched with deeds, Joice Mujuru (who during the war assumed the name Teurai Ropa, meaning "spill blood") was appointed to the ZANU Central Committee as Secretary for Women's Affairs. The following year her unit was expanded to become the Department of Women's Affairs. Although the Department was created to represent all women, Mujuru and two of the other primary leaders, including Sally Mugabe, the wife of ZANU's President, were married to high-ranking men. Mujuru became an effective spokesperson before external audiences; but she and her aides continually reminded women of their centrality to preserving "traditional" culture and shoring up the men who were fighting. In one meeting with female comrades, she explained her position: "Since we can't go home [to the front] we have a lot of duties to do here. We came here to help keep the well-being of boys, washing their clothes, cleaning their houses and treat them when they are sick. We also have the duty of carrying material for the boys."[15]

The grievances women expressed to Mujuru and other members of the Department were varied. Responding to their sexual vulnerability in the camps, many women demanded contraceptives and refused to accept the entire blame for becoming pregnant when childbirth automatically disqualified them from military service. They also rejected

[15] Quoted in Josephine Nhongo-Simbanegavi, *For Better or Worse? Women and ZANLA in Zimbabwe's Liberation Struggle* (Harare: Weaver Press, 2000), 54.

the gender stereotyped projects of the Department of Women's Affairs, "Coming to take us from the [military] camps to sew! We thought we were going somewhere abroad either to China, Romania or elsewhere ... to be pilots or some kind of qualifications."[16]

As in Namibia, sexuality became one of the major challenges for Zimbabwe's liberation movement. Initially ZANU forbade sexual relations and marriage in the camps and in operational fields, but these guidelines were changed as more and more recruits arrived. Codes of conduct notwithstanding, it was easy for high-ranking officials to manipulate their positions, sometimes using force and targeting young women for punishment when they turned down sexual overtures, at other times exploiting girls' willingness to trade sex for scarce food and toiletries. With contraceptives generally unavailable, and women who used them branded as prostitutes, the number of pregnancies multiplied. Although the party attempted to codify its policy relating to sex and marriage in 1978, the effort to reconcile the contradictory principles of local custom, Christianity, and Marxist revolutionary ideology advocating women's equality made these guidelines difficult to reconcile and implement. The separate, isolated camp created for pregnant women ended the revolutionary careers of most women and, by its reluctance to request contraception from outside organizations, the Department of Women's Affairs passively colluded with male leaders who resisted making birth control widely available.

Although ZANLA (the Zimbabwe African National Liberation Army) celebrated women's participation throughout the struggle, there were no significant moves to include them in decision making either during the war and transition or after independence. The ideology of gender equality was mere rhetoric. At the front, women served in feminized spaces that mirrored their marginalization after the conflict ended. And even the rhetoric was geared not to changing the status quo, but to appealing to women to support the struggle as mothers and cooks. This approach was pragmatic, reflecting the leaders' care not to antagonize either local patriarchal officials or spirit mediums when they entered a new area. Indeed, support of these religious officials, who represented the spirits of the land and supported women's subordination to the men in their families, was deemed essential to the movement's survival. Only as elections loomed did ZANU rely on

[16] From Nhongo-Simbanegavi, *For Better or Worse?* 55.

former female fighters to appeal to women voters and step up the discourse of gender equality to satisfy outsider observers.

In the first elections after Zimbabwe's independence, women won 8 percent of seats in the new Parliament, with three women appointed to Cabinet posts, two at the deputy level. Not unexpectedly, Mujuru at first became the Minister of Youth, Sport and Culture and later of the newly created Ministry of Community Development and Women's Affairs, which worked closely with the Women's League. As in other postindependence countries, Women's League projects were confined to the domestic sphere and did not address women's dependence for land on husbands or other male relatives. Legal reforms designed to meet the expectations of middle-class supporters quickly followed independence, however, creating a new framework for gender equity applicable especially to the educated minority of women. The Majority Act of 1982 gave legal majority status to both women and men at age eighteen, ending their position as lifelong legal minors. Other laws granted women maternity leave and possible custody of children in the case of divorce and ended sex-based discrimination in the workplace.

The armed struggle in South Africa lasted longer than elsewhere, from the early 1960s until 1990, with democratic elections occurring only in 1994. As in other liberation movements, part of women's difficulty as fighters came from the close connection between heroism and masculinity and the tendency to identify freedom with the restoration of African manhood. Despite these images, which relegated women to supporting roles as wives, mothers, and girlfriends, numerous women joined the ranks of soldiers and underground activists. Indeed, some estimates suggest that by 1989, as the struggle neared its end, women made up about 20 percent of cadres of Mkhonto we Sizwe (MK), the Spear of the Nation, the armed wing of the African National Congress (ANC). Although these female recruits received the same political and military training as men, they acted mainly as couriers and were excluded from traditional combat roles. Their position could also be difficult. Women were constantly challenged about their place in a man's world. In a report in 1987 women complained that "comrades are in a hurry to 'privatize' women because of the shortage of women in MK."[17] Thenjiwe Mtintso elaborated that,

[17] Quoted in Shireen Hassim, *Women's Organizations and Democracy in South Africa: Contesting Authority* (Madison: University of Wisconsin Press, 2006), 98.

"camps could dull your sharp gender mind, but you also dulled it deliberately. You didn't want to look at roles as exploitative … Life is tough … you wanted to make your life as comfortable as possible … I could benefit from having a relationship with commanding personnel. If I don't, life is going to be hell. All of us experience hell, but men bring things from town, goodies."[18] During the 1980s when women were transforming other areas of the ANC, MK, which was a hierarchical and authoritarian movement, was slowest to meet demands for greater representation of women in leadership positions or to advocate for women's emancipation.

Women also played an active role in the ANC in exile, first in Tanzania and later in Zambia. Their activities centered on the Women's Section, formed in 1969 to mobilize them as active members of the organization, but also to establish child care and nursery facilities, process donations of food and clothing, and look out for the well-being and education of exiled children. Although theoretically women members of MK were forbidden to become pregnant and women deployed in Angola had IUDs inserted as a matter of policy, the growing number of pregnant women and children, especially after the influx of young people to the camps following the Soweto Uprising in 1976, demanded new policies. In the wake of this flood of young recruits, older Women's Section members found themselves acting as surrogate mothers. They were drawn into resolving personal problems, organizing recreational and cultural activities for these young girls, conducting sessions on sex education and family planning, and taking action against violent and abusive men.

Women's long history of organizing, both independently and in association with the ANC, strengthened their presence in the struggle against apartheid. During the 1980s, as the underground military campaign intensified, regional women's organizations within South Africa, loosely allied with national groups, were beginning to build their own independent structures. Influenced in part by their travels overseas (in both Western and socialist countries) and by the rise of the international women's movement, these women, and those in exile, began to discuss more actively what national liberation would mean for women. They persisted even when many male comrades treated the issue as divisive and refused to accept women's liberation as an immediate goal of the struggle.

[18] From Hassim, *Women's Organizations*, 98–99.

In the midst of this political mobilization, the Nairobi conference of the UN Decade for Women in July 1985 proved a turning point, giving South African women in exile the opportunity to meet directly with activists within the country. Together these women led the opposition to the official delegates from the United States, who argued that apartheid and Palestinian rights should not be seen as women's issues, but as "political" questions that did not belong on the conference agenda. This controversy helped South African women to clarify their position on the relationship between national liberation and the liberation of women and to challenge the position that women's issues were secondary to the fight against apartheid. From this point onward, the younger members of the Women's Section began campaigning more aggressively to keep women's liberation and their representation in the forefront of debates within the ANC. A 1987 paper blasted "backward, conservative and chauvinistic" male attitudes as a "cancer that is slowly but surely eating through the ranks of our organization … The longer we nurse them like a terminal tumour, the deadlier they become both to ourselves and to the movement."[19] By 1990, when the apartheid government began to relinquish power and legalized the underground political movements, women strongly affirmed the need to struggle for their rights as the country moved forward. They still had scant representation in leadership positions, however.

Internationalizing women's struggles

In their memoirs and autobiographies many African women leaders credit international women's movements with helping to inspire their approaches to such problems as poverty, environmental degradation, and political disenfranchisement. Wangari Maathai was among those who made this connection. Thinking about how her concern with water, energy, and nutrition led her to launch a radically new women's environmental group, she wrote: "When I reflect on the years leading to the creation of the Green Belt Movement and the years of its emergence and growth, it also seems no coincidence that it was nurtured during the time the global women's movement was taking off, or that

[19] Hassim, *Women's Organizations*, 111.

it flourished during the decade for women (1976–1985) the United Nations declared in Mexico City."[20]

During the 1950s, as nationalist movements flourished, women leaders began to forge connections across countries and regions, holding periodic conferences in which Funmilayo Ransome-Kuti played a key role. Her papers and correspondence attest to a complex international network that predated the later feminist movements of Europe and North America. The driving force for these groups came jointly from women's nationalist organizing and from UN efforts through the Economic Commission for Africa (ECA) formed in 1958. By 1962, a year before the Organization of African Unity (now the African Union) was founded, women political leaders united to launch the All-Africa Women's Conference (AAWC), later the Pan-African Women's Organization (PAWO).[21]

The initiatives of the ECA during the 1960s were critical in laying the groundwork for the programs of the UN Decade for Women in the 1970s.[22] Although ECA conferences as early as 1960 agreed that women's voices needed to be heard, organizers perceived women primarily as mothers, confining women's issues to home and family. Nonetheless, by 1963 and 1964, as the ECA expanded its vision of "modernization" to encompass social and community development, the Commission was also beginning to acknowledge and document women's vital place in economic life. They discovered, for example, that women in Lesotho performed 90 percent of the road building under the food-for-work program, that on average Tanzanian men worked 1,800 hours a year as compared with 2,600 for women, and that in the late 1950s and early 1960s, women represented 83 percent of the sellers in urban markets in Lagos, Nigeria and 85 percent in Accra, Ghana.[23]

The UN Commission on the Status of Women (CSW), established in 1947, began the organization's involvement in promoting women's rights and equality. But, in the view of Margaret Snyder, the first director of UNIFEM (the United Nations Development Fund for Women), it was the independence of fifty-four former colonies, many of them in Africa, that prompted a new focus on poverty

[20] Maathai, *Unbowed*, 125.

[21] Interview cited in Snyder and Tadesse, *African Women*, 28–29.

[22] Snyder and Tadesse, *African Women*, 29–35.

[23] Figures from Snyder and Tadesse, *African Women*, 31.

and "development" and led to the founding of the United Nations Development Fund for Women (UNIFEM) in 1976.[24] The African Training and Research Centre for Women (ATRCW), formed in Addis Ababa, Ethiopia in 1970, became the first regional center in the world to work on articulating the role of women in international organizations, helping to facilitate women's participation in the UN women's conferences and formulating policies for women's economic and political empowerment.

From the 1970s onward, there were strong connections between global efforts to transform women's status and local and regional women's movements. In 1977, for example, just after the UN Decade for Women began, a small group of women formed AAWORD, the Association of African Women for Research and Development, to carry out and support research, training, and advocacy to promote women's rights. Nigerian-born scholar Amina Mama credits AAWORD with "ensuring the survival of a vibrant intellectual culture" at a time when African universities were deteriorating.[25]

The UN Conference in Nairobi in July 1985, which closed the UN Decade for Women, was a transformational moment for African women, however. Margaret Snyder sees the most important outcome of the official conference as the extraordinary consensus delegates reached in their unanimous adoption of the document, "The Forward-looking Strategies for the Advancement of Women." This comprehensive statement covered women's views on a variety of world affairs, including human rights, development, culture, family and children, and relationships between women and men. It also represented a dramatic change from the confrontational atmosphere at the previous gatherings in Mexico City and Copenhagen.

But the impact of the NGO (Non-Governmental Organization) Forum was even more dramatic. Fourteen thousand women from 151 countries took part in the Forum, in addition to the 6,000 official delegates from around the world. Forum attendees included 3,000 Kenyan women, mainly from rural areas. By comparison with the

[24] Margaret Snyder, "Unlikely Godmother: The UN and the Global Women's Movement," in *Global Feminism, Transnational Women's Activism, Organizing and Women's Rights*, eds Myra Marx Feree and Aili Marie Tripp (New York: NYU Press, 2006), 27.

[25] From Amina Mama, "Critical Capacities: Facing the Challenges of Intellectual Development in Africa," Wolpe Lecture, University of KwaZulu-Natal, Durban, June 23, 2005, ccs.ukzn.ac.za.

1980 conference in Copenhagen, there was a massive increase in the number of delegates from developing countries, women representing various Third World liberation movements, and black and immigrant women from Western countries. Particularly outspoken were women from the liberation movements in Namibia and South Africa, where white rule persisted. At this point women's groups in southern Africa associated with the main liberation movements (SWAPO and the Women's Section of the ANC) still opposed the idea of independent women's movements as counter-revolutionary. *Forum 85*, the newspaper published by the NGO group, addressed some of the contentious questions related to African women's presence: why (if peasant women were a major audience) sessions were not translated into Swahili, the local *lingua franca*; how best to address the question of female genital cutting; and the relationship between national liberation struggles and feminism – whether women's rights should take a back seat to achieving freedom from white colonial domination. A cartoon of gaunt dead bodies ironically entitled "Peace Under Apartheid" powerfully established the devastating impact of racial oppression on all South Africans.

Perhaps most significant for the future, however, were the articles about the new multi- (or trans-) national organizations in the global South launched during the UN Decade. Particularly important were AAWORD, discussed in an article pointedly entitled "Decolonized Research," and DAWN, Development Alternatives with Women for a New Era, founded in 1984 and planning to have a secretariat rotating among Asia, Latin America, and Africa. While some of the women's groups that formed in the wake of these international meetings began to claim the designation of "feminist," others rejected the label, affirming a consciousness different from that of many women's organizations in the West.

Conclusion

The lives of women nationalist leaders illustrate the complexities of independence for women. Born in 1900, Funmilayo Ransome-Kuti was among the most senior of the women discussed earlier. After Nigeria's independence, she continued her political activities and established several schools, including a secondary school, the Reverend Ransome-Kuti Memorial Grammar School, named for her late husband. She was also a fierce defender of her musician son, Fela Anikulapo-Kuti, a vocal Pan-Africanist and adamant opponent of Nigeria's successive military governments, whose home and nightclub were frequently raided. When 1,000 armed military personnel stormed Fela's compound on February 18, 1977, soldiers threw Funmilayo Ransome-Kuti from a second floor window. With severe injuries to her leg, she went into shock and remained ill, depressed, and withdrawn for a year until she died. Across the country, Nigerian newspapers published full-page eulogies, praising her activities as a visionary political activist devoted to the interests of women, children, and the poor. One headline announced: "The Voice of Woman Is Dead."[26] When her body was moved from Lagos to her hometown of Abeokuta, the thousands of mourners included a large contingent of market women, who had closed the town's markets and many other shops in her honor.

Twenty-six hundred miles to the east in Tanzania, Bibi Titi Mohamed shared the platform with the new President Julius Nyerere when independence was celebrated on December 9, 1961. Until 1967 she remained politically active as the Junior Minister for Community Development, a founder of the All-Africa Women's Conference, an international advocate for women's rights, and as President of the national women's organization, Umoja wa Wanawake wa Tanzania (Union of Tanzanian Women). She used her national office to fight for the development of rural women and to advocate for children's education. She also supported legislation to punish men who impregnated girls. Yet in 1965, Bibi Titi lost her seat in Parliament (along with many other TANU MPs) and two years later she resigned from the TANU Central Committee to protest against a provision in the Arusha Declaration, the blueprint for Tanzanian socialism, which banned committee members from renting property. For women with little formal education, renting property was among the limited ways to earn a stable income.

Now estranged from government and the ruling party, in 1969 Bibi Titi was accused of treason and sentenced to life in prison for allegedly plotting to overthrow the government – a charge she adamantly denied. During the trial Attorney General Mark Bomani asked Bibi

[26] Cheryl Johnson-Odim and Nina Emma Mba, *For Women and the Nation: Funmilayo Ransome-Kuti of Nigeria* (Urbana: University of Illinois Press, 1997), 170.

Titi to explain why she had refused to leave politics after her first husband's threats of divorce. He continued: "So you were not prepared to bow down to your husband? ... You seem to be a very tough woman."[27] After she had served two years of her sentence, Nyerere pardoned her, but she had already been abandoned by her husband and many of her friends and political associates. Life was difficult after Bibi Titi's release. At first she survived by selling paraffin oil, but in 1976 got back her house, which she was able to rent. By the late 1980s, however, the party found it useful to resurrect her. In a 1991 supplement to the government-owned newspaper celebrating three decades of independence, Bibi Titi appeared as "A Heroine of Uhuru [Freedom] Struggle."

Frances Baard's personal and political trials followed the trajectory of her country's liberation struggles. After the court appearance in 1964, when she denied the charges against her, she was sent back to prison for another five years. Rather than allow Baard to return to her home in Port Elizabeth at the end of her incarceration, authorities banished her to a tiny two-roomed shack in Mabopane, a township an hour outside Pretoria, far from her home and family. Her neighbors initially avoided her, fearing that she was a police informant. Persecuted for continuing her refusal to carry a pass (the identity document she had fought against for years), flung into a hostile environment, and newly released from prison, Baard was penniless and jobless. When the United Democratic Front, a new antigovernment coalition, was organized in the 1980s, Baard resumed her political activities against apartheid and against the corrupt "homeland" government of Bophuthatswana where she then lived; she also continued to work on local community projects, most notably launching a day care center called the Zenzeleni Community Center. She died in 1997, three years after the democratic transition to which she had devoted her life. In 2001 the Diamantveld District Council in Kimberley, the city of her birth, was renamed the Frances Baard District Municipality in her honor.

Throughout Africa during the 1960s and 1970s, women had high expectations that the fruits of independence, and later of national liberation struggles, would transform their lives in tangible ways. Some

[27] Susan Geiger, *TANU Women: Gender and Culture in the Making of Tanganyikan Nationalism, 1955–1965* (Portsmouth, NH: Heinemann, 1997), 183.

women, particularly the small numbers who benefitted from the expansion of secondary and university education, did see substantial improvements in their material lives, particularly if they were married to politicians or administrators, army officers, commercial farmers or traders, teachers or clergy, or men in other middle-class occupations. Yet for the vast majority of poor women in both rural areas and cities, life remained a struggle, exacerbated during the 1970s and 1980s by widespread drought, civil wars, military coups, government corruption, and falling prices for agricultural commodities.

Women and children also suffered disproportionately when austerity programs dictated that governments slash expenses for social services, health, and education. Yet even where social programs and development projects were successful, they often viewed women primarily as wives and mothers whose earnings supplemented men's wages, rather than acknowledging that their incomes were essential to feeding, clothing, and paying school fees for their families. And many of the women's organizations that had emerged from independence struggles remained closely tied to ruling political parties, their agendas set by elite, politically connected women who often neglected or misunderstood the issues that confronted their grassroots constituencies. These difficulties in the public arena meshed with women's struggles to adapt their personal lives in the context of rapidly changing societies. Now, however, African governments, women's groups, and international organizations became actively engaged in debating and seeking to transform longstanding social practices.

Women's conflicts with independent governments and liberation movements also might have led many women in sub-Saharan African countries to the same conclusions as Marie-Aimée Hélie Lucas, a former fighter in the lengthy and violent Algerian struggle for independence from France:

> We are made to feel that protesting in the name of women's interests and rights is not to be done NOW: it is never and has never been the right moment: not during the liberation struggle against colonialism, because all forces had to be mobilized against the principal enemy; not after independence, because all forces had to [be] mobilised to build up the devastated country, not now that racist, imperialist Western government[s] are attacking the Third World.[28]

[28] Quoted in Nhongo-Simbanegavi, *For Better or Worse?* 153.

6

"Messengers of a new design": marriage, family, and sexuality

In her first novel, *So Long a Letter*, Senegalese writer Mariama Bâ describes the dilemmas that confronted educated women in the decades following her country's independence. Written as a series of letters from recently widowed Ramatoulaye to her longtime friend Aissatou, the book contrasts the choices each of them made in her effort to reconcile local cultural and religious practices with those of her French-influenced formal education.

These exceptional girls were products of an elite school that drew competitively from all of former French West Africa. Their education was designed to lift them "out of the bog of tradition, superstition and custom" and to make them "appreciate a multitude of civilizations" without renouncing their own.[1] Referring back to their idealistic youth, Ramatoulaye recalls: "It was the privilege of our generation to be the link between two periods in our history, one of domination, the other of independence. We remained young and efficient, for we were the messengers of a new design."[2] "We all agreed," she writes, "that much dismantling was needed to introduce modernity within our traditions. Torn between the past and the present … We were full of nostalgia but were resolutely progressive."[3]

Despite their common idealism, the two women made contrasting decisions when confronted with the painful choices that reflected their

[1] Mariama Bâ, *So Long a Letter* (Harlow, Essex: Heinemann, 2008), 16.
[2] Bâ, *So Long a Letter*, 25.
[3] Bâ, *So Long a Letter*, 19.

country's complex blend of old and new realities. Aissatou married a doctor, whose mother, of royal origin, disapproved of his marriage to a goldsmith's daughter. While Aissatou took a job as a teacher and enjoyed life with her husband Mawdo, attending parties and picnics, and walking on the beach, her mother-in-law plotted revenge by taking Nabou, a young girl, under her wing, having her educated as a midwife, and preparing her to become a docile second wife to her son. To save his mother from shame, Mawdo agreed to the marriage, but assured Aissatou that he loved her and would see his new wife only every other night. Unconvinced by a combination of threats and promises and refusing to accept her demotion to co-wife, Aissatou left to forge a new life. In a letter to Mawdo, she explained, "I am stripping myself of your love, your name. Clothed in my dignity, the only worthy garment, I go my way."[4]

Ramatoulaye's crisis took a similar turn after a lengthy marriage when she learned that her husband Moudou had courted and wed a friend of their school-aged daughter. The Imam who announced the news to the stunned family explained, "He [Moudou] says it is fate that decides men and things: God intended him to have a second wife, there is nothing he can do about it. He praises you for the quarter of a century of marriage in which you gave him all the happiness a wife owes her husband."[5] Furious, their daughter urged her mother to leave, but Ramatoulaye was undecided. She wrote to Aissatou, "Leave? Start again at zero, after living twenty-five years with one man, after having borne twelve children? Did I have enough energy to bear alone the weight of this responsibility which was both moral and material?"[6] Much to the surprise and disapproval of her children, she decided to stay. But contrary to his assurances of equal treatment for both families, Moudou "never came again; his new found happiness gradually swallowed up his memory of us. He forgot about us." Her letter continued: "From then on, my life changed. I had prepared myself for equal sharing, according to the precepts of Islam concerning polygamic life. I was left with empty hands."[7]

As Ramatoulaye confronted her abandonment, her children sustained her as she learned to drive the car that Aissatou bought for her

[4] Bâ, *So Long a Letter*, 33.
[5] Bâ, *So Long a Letter*, 38.
[6] Bâ, *So Long a Letter*, 41.
[7] Bâ, *So Long a Letter*, 48.

and rejected several suitors after Moudou's death, including her husband's brother to whom she retorted, "I am not an object to be passed from hand to hand."[8] To an old friend, a former suitor, physician, and deputy at the National Assembly, she exploded, "Nearly twenty years of independence! When will we have the first female minister involved in the decisions concerning the development of our country? ... When will education be decided for children on the basis not of sex but of talent?"[9] Finally, exuberant with her long-delayed freedom, she wrote to her friend, "As for me, I was bolting like a horse that has long been tethered and is not free and reveling in space."[10]

Having rejected these two marriage proposals, Ramatoulaye finds solace in her independence, and also in her elder daughter Daba, who relies on reason rather than tradition to make decisions about her life and whose husband shares household work and insists, "Daba is my wife. She is not my slave, nor my servant."[11] But Ramatoulaye faces these questions again with her younger children, whose lives challenge her to seek her own personal balance between tradition and modernity. When her daughter becomes pregnant, she writes,

> The world is upside down. Mothers of yore taught chastity. Their voice of authority condemned all extra-marital 'wanderings'. Modern mothers favour 'forbidden games'. They help to limit the damage and, better still, prevent it ... All the same, I insist that my daughters be aware of the value of their bodies ... the sublime significance of the sexual act, an expression of love.[12]

In the concluding section of the novel, as Ramatoulaye awaits a visit from her dear, longtime friend, she reflects on the balance between women and men, the old and the new. Articulating her own continued quest, she poses a question to Aissatou:

> So, then, will I see you tomorrow in a tailored suit or a long dress? I've taken a bet with Daba: tailored suit. Used to living far away, you will want – again, I have taken a bet with Daba – table, place, chair, fork.
>
> More convenient, you will say. But I will not let you have your way. I will spread out a mat. On it there will be the big, steaming bowl into which you will have to accept that other hands dip...

[8] Bâ, *So Long a Letter*, 60.
[9] Bâ, *So Long a Letter*, 63–64.
[10] Bâ, *So Long a Letter*, 64.
[11] Bâ, *So Long a Letter*, 77.
[12] Bâ, *So Long a Letter*, 92.

> I would so much like to hear you check or encourage my eagerness, just as before, and as before, to see you take part in the search for a new way…[13]

With her own life as a metaphor for society, Ramatoulaye explains, "Despite everything – disappointments and humiliations – hope still lives on within me. It is from the dirty and nauseating humus that the green plant sprouts into life, and I can feel new buds springing up in me."[14]

Although they make divergent choices when confronted with their husbands' polygyny, unlike Nnu Ego a generation earlier, Ramatoulaye and Aissatou both understand the conflicting forces that destroyed their marriages and the new lives their children are forging. Rather than Nnu Ego's premature death in the village of her birth – refusing to renew a society she no longer comprehends – Ramatoulaye and Aissatou, well-educated and economically secure, actively engage in creating a new and complex blend of "tradition" and modernity. But this balance was challenging throughout the continent (as it has been worldwide), where contestations over marriage, family life, and sexuality continued to be as controversial and divisive in postcolonial Africa as they were under European rule.

What changed from the 1960s onward, however, were increasing numbers of people migrating from the countryside to the cities, a growing number of educated young people more detached from the authority of rural families, and greater exposure to international popular culture. Nonetheless, efforts to legislate uniform family codes faced the intransigence of established cultural practices and the inclinations of both women and men to experiment and adapt creatively in a time of rapid change. Further complicating family life, Western forms of birth control, international feminist campaigns against women's oppression, and – from the early 1980s – the HIV/AIDS crisis awakened new attention to African rites of passage and sexuality. Although religion remained an important arena of women's solidarity, men (newly empowered in African governments) were moving into leadership positions in many religious groups.

[13] Bâ, *So Long a Letter*, 94.
[14] Bâ, *So Long a Letter*, 94–95.

Politics of the family

Following independence, family law and domestic partnerships remained as contentious and complex as under colonial rule. Furthermore, changes intended to transform marriage were difficult to enforce and often had unintended consequences. Supported or prompted by women's organizations, some African governments sought to "modernize" marriage by challenging polygyny, raising the age of legal marriage, establishing new courts to replace lineage authorities in handling conjugal disputes and, particularly during the economically distressed 1980s, defining more clearly men's responsibilities to provide for their families. But such changes rarely settled the issues they intended to legislate and often raised new questions about who had the power to settle disputes; whether customary, Islamic, Western law, or a pluralistic system would prevail; and whether women should be granted legal equality. Other contested questions included the age of marriage, the definition of a "legal" marriage, the relationships between formal and informal unions, the obligations of both married and divorced men to their families, and whether and how governments should intervene in private life. With the economic challenges of the 1980s, these issues of family responsibility often took on greater urgency.

Even where governments sought to enact changes in marriage law, long-established practices continued to prevail, and some states resisted any efforts at change. In the Maradi area of Niger, family relations were governed by Maliki Islamic law that guaranteed a man's right to four wives, custody of children in case of divorce, and the right to repudiate wives at will. During the early independence period, the Union de Femmes du Niger, the women's branch of the ruling party, took on some of the same issues that had preoccupied the colonial government – women's consent to their marriage partners and the high cost of matrimony. Responding to the latter issue in particular, the women's union favored reducing bridewealth payments (*sadaki*), which had to be returned to the husband in case of divorce. They also urged the government to adopt a family code that would end polygyny and guarantee divorced women's rights to their children. But, despite continuing debate over marriage practices, successive governments failed to change the law, and by the late 1980s these disputes became even more explosive as Islamic sentiment from northern Nigeria spread into the country.

Extensive debate notwithstanding, the issue of women's choice of husbands and the age of marriage remained unresolved legally, although there seemed to be a consensus that girls younger than thirteen should not be married; for girls not in school, however, marriages were arranged as soon as their breasts began to develop. As in the past, these first marriages remained extremely fragile and often ended within a year. Thus, there were two peaks in marriage age – at thirteen when most girls reached puberty and at fifteen, when many failed the entrance exams for the *lyceé* (secondary school). Only after the age of fifteen were most women able to marry a man of their own choice. For the overwhelming majority of girls, however, these trends meant little, since in the 1977 census, 97 percent of women over ten in Maradi had received no schooling at all.

Not all French-speaking countries followed the traditionalist path of Niger. In the early 1960s, both Guinea and Côte d'Ivoire formally abolished polygyny, while laws in Mali, Senegal, and Togo allowed a choice of systems. But even where the practice was abolished, the number of plural marriages continued to be high. In predominantly Muslim Senegal, the home of novelist Mariama Bâ, the proportion of polygynous marriages remained among the highest in Africa. Here the family code followed Islamic precepts that a man could not marry more than four wives and that all wives must be treated equally. With Western education significantly more widespread than in Maradi, by the 1990s, the age at first marriage had risen to 18.8 from 15.9 a generation earlier and rapid remarriage after divorce or widowhood remained the norm. During the period from 1978 to 1986, 60 percent of women over the age of thirty were in a polygynous marriage, though the percentage was lower for women with higher levels of education. Interviews in the capital city of Dakar suggested that men remained in favor of plural marriage regardless of education, continuing to see it (as did Mawdo and Moudou) as one their "privileges," a mark of success, and an ambition to strive for as soon as one has the means. By contrast with educated women, many educated, intellectual men also favored the practice as more in keeping with Islam or with African values. In addition, for some men, polygyny might be imposed by the family, as was Mawdo's second marriage in *So Long a Letter*.

Although women generally opposed polygyny, their ambivalent attitudes – and the social disapproval of single women – reinforced the institution. Society presented marriage and motherhood as women's "destiny" and the strong pressure of religion and family all made marriage urgent for women; despite a relatively high divorce rate in Dakar, most divorcees remarried rapidly. Many women also preferred polygyny for reducing the burden of domestic chores and social obligations and for leaving more time for economic activities such as trade. One migrant woman in a polygynous household explained: "One woman in the house is not enough. Between two it is better, since you share the daily work. I come from a big family, I have half brothers and our mothers get along well. We don't differentiate between our mothers."[15] The most unfavorable attitudes toward plural marriage came from women in monogamous unions who feared the arrival of a second spouse. A twenty-five-year-old woman explained her position: "I chose monogamy because there are good and bad women. When you share your husband with these bad women, they will create all sorts of problems. They can stab you with a knife, they can embroil you in all kinds of scenes."[16] Another woman, thirty-five and unmarried, took a more positive attitude toward plural marriage that included a religious justification. She explained: "Everyone should opt for polygyny ... We must realize we are Muslims and the religion permits men to have as many as four wives ... If you find a husband, thank God and content yourself with what comes afterward."[17] Once women had adult children who could provide for them, the urgency of remarriage diminished. But, despite women's conflicting attitudes toward polygyny, the practice benefited from official religious and social approval and, for men, remained a prime way of broadcasting their social and economic success and controlling and dominating women.

The case of Côte d'Ivoire offers an important illustration of the difficulties involved in imposing wholesale changes in family life from above. The country's first postindependence president, Félix Houphouët-Boigny, sought to create a unified legal system with one set of modern laws regulating women's marital status and their rights and privileges vis à vis their husbands. By the 1990s, however, many women from all backgrounds were debating the implications and contradictions of a unified family code as opposed to a system that allowed

[15] Philippe Antoine and Jeanne Nanitelamio, trans. Laura Mitchell, "Can Polygyny Be Avoided in Dakar?" in *Courtyards, Markets, City Streets: Urban Women in Africa*, ed. Kathleen Sheldon (Boulder: CO, Westview Press, 1996), 145.

[16] Antoine and Nanitelamio, "Polygamy," 146.

[17] Antoine and Nanitelamio, "Polygamy," 146.

for greater legal pluralism. After nearly thirty years, it was not clear which legal system would promote greater social change for women.

The new civil code adopted in 1964 emphasized monogamy and made the conjugal family the only legitimate marital unit. The aim was to make every married man the head of household, thereby liberating the family from dependence on lineage heads who might pose obstacles to development. The impact of legal changes on women was considered secondary. Both women and men were expected to contribute economically to household expenses, but women remained dependent on their husbands, as they had been on lineage heads, and still required male authorization to open a bank account or to hold a job. Only women with their own businesses were exempt from these regulations. Married women thus became "strangers" in their husband's community while matrilineal inheritance was phased out. Despite this new "modernized" legal code, and despite some changes in 1983 giving women somewhat greater control over joint property, most marriages continued to be ratified outside the formal legal system as they were during the colonial period and customary, Islamic, and secular law persisted side by side.

Furthermore, the unintended consequences of these apparently modernizing reforms continued to reverberate, particularly through the law's inability to prevent extramarital sexual relationships. By insisting on monogamy, the postcolonial legal system encouraged the proliferation of informal unions that were controlled by neither the state nor tradition, thereby jeopardizing the financial security of both married women and more casual domestic partners. And, although married women could opt to separate their assets from those of their husbands, women who did so often were condemned as selfish.

Legal changes notwithstanding, a plural system continued to prevail, with marriages often beginning under customary law and being legalized only after many children and years of cohabitation. Thus, despite government efforts from the early years of independence to adopt a marital regime seen as more "modern" and conducive to national development, few efforts to implement reforms were successful and most had unintended consequences that had not been foreseen.

Alongside the efforts of postindependence governments to legislate changes in family life, local courts increasingly replaced customary family courts as the arena for settling marital and other family disputes. The experience of Akan women in the Ghanaian city of Accra and women in Lusaka, Zambia illustrate women's varied challenges when such cases came to court. Living in a matrilineal community, women in Accra were accustomed to a high level of economic independence and control over their children. They also had the right to bring domestic disputes before specially designated family courts. The need to seek legal intervention in marital conflicts increased from the 1980s onward as a drastic decline in the price of cocoa led to economic collapse and stringent structural adjustment programs slashed government subsidies for social programs. One woman lamented, "Before 1983, we were hesitant to bring the men to court and ask for maintenance … our mother would never support this. But things got so bad in 1983, then I knew that I had to do it."[18]

High levels of female unemployment and impoverishment forced women to confront a new dilemma: asking courts to make men more responsible for their families would assist them economically, but also opened the door to increased male domination, threatening their autonomy and control over their children. Until the 1980s, domestic problems had been handled through lineages outside of state control. But in response to the severe economic problems of the decade, the government began to encourage women to use the family courts to alleviate their problems. New laws also were adopted to regulate marriage, divorce, inheritance, and wills. One of the greatest challenges of the period was the growing number of single-parent households in Accra. Women's claims in the courts were generally applications for maintenance of their children.

In face of these challenges, the cases brought to the Ghanaian courts reveal changes in attitudes toward marriage. They show urban women during the 1980s as less willing to tolerate a second wife with children because of the financial burden involved, including educational and medical expenses for the children, and less willing to bear additional children themselves. Without subsidized medical services and with the cost of food soaring and infant mortality rising, women also stepped up demands on their husbands to treat health care as a paternal responsibility.

The court's intervention in the previously private household arena, particularly giving men social responsibilities monitored by the state, also transformed concepts about the private nature of

[18] Gwendolyn Mikell, "Pleas for Domestic Relief: Akan Women and Family Courts," in *African Feminism: The Politics of Survival in Sub-Saharan Africa*, ed. Gwendolyn Mikell (Philadelphia: University of Pennsylvania Press, 1997), 96.

family relationships. While reluctant to confront the major principle of Akan family relationships – women's right to "own" and control their children – the courts sought to expand men's responsibilities to their conjugal families in response to the economic crisis. In a further change from the past, these court decisions also confirmed the emerging consensus that individuals rather than lineages bore responsibility for handling family difficulties.

As some women feared, legal involvement in domestic life had unintended consequences. As men began to figure out the dynamics and rulings of the "women's courts," they tried to avoid acknowledging paternity and marrying the women they impregnated, thus defying traditional norms and stigmatizing the children. Women were also worried that, with courts giving custody to men more often than in the past, women's autonomy might be diminished. These contradictions posed a dilemma for the courts and the state: to insure that in creating new paternal responsibilities they did not radically shift the balance of marital power in ways that could not be reconciled with other aspects of Akan culture.

As in Accra, local courts in Lusaka, the Zambian capital, also became a site for renegotiating "customary" law, a system of legal relationships being constantly adapted and created from practices not necessarily recognized as part of the "traditional" past. Unlike the situation in Accra, however, in urban Zambia, wives expected their husbands to "keep" them and their children, providing them with shelter, clothing, and a household allowance in a context in which housing, land, and credit were allotted only to men. Yet contrary to these expectations, husbands' earnings were not considered household income and wives had no assurances that their husbands would support the family's daily needs or children's education rather than spending part of their earnings on a "wife on the side" and drinking. And when a husband died, his matrilineal relatives might grab all the contents of the house, and sometimes the dwelling itself. In case of divorce, he had no continuing obligations to his family.

Here both women and men brought civil disputes to the local courts, women taking men to court mainly for divorce and for chasing them from the home, men accusing women of deserting the home for other men, and for committing adultery with their partners. In these cases, the outcome generally depended on whether bridewealth (legally termed dowry) had been transferred, the measure of a "proper" marriage. As in 1980s Accra, however, with a severely strained economy, these proper marriages were increasingly difficult to maintain. Men relied on women for cooking, cleaning, and providing them with sex, and expected women to obey them and treat them as heads of the household, whereas women counted on men to provide for them and their children. In cases of adultery, husbands took the men involved to court, but one woman with the same complaint was told that she could not stop her husband from going out with other women since that was the "nature of men." Wives who deserted their homes were accused of being "bitches."

The tight economic situation also intensified tensions among women, since girlfriends were often the cause of domestic strife. But the outcome of these cases was informed by legal definitions of men as those with authority and women as dependents. One woman who sued her husband for divorce confirmed this interpretation when she said: "I hope they [the court] will grant me freedom, [but] I don't think I stand any chance because according to our Zambian law a woman should not say, 'I don't want marriage,' but a man has got all the right to say, 'I don't want my wife.'"[19]

In the ongoing changes reflected in the courts, legal "marriage" was increasingly transformed from a series of processes involving transfers of wealth as in the case of customary bridewealth, to a determination of whether "dowry" had been paid. Relationships with no formal dowry were considered "friendships" in which men had no obligation to support women and their children in case of divorce. Nonetheless, as in Accra, the courts continued to provide a forum for both women and men to contest and redefine the meaning of conjugal relationships.

One marital conflict from Tanzania illustrates the potential power of laws that treated women as citizens rather than as subjects of patriarchal authority. Although women had formal equality in most countries, local practice did not necessarily reflect this legal status, particularly when faced with challenges from customary law. The case concerned a Maasai man, Aladala, who had expelled his wife from her home after their first three children died in infancy. She then moved to the homestead of her brother Ronda, where she bore four healthy children whom Ronda helped to feed and clothe; he also financed

[19] Karen Tranberg Hansen, "Washing Dirty Laundry in Public: Local Courts, Custom, and Gender Relations in Postcolonial Lusaka," in *Courtyards, Markets*, Sheldon, ed., 121.

their school fees and ritual occasions. When one of the daughters, Aloya, reached adulthood she became involved with a young man with whom she had a son. When he began making bridewealth payments to Aloya's mother and uncle, Aladala (who considered himself her "father" since he had transferred bridewealth for her mother) intervened and arranged a marriage for her with another man, negotiating a settlement with the elders to re-establish his rights over Aloya and bringing her and her son to his homestead to prepare for the marriage. Eventually Aloya decided to challenge the authority of the elder Maasai men; she approached the police, accusing Aladala of forcing her to marry someone against her will and threatening to commit suicide if he persisted.

Fortunately for Aloya, the law was on her side, regarding her as a citizen not as a daughter and offering a forum in which she and her "father" would be treated as equals. According to the Marriage Law of 1971, free and voluntary consent was necessary for a marriage, though there was some leeway for a local magistrate to interpret the law's application. Most people expressed shock and anger that a young woman would take her father to court; but Aloya had the advantage of speaking fluent Swahili, the national language, and was able to testify that Aladala had neglected her during her childhood and had tried to force her into an arranged marriage only after she had wed a man of her choice and given birth to a child. In the end (as in the Lusaka courts), the case rested on the bridewealth payments that legitimized her marriage and on who had fulfilled the social obligations of fatherhood. In expressing judgment, the magistrate discussed the case in terms of a conflict between competing marriage practices, but included a strong statement on the evils of forced marriage. He not only sided with Aloya, but sentenced Aladala to a fine of 5,000 shillings or a six-month jail term. Outraged, Aladala yelled, "Take my daughter then, she is yours, she belongs to the government now … I disown her here and now."[20] In this case, the judge determined that the rights of daughters as citizens of the nation state superseded the rights of Maasai fathers and the prescriptions of "tradition."

[20] Dorothy L. Hodgson, "'My Daughter … Belongs to the Government Now': Marriage, Maasai, and the Tanzanian State," in *"Wicked" Women and the Reconfiguration of Gender in Africa*, eds Dorothy L. Hodgson and Sheryl A. McCurdy (Portsmouth, NH: Heinemann, 2001), 161.

Despite the difficulties of changing established gender relations, by the 1980s and 1990s, in a pattern documented for Nigeria and Kenya, small numbers of highly educated women were beginning to initiate change on their own. Anxious to have children, but without the constraints of a traditional marriage, some Nigerian graduates were marrying into polygynous households. As described by literary scholar Chikwenye Ogunyemi, "These women manipulate the system so that their children can have access to their father ... The women, like the men, are free to come and go. With such an arrangement they do not have to do housework for the man and the extended family."[21] Reflecting a similar pattern of liberation from customary norms, Kenyan women were opting to have children with a married man, giving the children a recognized father, but retaining their freedom.

Love and sexuality

At the same time that African states as well as individual women and men were grappling with the difficulties of transforming customary ceremonies and practices, films, popular magazines, and music were challenging established institutions in other ways – by popularizing the idea of romantic love among new generations of young people, both women and men. With literacy more widespread after independence and new forms of popular culture proliferating, African youth were exposed not only to the romantic ideas in classical and popular European literature, but to Hindi romance films and their "Nollywood" (Nigerian) successors. In addition, a wider variety of music and film became increasingly accessible as new media – audiocassettes, videos, the Internet, DVDs, cell phones, and satellite television – burgeoned from the 1970s onward.

Like Ramatoulaye's daughter Daba, many young women embraced ideas of romantic love, which held out the promise of greater equality in their relationships and more independence from their husbands' families during both courtship and marriage. Enhanced intimacy between spouses also seemed to offer women protection from polygyny. In English-speaking areas, one of the publications that sparked

[21] Susan Arndt, "Gender Trouble and African Womanism: An Interview with Chikwenye Ogunyemi and Wanjira Muthoni," *Signs* 25, 3 (2000), 716.

intense popular discussion of sexuality and romance was *Drum* magazine. Originally published in South Africa, *Drum* expanded in the early 1960s to produce separate monthly issues in Ghana, Nigeria, and Kenya. The publication achieved immediate popularity, selling as many as 300,000 copies a month.

Among the most popular columns in *Drum* was "Dear Dolly." "Dolly," responding in a witty and often ironic style, answered young men's and women's questions about courtship and sexuality. Although the replies, written collectively by the mostly male staff, were designed to entertain and titillate readers, the photo of Dolly Rathebe, a famous South African music and film star, at the top of the column lent the advice a combination of sexuality, authority, and modern wisdom. Men tended to read the column aloud in the company of male friends, women generally in private as a source of romantic vocabulary for letters to their boyfriends. Most of the letters were standard fare for the period, featuring "lustful young men" eager to have sex with "reluctant or bashful" young women. Reacting to these pressures and fearful of pregnancy, women sought advice on how to resist. The few letters concerned with homosexuality asked about the legality of their relationships and how to end them.

These letters and the editors' responses represented the changing sexual mores in English-speaking Africa during the 1960s and 1970s. They illustrate that, at least in the cities, courtship was becoming less an issue for family negotiation and more an independent preoccupation of young people themselves. "Dolly" often advised writers to ignore the wishes of their parents and to do what they felt was right for themselves. While discouraging premarital sex as immoral, the column also warned that unintended pregnancy might endanger a woman's chances of marrying and having more children. Advice about homosexuality echoed this pronatal emphasis, reacting more negatively to women's queries than to men's.

One letter from a seventeen-year-old young man in Nairobi who loved a fifteen-year-old girl was typical. He lamented, "I am in love with her and I have spent a lot of money on her. But whenever I ask her for sex she tells me she is ill ... Advise me on how I can get this girl to bed and then leave her."[22] The editors chastised him: "Nothing

[22] Kenda Mutongi "'Dear Dolly's' Advice: Representations of Youth, Courtship, and Sexualities in Africa, 1960–1980," in *Love in Africa*, eds Jennifer Cole and Lynn M. Thomas (Chicago: University of Chicago Press, 2009), 95.

doing, chum. Even if I did know the secret of luring young girls to bed for adolescents who mistake lust for love, I would not tell you. You should be ashamed of yourself."[23]

If "Dolly" tended to criticize rapacious male behavior, the column sometimes blamed women who became pregnant for their plight. To one nineteen-year-old in love with a twenty-four-year-old man who refused to reimburse her for the abortion he had requested, the editors wrote: "It is your fault that you are in this mess. The man has taken you for a ride and you have lost your honor, money, and the baby. You would be a fool to continue with him." [24]

Films also sparked subversive new ideas about courtship and love. On Zanzibar and in other Swahili coastal societies, Hindi films came to displace poetry and song as the most popular venues for prompting debates among family and friends about the meaning of love and romantic relationships. These melodramatic narratives provided both young women and men the vicarious experience and the language for discussing romance, sexuality, and marriage. In an area with some of the highest divorce rates in the world, such discussions were a long-established cultural idiom; even before the 1980s and 1990s, when some couples began to choose their own first marriage partners, second and subsequent unions were often initiated by the couple themselves and rooted in romantic relationships. In the words of one taxi driver in Dar es Salaam, "One of the things about these Indian movies was that when you see them they force you to talk about love, about what real love means and how to love each other."[25]

The themes of these films and the experience of viewing them challenged family control over courtship and marriage. Bollywood films emphasized young people's desire to marry for love, often complicated by a commitment to one's extended family. Characters that too openly flaunted cultural norms brought difficulties on themselves and their families. Large movie theaters also offered one of the few public spaces where women and men could gather informally with members of the opposite sex, or where couples might be alone together, or even sit near each other in public.

[23] Mutongi "'Dear Dolly's' Advice," 95.

[24] Mutongi "'Dear Dolly's' Advice," 94.

[25] Laura Fair, "Making Love in the Indian Ocean: Hindi Films, Zanzibari Audiences, and the Construction of Romance in the 1950s and 1960s," in Cole and Thomas, *Love in Africa*, 72.

One woman described the experience of watching a film with her lover, who sat apart from her. "We would glance at each other, and make love with our eyes before the show started and during intermission. It was all so romantic! … And the entire time you and your lover were watching the movie you were experiencing together the love you saw on screen."[26] For couples seeking extramarital encounters, the "Ladies Show" became so popular a venue for romantic trysts that the phrase became a euphemism for having an adulterous affair.

In the Igbo area of eastern Nigeria oral histories, fables, and older literary traditions document a long history of romantic love despite the prevalence of arranged marriages. By the late twentieth century, the idea that marriage should be based on romantic love had become widespread, but without diminishing the importance of couples' relationships with their extended families. Nor did individual choice and romantic love reduce the widespread acceptance of the idea that men wanted or needed multiple sex partners. One older man captured the widely acknowledged double standard when he explained, "If I catch my wife, she is gone; if she catches me, she is gone too,"[27] implying that she had no right to object to his extramarital encounters.

Yet, by contrast with the Swahili coast, divorce in Igbo society was so highly stigmatized that women whose husbands had extramarital relationships often were forced to accept this behavior if the man was discreet, continued to treat his wife well in public, and take responsibility for his family. This level of tolerance was particularly prevalent in relationships based on romantic love since these women were less willing to appeal to their kin and in-laws for support. Furthermore, in face of beliefs that connected a man's happiness to his wife's capacity to please him, friends and family might hold her responsible for his infidelity. As one woman observed, "In this our society, when a man cheats on his wife, it is often the wife who will be blamed. People will say it is because she did not feed him well, she refused him in bed, or she is quarrelsome. And it is often our fellow women who are most likely to blame the wife."[28] Ironically, then, in a context where women's reputations rested in part on a stable relationship, the idea

[26] Fair, "Making Love," 73.

[27] Daniel Jordan Smith, "Managing Men, Marriage, and Modern Love: Women's Perspectives on Intimacy and Male Infidelity in Southeastern Nigeria," in Cole and Thomas, *Love in Africa*, 167.

[28] Smith, "Managing Men," 179.

that marriage should be based on love often forced them to tolerate or even cover up their husbands' unfaithfulness. Even more threatening, by accepting infidelity, many women increased their risk of contracting HIV/AIDS from their husbands.

Coming of age

During the 1980s, Watoro, a Kikuyu woman then in her fifties, reflected on her life and shared her critical perceptions of young people who had not gone through formal initiation ceremonies. She explained:

> Nowadays, girls are getting pregnant when they are still at their parents' home. This is because they have no way of knowing when they are grown-up. Now, a boy of my son's age [twelve years old] can abuse me and give no respect. It is not like long ago, when we refused to have any dealings with anybody who was not an age-mate. And now, young uncircumcised boys are being called "men" by girls, so they feel grown-up and can joke about with the girls. All this was brought about by school and when we threw away the traditional way of becoming adults through *Irua* [circumcision].[29]

In the words of Wanoi, another woman about the same age, "*Irua* was like being given a degree for going from childhood to womanhood."[30]

For Nyambura, then in her twenties, life passages were very different. She explained: "Did I go through *Irua* before I was married? *Wĩ* [you], those days are over! You know, I am a Christian, and we do not believe it is a good thing. Why? Because it was a thing of the past. Going to school and learning some things helped us see the difference. We learned that we no longer needed *Irua* – that was for the old people."[31]

In place of excision and its accompanying ceremonies, then, for Nyambura and women of her generation, childbirth became the event that separated girlhood from womanhood. She explained, "Things really changed for me after I had Mwangi [her son] because I suddenly became conscious that I was totally responsible for this tiny

[29] Jean Davison, *Voices from Mutira: Changes in the Lives of Rural Kikuyu Women, 1910–1995* (Boulder, CO: Lynne Rienner), 1996, 98.

[30] Davison, *Voices from Mutira*, 149.

[31] Davison, *Voices from Mutira*, 178–79.

human being and what the future holds for him … Now I knew I was a *mũtũmia* – a full-grown woman. When you are a girl and then give birth, you find that you are changed … So you have gone from girlhood to womanhood."[32]

Rites of passage were more contentious in the Kikuyu area of Kenya than in many other African societies because female genital cutting formed an important aspect of girls' coming-of-age ceremonies. Yet, here as elsewhere, generational transformation and Western education were prompting changes in the transition from childhood to adulthood.

During the 1970s debates over these rituals were reignited both within African communities and in international debates over women's rights when feminist activists, both African and Western, took up the critiques of excision that missionaries had voiced earlier in the century. In 1975, Les Femmes Voltaiques, a feminist group in Burkina Faso (then Upper Volta), initiated radio broadcasts against excision and in 1977, the Sudanese Obstetrical and Gynecological Society organized a local meeting to discuss the practice. Egyptian opponents of female genital cutting (FGC) also became connected with international movements at this time. In 1979, Africans were among those who attended an international meeting in Khartoum, Sudan sponsored by the World Health Organization (WHO) on Traditional Practices Affecting the Health of Women and Children. Conference recommendations focused on the importance of education and grassroots involvement in campaigning against genital cutting. Western critiques were not warmly welcomed, however. At the NGO Forum that paralleled the 1980 Second World Conference on Women in Copenhagen, African women boycotted a panel on FGC for its insensitivity to local perspectives on the topic. When the WHO and UNICEF sponsored a consultative meeting in Cairo the same year, African and Asian delegates dominated the discussion, criticizing the one Western delegate who spoke out.

By 1984, African women organized their own meeting in Khartoum with delegates from twenty-six countries, entitled, "African Women Speak Out on Female Circumcision." Throughout these efforts, Egyptian feminist physician Nawal El Saadawi remained one of the most vocal African voices against the practice; in 1983, Asma El

[32] Davison, *Voices from Mutira*, 179–80.

Dareer, a Sudanese doctor, published her powerful book, *Woman, Why Do you Weep?* And other African women and women's organizations began to organize educational campaigns, often working in cooperation with UNIFEM (the UN Development Fund for Women). During the following decade, numerous local projects were initiated to continue these efforts, with many African women's organizations experimenting with ways to retain the educational messages and cultural bonding of these rituals without the ceremonial cutting.

Family planning, family threats

Rapid population expansion provided the backdrop to debates about marriage, rites of passage, and family life. Rates of growth began to recover between the wars, probably a response to declining death rates rather than to rising birthrates. From about 1950s to 1990, however, population growth accelerated rapidly as did average life expectancy – from thirty-nine to fifty-two years. Widespread vaccinations (especially against smallpox) and newly discovered cheap synthetic drugs that offered protection against common childhood illnesses such as pneumonia and malaria accounted for much of this improvement in public health. Population growth was also fueled by the desire for large families that parents continued to regard as symbols of virility and success, as economic assets, and as sources of support in their old age. Furthermore, until the 1980s, breast feeding for eighteen to twenty-four months, the conventional means of birth spacing, remained the main form of family planning.

By the early 1980s, however, modern contraceptives grew more popular and overall fertility rates began to decline. In Kenya, with funding from the United States Agency for International Development, the number of official family planning clinics increased from fewer than 100 to 465 between 1981 and 1988. In the late 1980s, condom sales in Zaire soared from 20,000 to 18,300,000 and in Zimbabwe, Botswana, and Kenya anywhere from one-quarter to over a third of married women or their husbands were using contraceptives. A 1989 survey in Kenya found both men and women supporting family planning, mainly because of the cost of school fees and the reluctance of families with many sons to further subdivide their land. In southern Nigeria, by contrast, women were stronger proponents of contraception than men, either for career reasons or as an alternative to breastfeeding and sexual abstinence as a means of spacing childbirth. Campaigns to protect people from HIV/AIDS, with the message of ABC, abstinence, be faithful, and use condoms, also may have contributed to contraceptive use.

Women often used modern forms of family planning in conjunction with more established methods. In an Islamic area of rural Gambia, despite an enthusiastic contraceptive campaign and contrary to Western assumptions, older women without education were more prone to use the birth control injection Depo-Provera than younger women, who relied more on herbs, charms, and abstinence. But most importantly, these rural women were not using contraceptives to curtail fertility, but alongside older methods of birth control to maintain the accepted two-year interval between children and to enable them to continue breastfeeding the older child.

In Zimbabwe, complex struggles between white settler governments and African nationalists, elders, and young women, and between husbands and wives, shadowed the history of birth control. Ideas of family planning were first introduced in response to the anxieties of the white minority about an expanding, politically explosive African population. Reacting to this racially tainted history, during the anticolonial military struggle, nationalists portrayed contraception as part of a European plot to decimate the African population.

On a more personal level, opposition came not only from individual husbands, but from a wider group of family members for whom new ways of controlling fertility violated the spirit of bridewealth, which obligated women to bear children for their husbands' lineage. Family planning also threatened to turn over the power of elders, who had previously regulated fertility, to those trained in Western biomedicine.

Yet for many individual women, new ways of regulating childbirth were extremely attractive, especially methods such as Depo-Provera that could be hidden from their husbands. According to one Zimbabwean woman, Mrs Mbizi:

> They were happy, especially women, because they liked the injection. You can have it privately like what I did. Traditional methods you will be given by aunt or grandmother and they will say it out [reveal it] some day, but injection is for me and that's all."[33]

[33] Quoted in Amy Kaler, *Running After Pills: Politics, Gender, and Contraception in Colonial Zimbabwe* (Portsmouth, NH: Heinemann, 2003), 173.

Another, woman, Mrs Mhane, agreed:

> They liked modern methods, especially women, because it was easy to hide and secret from men. Traditional methods you have to consult someone and so there was a lot of gossip.[34]

Just as new forms of birth control were spreading during the mid 1980s, a devastating human and demographic threat emerged in the form of the HIV/AIDS virus. Taking root in western equatorial Africa, where its virulence was mitigated by high levels of male circumcision and low levels of sexually transmitted diseases, the virus rapidly spread to the east and south. Within a few years the continent had nearly two-thirds of the world's cases and some countries such as Uganda were particularly devastated. Within less than a decade, some 1,300,000 Ugandans were infected, 60 percent of them women, including 25–30 percent of the residents of the country's largest city, Kampala. Pregnant women had a high chance (from 30 to 40 percent) of transmitting the disease to their babies. Spread by commercial truck drivers and migrant workers returning to their rural homes, the epidemic then rapidly advanced southward. By the early 1990s, the consequences were particularly devastating in the densely packed townships of South Africa, whose migrant workers became catalysts for diffusing the disease into the countryside. As the outbreak swept across country after country, residual opposition to condom use and the widespread acceptance of polygyny made containing the scourge of AIDS more difficult, while its association with sex workers reignited the scapegoating of urban women, who were often stigmatized as the immoral polluters of men (Figure 5).

Widows

At the other end of the life cycle, the lives of widows were also transformed. In Kenya, their position was directly related to new laws governing land ownership that were introduced during the late colonial period and reinforced under African control. This national program of land consolidation, designed to modernize agriculture, had unintended consequences for widows. In many cases, having their land

[34] Kaler, *Running After Pills*, 174.

FIGURE 5 This banner was displayed along the border between Botswana's capital, Gaborone and Naledi, the city's oldest low-income housing area. It publicizes the awareness campaign adopted for AIDS prevention by the Botswana government in the late 1990s. By then more than one in four adults in the country was infected with the HIV/AIDS virus. The ABC approach began in Uganda in the late 1980s. Young people were encouraged to wait before having sex and sexually active people to be faithful to their partners and to use condoms. The campaign's success in Uganda rested not only on persuading people to follow these guidelines, but on a national campaign of testing, treatment, and counseling as well as efforts to reduce the stigma of AIDS and to raise the status of women.
Source: Getty Images/Yoav Lemmer.

inspected and consolidated required giving up the land where their husbands were buried and being moved to new, larger plots that were difficult for them to cultivate successfully. Furthermore, the new government's unfulfilled promises to distribute land more equally was particularly harmful to women whose husbands had died. According to customary law, widows were allowed only to register land in their own names temporarily in order to safeguard it for their sons; thus their rights were easily challenged by male relatives or neighbors. Although widows contesting family claims to their husbands' land now could invoke the language of citizenship to support their applications, officials were no more inclined to hear their grievances than in the past when they had portrayed themselves as "poor suffering widows."

Lack of education and a new ideology of national responsibility for poverty also affected the claims of rural widows in significant, sometimes devastating, ways. Unable to read and write, many were easily deceived into giving their thumbprints to documents that transferred their land rights to rich and powerful men. Local elders who might have assisted them in the past now believed that widows were the responsibility of a newly elected government that had explicitly outlined its obligation to help the poor. Despite the attempts of many widows to appeal to the national government for assistance, by the late 1980s many still did not have their land registered. Indeed, according to a national survey fewer than 30 percent of peasants in western Kenya had title deeds and only 5 percent of them could afford to plant such profitable crops as tea and coffee. Whereas in the past, expressing "worries of the heart" in person to local patriarchs had provided widows with an effective way of voicing their grievances, the failure of letter writing to officials who had promised them rights as citizens left widows feeling bitter and betrayed.

In 1972, the Kenya National Assembly further complicated issues of land inheritance by hastily passing the Law of Succession, a bill governing inheritance that failed to define the meaning of key terms such as wife, co-wife, cohabitants, or divorcees. The legal ambiguities meant that controversies over inheritance were fought out in court, where rural widows often had to confront city widows (or women with whom their husbands had had affairs) whose fluent Swahili gave them greater chances of success. In the words of one woman whose husband had died in a car accident, "My Swahili was the stammering kind, so I just mumbled through the court, and that is why that woman won the case."[35] Many women had visited Nairobi only occasionally, and found the experience of traveling to court there intimidating. According to another widow, "I waited for a long time before I could cross the road; the speeding cars, the crowded streets of people pushing you back and forth, scared me. Eeeh! It was not easy."[36]

These conflicts centered both on who was a legitimate wife and also on the failure of most men to write wills at all. With large numbers of men moving to the cities after independence and engaging in extramarital romantic relationships, often with women from different

[35] Kenda Mutongi, *Worries of the Heart: Widows, Family and Community in Kenya* (Chicago: University of Chicago Press, 2007), 186.

[36] Mutongi, *Worries of the Heart*, 186.

ethnic groups, the definition of "legitimate" marriage grew murky. So also did the division of modern forms of property such as furniture, gas stoves, refrigerators, and music systems. Given these difficulties of survival, many widows interviewed in the 1990s were adamant that life was better in the colonial days and that their own people were unable to govern in the interests of ordinary Kenyans. In the words of one woman, "it is hard to persevere when our own people are treating us badly, when they are supposed to take care of us like they are our own people."[37]

Religion, healing, and empowerment

As Africans in most of the continent seized control of their own institutions, religious communities quickly adapted to new conditions. Most striking was the blossoming of independent churches, whose numbers soared from 3,000 to more than 70,000 between 1968 and 1985. By the 1990s, membership in these churches exceeded 32 million, 15 percent of Africa's Christian population. But established Christian churches and Islam also adapted to the new political environment. In all cases, the results for women were mixed, as they lost ground in some religious groups and gained it in others. Women continued their primacy in ceremonies connected with health and healing, however, thereby connecting their religious practice closely to the lives and health of their families. Indeed, for many women, religious groups provided social bonds that supported or supplemented their family lives. Their healing powers also assumed a new importance in the wake of the AIDS crisis.

In the Roho church in western Kenya, for example, women's opportunities for leadership were systematically reduced as the church adopted a more male-dominated model for leadership that valued Western education and experience in colonial institutions. Although the church remained apolitical, for some young men with political aspirations, Roho (and other African-initiated churches) became a means of mobilizing popular support and creating broader opportunities for advancement. Women were apparently unconcerned about this change from the active leadership of their forebears in the church's early years. They expressed no desire

[37] Mutongi, *Worries of the Heart*, 195.

to become pastors or teachers, insisting on their primary importance in singing, entering trance states, praising God – and most especially healing.

The position of women was similar among the Apostles of John Maranke (the Bapostolo or Vapostori), one of the largest indigenous churches in central Africa, where women were the majority of members, but were excluded from the decision-making hierarchy. Since the group's founding in 1932, their leadership had remained ceremonial. During the 1940s and 1950s, while based in Zimbabwe, the group expanded along the rail lines; by the 1970s its 500,000 members were spread across central Africa. Respected as prophetesses, a select number of women were able to challenge and check the decisions of the male council of elders, expressing their leadership through song, healing, and mediumship – communicating directly with spiritual powers. Interrupting sermons with impromptu singing also allowed women the indirect power to refocus discussion on moral lessons that criticized men's wrongdoing. During healing ceremonies women expressed their influence directly.

As in many such churches, women's theraputic power was central to the church's activities. At the end of each Sabbath service, women stood in rows to receive patients, mainly women and children. Indeed, many women explained that they had joined the church to treat and care for their families. Midwives, usually elder women, also relied on these religious powers – since, as elsewhere in central Africa, childbirth was not simply a medical procedure, but a ceremonial process that began with prayer and the mother's confession of her sins, and involved prayer, ritual healing, song, and dance. While faith was the basis of therapy, healers were taught to touch nodes of the body in which physical problems might arise. Ceremonies were public, with healers surrounded by women bystanders and healers, all praying and singing. Healing was considered a spiritually inspired activity that required special gifts since all illness was perceived as caused by the evil action of demons that needed to be exorcised. As in many other churches, women bolstered their claims to spiritual power through stories of their close association with male leaders.

Unlike many other religious communities in the postindependence years, in the Catholic Church in Congo-Brazzaville women became more important as the church changed from being missionary dominated to a "church of the people" centered on women's associations. This increase in women's importance flowed from many changes, both internal and external, including the directives of the Second Vatican Council in 1962–5 that allowed for more local religious expression and services in vernacular languages. The expansion of girls' education often occurred in schools run by Catholic sisters. By the mid 1960s, when the number of women and men in Brazzaville had reached near parity, the church was predominantly an urban institution. Women assumed leadership positions through the establishment of local groups of Catholics called *mabundu* ("community" or "family"). These communities became the basis for the spiritual and well-being of their members by organizing prayers, hymn singing, and discussions of talks by catechists and visiting priests. Members also visited widows and sick members, helping with family expenses and communal projects, and arbitrating local disputes. Even under the country's radical socialist regimes, the church continued to grow, as did women's engagement in these religious communities.

For women in towns, these communities, known as "fraternities" despite the male association of the word, offered women an alternative source of spiritual and social empowerment, as well as protection from witchcraft, in societies where men held economic and political power. Women were welcomed regardless of whether their lives would qualify them as full members of the church – those who were divorced, or had customary marriages or children from more than one father. Fraternities also functioned as mutual aid groups, whose members assisted each other with the costs of illness, death, burials and wakes, and mourning. Drawing on their ability to meet women's spiritual and social needs, fraternities grew rapidly after their founding in 1964. The choice of particular patron saints gave organizations their identity, with women drawn to the stories of saints who, like them, had suffered physical and emotional pain and anguish. In explaining the popular choice of Saint Rita, one woman explained: "She was married and had children and she became a nun after the death of her husband. She had experienced great suffering and lived through many problems like we do. Her intervention in our lives can help us."[38]

Though these fraternities shared many characteristics of the mutual aid societies common throughout urban Africa, they were

[38] Phyllis M. Martin, *Catholic Women of Congo-Brazzaville: Mothers and Sisters in Troubled Times* (Bloomington: Indiana University Press, 2009), 156.

also deeply religious and spiritual, drawing both on Catholic faith and on the healing cults common to the region and still flourishing in rural areas. These older therapeutic ceremonies concerned especially with fertility continued to flourish in the rural areas of Congo-Brazzaville, as they did elsewhere on the continent. In the Kongo region, these groups were based on a water spirit believed to have powers to treat such misfortunes as illness and infertility and to fight off witchcraft. The new relationships and networks of women that formed after possession and treatment were similar to those in the Catholic fraternities.

Despite the success of these groups, the church continued to have difficulty in recruiting African women as nuns. Even in devout families, there was strong opposition to daughters choosing a religious vocation in societies in which motherhood was so critical to adult womanhood. In the words of a Congolese nun in Pointe-Noire:

> At present, a young girl who goes to the convent is very strange, she will not marry, she will not have children, and my parents will never cradle my small child. That is very hard for certain parents to accept. I was sure of my choice. I decided to stick with my decision in spite of opposition from my family.[39]

Gradually, however, as the rites of incorporation to religious orders became more Africanized, and drew more heavily on earlier rites of passage, some of the opposition dissipated. A woman's kin were included in the process of entering religious life through the metaphor of a marriage agreement between families, with a young woman walking down the aisle of the church escorted by her mother and father, and a ritual in which the young woman knelt before her father and asked his consent. After her father poured wine on the ground for the ancestors and drank a little before passing the glass to his daughter, she then did the same with the head of her maternal family.

In 1989, the rite of profession for five African sisters was conducted at the cathedral by the archbishop of Brazzaville with other priests, sisters, and high officials attending as well as more than 2,000 other people. By the end of the century, more families had come to see the educational and professional advantages of a religious life and some women explained that by choosing a religious vocation, they had opted

[39] Martin, *Catholic Women*, 139.

to be "mothers of all the people." Indeed, it became common for nuns to be addressed as "*Mama*," a term of address usually reserved for a Kongo woman who had borne children.

After independence, many Muslim women continued their relative invisibility in religious practice, although in some areas social and political changes challenged the stability of Islamic rituals. French colonial authorities in Niger considered Islam a corrupting influence, situating it somewhere between what they considered the "civilized" influence of Christianity and "primitive" African religions. In the semirural town of Dogondoutchi, not far from the Nigerian border, conversion to Islam increased after independence, but intensified still further following a coup in 1974, when the new ruler tried to turn Islam into a shared national identity. In this environment, visible Islamic practice, particularly participation in public prayer, became the key indicator of social and economic success for men. By the late 1980s, however, women remained second-class Muslims. The small number of girls who attended Quranic schools rarely went beyond the first stage of study in which they memorized the Quran, but without understanding the words they recited. Women rarely prayed regularly and, despite the disapproval of their husbands, most women followed the patterns of West African Islam by continuing their visits to local healers associated with *bori* spirits. Women prayed in their homes, if they were not too busy attending to domestic chores and, although postmenopausal women were allowed to take part in public worship, most never did so. Nonetheless, women generally observed the holy month of fasting known there as *azumi*, regularly gave alms, and considered themselves practicing Muslims.

Elsewhere, however, women challenged their subordination. In the Burkina Faso community of Bobo-Dioulasso, by 1960 a town of 70,000 people, a conflict erupted between women and men over the continuation of the Kurubi. Traditionally both women and men descended from the warrior elite attended this dance on the night before the twenty-seventh day of Ramadan, when they believed that angels descended to earth to distribute happiness for the coming year. Men enjoyed the opportunity to dance boisterously and competitively, while women competed in displays of their jewelry and beauty. Muslim clerics gathered more formally to read the Quran. As French colonial influence challenged militaristic masculine culture, elite men gradually adapted new ideals of masculinity centered on professional success, Muslim observance, and having pious, docile wives. After independence, however, when many women came to earn more than their husbands, some became increasingly independent. The conflict came to a head in 1969 and 1970. During the previous decade, most men had ceased Kurubi dancing, opting instead to attend readings of the Quran. Many women insisted on their right to continue dancing, flaunting the wishes of men, who feared that their wives might be using the opportunity to spend time with their lovers.

Conclusion

After independence, issues such as polygyny, bridewealth, rites of passage, and inheritance laws continued to provoke passionate, sometimes bitter debate. Now, without colonial dictates from above, both governments and individuals grappled with how and whether to challenge and reshape customary practices under rapidly changing economic, political, and social conditions. Particularly for young people, film, music, magazines, and other forms of popular culture were accelerating the pace of change in ways difficult to control. Although some women remained silent about the inequities they faced, others felt newly empowered to speak up.

Kenyan nationalist leader Wambui Waiyaki Otieno was involved in one of the most heavily publicized cases involving the clash between a widow and her husband's family. When her husband S.M. Otieno, a prominent criminal lawyer, died of a heart attack in December 1986 without leaving a will, she made plans to bury him in Nairobi, where they had lived, worked, and together raised their children – and where he had verbally requested to be interred. Unlike Bibi Titi, Wambui Otieno's public career continued after independence. She ran unsuccessfully for Parliament in 1969 and 1974, but continued as a leader of Maendeleo ya Wanawake and the National Council of Women of Kenya. She was also a delegate to the UN Decade for Women Conference in Copenhagen in 1975 and an official of the NGO Forum in Nairobi a decade later.

Responding immediately to her announced burial plans, members of her husband's Luo clan, who had disapproved of his interethnic marriage from the beginning, sued to prevent the burial. They insisted that Otieno's birthplace in western Kenya must be his final resting place. After an emotional, highly publicized trial that lasted seventeen days, she lost her case, which was also denied on appeal. Both times, the court privileged local customary law over the common law of the country. Wambui Otieno only managed to block his family's claims to his entire estate because she and her husband had jointly registered the property acquired during their twenty-three-year marriage.

In response to the verdict, Richard Otieno Kwach, the lawyer representing Otieno's Luo clan said: "This is a very fantastic ruling by the court. This goes a long way to confirm the fact that a woman cannot be the head of an African family. Customary law must prevail. I always knew from the start that common law was irrelevant in this case."[40] Furious, Wambui Otieno charged that the decision represented discrimination against women, arguing, "Every woman in Kenya should look at this case keenly. There is no need of getting married if this is the way women will be treated when their husbands die."[41]

Despite such struggles, the fictional story of a recently widowed Zambian woman, Mrs Moya Mudenda, threatened with losing her home and small farm to her late husband's elder brother, captured another woman's emerging confidence in women's ability to fight against customary practices and the "code of silence" that disadvantaged them. At the end of the process of fighting through the courts for her right to retain her land after her husband died, she acknowledged to herself that, in the end, only the judge would decide. She then thought:

> The judge.
>
> I almost laughed as it dawned on me that it was yet another man who was going to decide my future. It seemed that all my life there had always been a man who decided what was good for me, and every time I had meekly accepted. But not this time. This time I was fighting for what belonged to me and my children. I had earned it and I wasn't going to give up without a fight, as I had done in the past.[42]

[40] Sheila Rule, "Kenyan Court Rules Tribe, Not Widow, Can Bury a Lawyer," *New York Times*, May 16, 1987.

[41] Quoted in Patricia Stamp, "Burying Otieno: The Politics of Gender and Ethnicity in Kenya," *Signs* 16, 4 (Summer 1991), 808.

[42] Tsitsi V. Himunyanga-Phiri, "Fighting for What Belonged to Me," in *Women Writing Africa: The Eastern Region*, eds Amandina Lihambi, Fulata L. Moyo, M. Mulokozi, Naomi L. Shitemi, and Saïda Yaha-Othman (New York: The Feminist Press, 2007), 307.

7

Women's rights: the second decolonization?

In April 1994, mile-long lines stretched outside South Africa's polling stations as black and white voters waited, often for more than six or seven hours, to cast ballots in the country's first democratic election. Political activist Albertina Sisulu told her daughter-in-law, "The excitement was unbelievable – going to jail, being forced to leave my children – it was all worth it to live to see this day."[1] As an antiapartheid campaigner and wife of prominent nationalist leader Walter Sisulu, she had suffered frequent arrests and imprisonment, solitary confinement, and years of banning, when her movements and social contacts were severely restricted.

Amid the excitement over this remarkable transformation, commentators rarely noted that the elections were an extraordinary step not only toward racial equality, but also toward equality between women and men. Only a few years earlier, Albie Sachs, a prominent legal figure in the antiapartheid movement, had called patriarchy one of few established nonracial institutions in South Africa. Until the 1980s, black women were legal minors and white women, once married, came under their husbands' protection. Regardless of race, women had no right to open bank accounts, take out mortgages, or sign official documents in their own names; for many years, teachers who married had to give up their jobs. Transcending this history of legalized subordination, after the

[1] Quoted in Elinor Sisulu, *Walter & Albertina Sisulu: In Our Lifetime* (Claremont, South Africa: David Philip, 2003), 621.

1994 election, women won 106 of the 400 seats in the new National Assembly and South Africa jumped from 141st to 7th place worldwide in the representation of women in the national legislature. Two years later the country adopted one of the most egalitarian, gender-sensitive constitutions in the world, a document that prohibits discrimination not only on the grounds of gender and race, but also on the basis of sexual orientation, motherhood, pregnancy, ethnicity, age, and disability.

Acting quickly and creatively as a follow-up to their electoral success, women activists grappled with a number of key issues. Anxious to establish a strong voice in government without ghettoizing and marginalizing women's concerns, they recommended against creating a separate women's cabinet position. Instead they adopted a policy of "gender mainstreaming," which mandated that all government agencies diversify their personnel and establish gender-sensitive programs. Directly confronting the country's high level of social conservatism, women also pushed through a new law in 1996 affirming a woman's right to reproductive choice, seeking to end the country's estimated 300,000 backstreet abortions each year. They also challenged rural traditional leaders over whether protection granted to customary law and culture would be subject to the equality provision of the constitution. The heated debate that ensued raised, but did not settle, culturally sensitive questions such as whether daughters and sons should have equal inheritance rights and whether co-wives in polygynous marriages, normally ranked by seniority, had to be considered as equals.

Elsewhere women's movements generated equally significant political transformation during the 1990s. By the early 2000s, a number of African countries had among the highest rates of female parliamentary representation in the world, generally (as in South Africa) through the use of quotas; women moved into leadership positions in political parties, legislatures, and NGOs and actively challenged discriminatory laws and constitutions. Women's groups also assumed leadership roles in critical health issues, campaigning against female genital cutting and organizing programs to prevent the spread of HIV/AIDS.

Intellectual climate in the 1990s

These dramatic transformations in South Africa occurred during a decade that offered both new challenges and new opportunities for women in Africa. What might be called the long 1990s, stretching from the late 1980s into the early twenty-first century, drew Africa into a new phase of globalization and contradictions. The continuing spread of HIV/AIDS, structural adjustment programs that slashed government funds for social services, and periodic, often unspeakably violent, political crises threatened women's health, economic position, security, and often their lives. Alongside these difficult, sometimes catastrophic events, the fall of the last two bastions of white domination in South Africa and Namibia, the continent-wide push for democratization, the reorganization of government in former conflict zones, and the growing international interest in gender equity opened up new possibilities for political action. With a variety of dynamic women's groups in many countries, issues such as sexual harassment, rape, and domestic violence took their place alongside political participation, clean water and sanitation, and access to land as issues that prompted women's organizing. In this new climate, some women's groups began to claim the designation of "feminist," an identity often rejected in the past as a foreign import.

International influences from United Nations-sponsored organizations, filtered through independent local and regional women's groups, were critical to creating this new political and conceptual climate. The United Nations Fourth World Conference on Women, held in Beijing in 1995, gave African participants the opportunity to engage in formulating a strong political agenda to protect the interests of women and girls. The appointment of Gertrude Mongella, a former Member of Parliament in Tanzania, as Secretary General of the gathering affirmed the central role of African women in these meetings. Although before the 1990s, many African women had criticized independent women's movements as corrupting Western influences, these attitudes changed as UN conferences and agencies began to reflect the voices and concerns of women from across the global South and as regional women's organizations on the continent became stronger and more vocal, gaining in importance and prestige during the 1980s as many established academic institutions deteriorated.

The preparation for the 1995 United Nations Fourth World Conference on Women, including regional planning meetings and an Africa-wide UN Women's Conference held in Dakar the preceding year, offered women's representatives the space to mobilize and define their collective objectives. In preparation for these meetings, women in many countries launched new national organizations to promote networking and to formulate collective goals and action plans. Typical of these groups were the Uganda Women's Network (UWONET) and the Tanzania Gender Networking Programme (TGNP). In Beijing, as in Nairobi, African women also took full advantage of the NGO Forum, attending workshops on such critical issues as fundraising, engaging and working with foundation representatives, and using new technologies to publicize their activities.

Enhancing the importance of international networks were other UN conferences during the early 1990s focused on human rights, the environment, social development, and population. The International Conference on Population and Development held in Cairo in 1994 was a particularly important milestone in the history of women's rights. For the first time an international group of delegates, both men and women, reached a consensus that women's access to reproductive health was critical to their equality and empowerment. Despite this general agreement on principles, participants failed to reach a consensus on the contentious issues of birth control and abortion. That these questions remained controversial was demonstrated a year later in Beijing, when all the African delegates (except those from South Africa) were opposed to including sexual and reproductive rights in the final declaration.

As women from the global South became more empowered, they also contributed to significant changes in the way women's issues were conceptualized. Key to these transformations was the idea of reframing women's rights as an aspect of human rights, an idea first proposed in 1990 by Charlotte Bunch and confirmed by the UN World Conference on Human Rights in Vienna in 1993. Bunch, a feminist scholar and activist, described the relevant issues in a path-breaking article. She explained:

> Significant numbers of the world's population are routinely subject to torture, starvation, terrorism, humiliation, and even murder simply because they are female. Crimes such as these against any group other than women would be recognized as a civil and political emergency as well as a gross violation of the victims' humanity. Yet, despite a clear record of demonstrable abuse, women's rights are not commonly classified as human rights.[2]

[2] Charlotte Bunch, "Women's Rights as Human Rights: Towards a Re-Vision of Human Rights," *Human Rights Quarterly* 12, 4 (November 1990), 486.

The UN World Conference on Human Rights, held in Vienna in 1993, confirmed this conceptual expansion by defining the human rights of women and the girl-child as an "inalienable, integral and indivisible part of universal human rights" and committing the international community to work toward the eradication of all forms of discrimination on the grounds of sex, including gender-based violence and exploitation and sexual harassment.

The move to understand women's rights as human rights created a new framework for combatting the abuses that African women were experiencing in the context of civil wars and political unrest. As Bunch observed, female victims of political repression were often invisible because the dominant image of the political actor was male. The concept also allowed women activists to link public and private violence against women as equally significant infringements of human rights.

Alongside the breakthrough in applying the discourse of human rights to women, many scholars and activists during the late 1980s and early 1990s also began to interpret women's issues in new ways. Their work focused not simply on "women" but on analyzing gender – the relationships between women and men – across space and time. Prominent African anthropologists Ifi Amadiume and Oyèrónkẹ́ Oyěwùmí pioneered in applying these ideas to Igbo and Yoruba communities, respectively.

African women's organizations, both political and academic, quickly adopted the concept of gender equity as a critical organizing principle for their work and as the framework for new research and teaching programs at African universities. Although African women initiated these efforts, most of them were made possible only by external funding, which meant a focus on practical, present-oriented development issues as opposed to more basic research in such areas as history and the humanities. Nonetheless, the development of women's studies and gender studies programs and institutes added a dynamic new element to the local intellectual climate. These centers offered innovative courses to new generations of college students, sponsored research projects aimed at improving the lives of women and girls, and sought to enlist men in the struggle for gender equity. Created in 1991, the Department of Women and Gender Studies at Makerere University in Uganda (now the School of Women and Gender Studies) was among the first such programs in sub-Saharan Africa.

By the mid 1990s, these initiatives also included the Women's Research and Documentation Centre at Ibadan University, the Network for Women's Studies in Nigeria, the Development and Women's

Studies group at the University of Ghana, the Women's Research and Documentation Project at the University of Dar es Salaam, the Gender Unit at Eduardo Mondlane University in Mozambique, the African Gender Institute at the University of Cape Town, and the Women and the Law in Southern Africa network. Helping to support and sustain these local projects, the prestigious, continent-wide research group CODESRIA (Council for the Development of Social Science Research in Africa) launched a Gender Institute in 1996 that sought to integrate greater gender analysis and awareness into African social science research.

African women also launched additional new initiatives to support and generate research and activism. Unlike earlier generations, many of these women openly identified their programs as "feminist," although with varied interpretations of the term's meaning and their goals as feminists. Some scholars defined African feminism as different from its Western counterparts in emphasizing pronatalism, heterosexuality, and a greater concern with economic inequality. *Feminist Africa*, first published in 2002 and based at the African Gender Institute at the University of Cape Town, had a different agenda. Drawing its contributors from across the continent, the journal was concerned to challenge research projects driven by international funding and narrowly focused on economic development. Other scholars continued to reject the feminist label and adopted various alternatives, most prominently African womanism, which according to one its primary theorists, Chikwenye Okonjo Ogunyemi, emphasized "the African obsession to have children,"[3] rejected lesbianism, and incorporated the complexities of women's lives. These complexities included not only racial, cultural, economic, national, and political considerations, but also ethnic conflicts, religious fundamentalism, gerontocracy, and relationships with in-laws.

New initiatives continued in the early twenty-first century. Attracting more than a hundred women from sixteen countries, African Feminist Forum, an activist group, held its first biennial conference in Accra, Ghana in 2006. Delegates adopted a wide-ranging program of social, economic, and political transformation designed to transcend the goals of NGOs and international development. The group's Charter of Feminist Principles for African Feminists

[3] Chikwenye Okonjo Ogunyemi, *African Wo/Man Palava: The Nigerian Novel by Women* (Chicago: University of Chicago Press, 1996), 133.

declared, "By naming ourselves as Feminists we politicise the struggle for women's rights, we question the legitimacy of the structures that keep women subjugated, and we develop tools for transformatory analysis and action."[4]

A decade of civil conflict

Casting deep shadows over these positive changes for women, this new gender sensitivity coincided with horrific conflicts in a number of countries. They included Sierra Leone and Liberia, wracked by civil war throughout the 1990s, and Rwanda, where during the 1994 genocide an estimated 800,000 Tutsi and moderate Hutu were massacred in the course of three months. Women in these countries suffered from terrifying violence, although no one was exempt from the mayhem and brutality.

On April 6, 1994, resentment against Rwanda's Tutsi minority erupted into full-scale ethnic slaughter after the country's Hutu President was killed in a plane crash while returning from negotiations with the Tutsi group (the Rwandan Patriotic Front) that was invading the country from the north. The Tutsi minority, rulers of the country's precolonial kingdom, favored under Belgian colonial rule, and ousted from power during a revolution in 1959, now became the target of brutal killings. This genocidal violence was incited by radical Hutu groups that sought not only to keep them out of power, but to eradicate the Tutsi population.

In the months preceding the genocide, extremists used violent sexual imagery of Tutsi women and men to incite anti-Tutsi sentiment and sexual brutality against Tutsi women increased. Some accounts cite the widespread intermarriage, particularly between Hutu men and Tutsi women, to suggest that Rwandan society was becoming less aware of ethnic boundaries. Yet, in part, it was these eroding boundaries that drove the violence against Tutsi women whose children from mixed relationships were legally Hutu, but considered ethnically impure. In addition, many Hutu extremists had Tutsi wives or mistresses, a result in part of lingering colonial representations of Tutsi women as more beautiful and intelligent than Hutu women. Although women had been disproportionately spared in past conflicts, during

[4] Charter of Feminist Principles for African Feminists, awdf.org/wp-content/uploads.

the genocide, women of childbearing age were particularly targeted through rape, brutal sexual violence, and mutilation.

Even after the slaughter ceased, bands of uncontrolled militias from Rwanda, many of them child soldiers, crossed the border into the Democratic Republic of Congo. Here, seeking control over an area overflowing with mineral wealth, they continue to terrorize the civilian population, leaving thousands of rape victims to suffer from devastating physical and psychological trauma.

By contrast with the ethnically based Rwandan genocide, a power struggle between a changing cast of governments and insurgents characterized the brutal war in Sierra Leone, which lasted from 1991 until 2002. The conflict began when a small rebel group, the Revolutionary United Front (RUF), invaded the country from Liberia, enacting a death toll variously estimated at 50,000 to 75,000 people. Targeting civilians, the conflict quickly became a war over which group would control the country's abundant diamond mines. In a struggle marked by extreme brutality, an estimated 215,000 to 257,000 women and girls became victims of sexualized violence, a primary means of asserting power and spreading terror. During the decade-long mayhem, many women were raped multiple times, forced into working for armed units, terrorized into joining in the slaughter of their own relatives, and married against their will to male fighters. In a deliberate effort not only to violate individuals, but to demonstrate their contempt for cultural norms, armed groups often raped women in mosques, churches, and at sacred initiation sites. Although women and girls made up an estimated 10–30 percent of fighters in the war, joining armed units was often the only way to survive in a treacherous and turbulent situation. As one woman named Aminita explained: "The commander or group leader will just tell you to kill so-and-so person. If you refuse they will kill you. So you just do it."[5]

In a similar conflict in neighboring Liberia, women, weary of war, made history by banding together to stop the violence. Here two bloody civil wars lasting more than a decade had left 250,000 people dead and one-third of the population displaced. In the midst of this terror, Leymah Gbowee, a social worker who counseled people traumatized by war, decided that only mothers could bring down Charles Taylor's brutal dictatorship. Gbowee's autobiography reports that after having a

[5] Chris Coulter, "Female Fighters in the Sierra Leone War: Challenging the Assumptions?" *Feminist Review* 88 (2008), 59.

dream in which Christian and Muslim women joined together to pray for peace, she and other women began mobilizing members of local churches and mosques to wage an aggressive campaign to end the violence. Clad in white shirts and headscarves to symbolize peace, they began daily sit-ins at the fish market in Monrovia holding banners that read, "Women of Liberia want peace now." As the bonds among the women grew, they became bolder, deciding that only a sex strike would force men to join them in confronting the country's warlords. In June 2003, when peace talks between Taylor and rebel groups finally began, women peace activists camped outside the hotel in Accra where the delegates were meeting.

Finally, impatient with the lack of progress, several hundred women marched into the building, gathered outside the negotiating sessions, and informed the chief mediator, Nigerian General Abdulsalam Abubakar, that they would hold the delegates as hostages until the opposing sides reached a settlement. To demonstrate their resolve, they resorted to one of African women's most powerful protest strategies, shaming men by threatening to rip off their clothes if the negotiators tried to leave. Under these threats, the talks turned serious and a peace agreement was signed within weeks.

These dramatic events were brilliantly captured in the film *Pray the Devil Back to Hell*. In the words of the film's broadcasters, "As the rebel noose tightened around the capital city of Monrovia, thousands of women – ordinary mothers, grandmothers, aunts and daughters, both Christian and Muslim – formed a thin but unshakeable line between the opposing forces. Armed only with white T-shirts and the courage of their convictions, they literally faced down the killers who had turned Liberia into hell on earth."[6] The fearless grassroots actions of these women forced Charles Taylor into exile and laid the groundwork for the choice of Ellen Johnson Sirleaf as African's first elected woman head of state. In 2011 both Sirleaf and Gbowee received the Nobel Peace Prize (Figure 6).

Postconflict politics

Liberia was unique in having a well-qualified woman candidate run for the presidency in the wake of civil war. But elsewhere as well

[6] www.pbs.org/wnet/women-war-and-peace/fullepisodes.

FIGURE 6 Liberian women from the Women in Peacebuilding Network (WIPNET) praying for God's intervention in ending the deadly Ebola virus in August 2014. WIPNET was founded in 2001 to enhance women's participation in promoting peace in postconflict west Africa by training them in mediation, advocacy, and conflict resolution. Launched by Nigerian lawyer Thelma Ekiyor through the West African Network for Peacebuilding, WIPNET helped to train Leymah Gbowee and the other women who organized the massive protests that ended Liberia's civil war.
Source: EPA/Ahmed Jallanzo/Alamy.

women positioned themselves to take advantage of the local and international pressures for democratic constitutions and multiparty elections during the 1990s and early twenty-first century. In the post-conflict reorganization of government that took place from South Africa, Namibia, Mozambique, and Uganda to Sierra Leone, Liberia, and Eritrea, women banded together to insure that their voices were not silenced in the new political systems. As in South Africa, one of their chief tactics was to demand greater parity between women and men in law-making bodies by setting quotas for women's representation in national (and sometimes regional) legislatures. By 2003, Rwanda, with close to 49 percent women in its Parliament, topped all other countries in its proportion of women representatives. Women also held more than 30 percent of seats in Mozambique, South Africa, Namibia, Tanzania, Uganda, and Burundi.

Except for Tanzania, all of these countries had emerged from civil strife since the mid 1980s, opening up spaces for political activists to push for political and constitutional frameworks that reflected contemporary concerns for protecting women's rights. By the end of the first decade of the twenty-first century, women across the continent were moving into leadership positions in political parties, legislatures, NGOs, and other voluntary organizations and actively challenging discriminatory legislation and constitutions. Women in many countries also were debating and implementing the most effective ways to integrate advocacy for women into government programs, including such measures as gender budgets, an effort (initially adopted from Australia) to clarify the implications for women of government resource allocation and spending.

Despite these remarkably high levels of political participation and activism, laws governing family life, property rights, and women's reproductive health proved difficult to change. Women's right to own land, critical to their economic survival, remained a contentious issue. Particularly heated debate occurred in Uganda, where parliamentary procedure quashed an amendment to the 1998 Land Act that would have given women co-ownership of land with their husbands. In Mozambique, by contrast, an active civil society campaign insured that land legislation introduced in 1997 protected the rights of widows, divorced women, and single mothers. By also recognizing customary law and land tenure systems, however, the law left some ambiguity about women's position.

The discussions at a workshop for women legislators in Uganda in 1996 illustrate the complex issues they faced learning how to exert power in an established patriarchal institution. Acknowledging their need to fit in, the women discussed how to adapt to the male political world – dressing as parliamentarians without reminding men of their beauty, not stepping on men's toes, and reading newspapers (including the sports page) so they could take part in any conversation. But other topics revealed their clear feminist agenda – opposing gender discrimination and institutional sexism, implementing gender budgeting, and scrutinizing government bills and policies for gender sensitivity. Assessing the impact of these elected representatives, James Wapakhabulo, the Speaker of the National Assembly, explained: "At first when women came in they … didn't know each other really … but as time when on, they began forming into a caucus and I dare say that that caucus achieved a lot of things. If one reads the constitution in areas of property, when it comes to divorce or death of partners, in areas of establishing affirmative action institutions … that really was something that came straight from the pressure of women."[7]

As in South Africa the political pressures that led to greater parity in legislative bodies also came from women activists. Fearful of being ignored when constitutions were written and political systems redesigned, they formed new political groups to insure women's representation. Unlike many earlier women's organizations that were affiliated with ruling political parties, these new women's movements claimed the freedom to select their own leaders, set their own agendas, mobilize women from both rural and urban areas, and to build coalitions that crossed ethnic, educational, and religious lines. Exempt from the control of male-dominated political parties, they could also address politically sensitive issues such as violence against women, reproductive rights, sex education in the schools, and sexual harassment. This emphasis connected them more to the concerns of international feminism than to the domestic and development-oriented goals of official women's organizations that dominated the 1960s and 1970s. In a few sporadic instances men joined in to oppose violence against women, marching in Botswana with banners proclaiming "Men against Rape," and in Cape Town to protest the abuse of women and children. But more commonly women activists faced the kind of ridicule that erupted during the 1996 national election in Uganda. Provoking raucous applause, a man at a campaign rally interrupted a woman candidate with the old local saying, "Have you ever heard a hen crow?"[8]

In Namibia, as in South Africa, women mobilized for change as the decades-long liberation struggle came to an end. Namibia Women's Voice, organized by churches in 1985, brought women together around small income-generating and development projects and also took action opposing the controversial birth control injection Depo-Provera. However, this group, the first major women's organization independent of a particular political party or church, dissolved in 1989, a year before Namibia won its independence, possibly because it posed a threat to established interests. By the mid

[7] Sylvia Tamale, *When Hens Begin to Crow: Gender and Parliamentary Politics in Uganda* (Kampala: Fountain Publishers, 1999), 109.

[8] Tamale, *When Hens Begin to Crow*, 1.

1990s urban-educated black women dominated most formal women's organizations. These women advocated successfully for national-level policies favorable to women, although groups promoting the interests of grassroots women were slower to emerge.

Despite the absence of a strong grassroots women's movement, relationships between women and men were under pressure to change in the Namibian countryside. In the northern area of Owambo, a major site of fighting during the independence struggle, chiefs and headmen were discredited for collaborating with the colonial regime. Here the churches and the South West Africa People's Organization (SWAPO) became the main sources of local power. Popular loss of confidence in traditional authorities left them unable to resist the pressure to reform their structures and policies, including striving for greater gender balance in decision making. Government recognition of chieftainship and customary courts under the Traditional Authorities Act of 1995 also gave rural chiefs an incentive to change in order to protect their position in the new order.

Even without a strong national organization, however, women activists in Namibia were able to gain political influence in important ways. They insured that CEDAW (the Convention on the Elimination of All Forms of Discrimination against Women), adopted in 1979 by the UN General Assembly, was ratified. They also pushed successfully for constitutional provisions that forbade sex discrimination, authorized affirmative action for women, and recognized customary practices only if they did not violate constitutional guarantees of women's equality. By the late 1990s, 40 percent of city, town, and village council representatives were women as well as one-quarter of members of the National Assembly. The national government also adopted a three-month paid maternity leave policy and broadened the definition of rape to include marital rape and sexual violence against men and boys. Most controversially, the Married Persons' Equality Act of 1995–6 abolished the husband's automatic "marital power," which made married women legal minors and insured a husband's control over his wife and her property and his legal position as the head of the family. Arguments for preserving the status quo based on the Bible and on "African tradition" were overcome when SWAPO insisted that all its representatives vote in favor of the Act.

Many of the statements made in Parliament when the Act was being debated emphasized the benefits of equality for both women and men: "The discrimination and oppression of women is a cancer in the flesh of humanity. Men are part of that humanity and therefore this deadly disease affects all of us, men and women," and, "The family which this Bill envisages would be a family based on partnership, mutual respect and consideration of the human worth of all its members."[9]

Postconflict challenges

While the adoption of new constitutions in the wake of conflict offered women some opportunities for reshaping political institutions, violent disruptions also created conditions that could make women's lives more precarious, particularly if they were poor and dislocated. By the end of the twentieth century, the UNHCR (United Nations High Commissioner for Refugees) estimated that more than six million refugees and displaced persons lived in sub-Saharan Africa, a majority of them women and children.

The situation of these women was complex and not open to easy generalization. For example, refugee camps might provide protection and a sense of community and offer some women opportunities to develop small-scale enterprises such as food production. At a conference in Dakar in 1998, women from Sierra Leone and Liberia demanded that they be allowed to stay in the camps for fear of facing difficult conditions as widows or single mothers if they returned home. Yet, exile in camps also separated families from the communal networks that allowed their poorest members to survive and the camps themselves could be dangerous. From 1991 to 1993, hundreds of thousands of Somali women fled across the border into Kenya to escape bloodshed and rape only to face sexual violence in the camps where they sought shelter.

But returning home after conflict ended could also be challenging. Given high mortality rates among men, many women were widowed and left caring for orphans or other family members. Without male protectors, they were vulnerable to losing access to land and other resources, including food aid, and being forced to adopt survival strategies such as prostitution, smuggling, and marrying men in their countries of refuge. Such unions were sometimes known as "marriages of hunger." And even in their former home communities, women faced

[9] Dianne Hubbard, *Guide to the Married Persons Equality Act* (Windhoek: Gender Research & Advocacy Project, Legal Assistance Centre, 2009), 4.

the continuing effects of wartime sexual assault, including gang rape (often by men infected with the AIDS virus), sexual abuse, mutilation, forced marriage, and unwanted pregnancy. In Rwanda, many women who had obtained land through their husbands before the 1994 genocide were left destitute. In addition, war widows who had suffered rape were stigmatized and found it difficult to remarry and widowed rape victims with children were cruelly ostracized. At a West African Workshop on Women in the Aftermath of War, women from Sierra Leone spoke of the impossibility of returning to villages governed by men who had raped them.

Ex-combatants in civil wars and liberation struggles, especially those in rural areas with little formal education, faced their own difficulties. In Sierra Leone women who had engaged in violence were perceived as impure for breaking sacred laws. In the words of Jeanette Eno, an activist from the country:

> Female ex-combatants had intended to return to their homes. But in many cases, these women and their families could not return. The fact is that while they were doing their combat training along with the boys, the girls had also committed rapes, torture and murder and had taken drugs. Viewed in terms of traditional values, they had broken sacred laws and were considered impure.[10]

A woman from Niger observed: "After the conflict, the men who have survived receive compensation. But the women, the[ir] sisters, the mothers and grandmothers of the dead, what compensation have they had?"[11] The return to civilian life was also difficult in Eritrea. In the words of one EPFL (Eritrean People's Liberation Front) fighter, "As for us, upon re-entering [civil] society, we find that we are liberated but not free. In the field we were not liberated, but [we were] free."[12] Of the 12,000 demobilized women combatants, half had divorced and were considered ineligible for marriage. The situation was challenging because the EPFL had espoused egalitarian views of women during the struggle for independence from Ethiopia. By the

[10] Quoted in Codou Bop, "Women in Conflicts, Their Gains and Losses," in *The Aftermath: Women in Post-Conflict Transformations*, eds Sheila Meintjes, Anu Pillay, and Meredeth Turshen (London: Zed Books, 2001) 29.

[11] Quoted in Bop, 30.

[12] Sondra Hale, "Liberated, But Not Free: Women in Post-War Eritrea," in *The Aftermath*, eds Meintjes, Pillay and Turshen, 138.

end of the war they made up 30 percent of fighting forces. Social relationships and gender divisions in the barracks were relaxed as was the social pressure for women to marry and have children. Once the war ended, however, women felt they were abandoned to cope with life alone in a highly traditional culture where both civilians and former combatants tended to romanticize "normal" private and family life.

Furthermore, the consequences of violence might linger throughout society in seriously disruptive ways. In many postconflict countries the aggression of warfare was transformed into high levels of crime. South Africa, with the highest incidence of rape in the world by the late 1990s, was a prime example of this trend. Official statistics in 1997 reported 134 women raped per 100,000 people (143 counting women who were raped more than once). In Namibia, the social disintegration during the lengthy war caused a high incidence of alcohol abuse and sexual violence against women and young children. During the conflict a stringent curfew had damaged the fabric of customary social life, especially the "moonlight dances" where young women and men had gathered under the supervision of their elders. In the absence of these communally controlled gatherings many young men turned to reckless drinking, a problem often blamed for a loss of respect for women and a scourge of gender-based violence in northern Namibia. A changing international landscape also contributed to continuing violence. Once the cold war ended, African countries received fewer heavy weapons, but more land mines, cheap rifles, and machine guns recycled from one conflict to the next. This proliferation of deadly weapons made it easier to arm child soldiers and intensified the threat of rape. In cultures that had paid great respect to elders, older women experienced rape by young boys as particularly humiliating.

Organization without equity: Kenya and Nigeria

Strong women's organizations, instrumental in sparking political transformation in many countries, did not guarantee a smooth transition to legislative parity or greater equality. In Kenya, with a long history of women's organizing, an estimated 27,000 women's associations with more than a million members were spread across the country by the mid 1990s. These small groups, often linked to national or international women's organizations, attracted many rural women with little or no education who came together to form businesses, run community projects, and oversee revolving loan programs. The most ambitious bought land and other property. Referring to the land she and her partners had purchased, one woman observed, "I am a free woman. I bought this piece of land through my group. I can lie on it, work on it, keep goats or cows. What more do I want? My husband cannot sell it. It is mine."[13]

These bodies as well as more formalized organizations such as the National Council of Women of Kenya (NCWK) and the YWCA had roots in earlier periods of Kenya's history. But during the democratization period of the early 1990s, they assumed a more activist stance. The YWCA organized voter education programs for women throughout the country. The NCWK launched the National Committee on the Status of Women to inform women about democracy and their political rights and to develop strategies to fight gender-based oppression. They also came together to combat desertification, which they defined as a women's issue.

Wangari Maathai took a leading role in these campaigns. In March 1992 a group of mothers who feared that their imprisoned sons were being tortured appealed to Maathai for assistance in securing their release. She was the only prominent woman to join them in a hunger strike that continued for eleven months. Suffering a violent police attack in the course of these protests, she landed in Nairobi Hospital's intensive care unit. Three months later, arguing that she could serve women better as an environmentalist than as a politician, she declined the endorsement of women delegates who urged her to stand as a candidate for president. The following decade she reconsidered her decision and won a seat in Parliament, serving from 2002 to 2007.

In her acceptance speech for the Nobel Peace Prize she affirmed the connections between the Green Belt Movement and the country's democratic struggles:

> Through the Green Belt Movement, thousands of ordinary citizens were mobilized and empowered to take action and effect change. They

[13] "The Mother of Warriors and Her Daughters: The Women's Movement in Kenya," in *The Challenge of Local Feminisms: Women's Movements in Global Perspective*, ed., Amrita Basu, with the assistance of C. Elizabeth McGrory (Boulder, CO: Westview Press, 1995), 199.

> learned to overcome fear and a sense of helplessness and moved to defend democratic rights.[14]

Yet this history of active women's organizing did not translate quickly or easily into effective political power. Although the 2010 constitution granted women equality in inheritance rights, made laws relating to marriage and child custody more equitable, and mandated that women make up one-third of the members of all elected public bodies, the Supreme Court mandated a slow-down in implementing these provisions. In late December 2012 the Court ruled against enforcing these changes for the 2013 election, deciding instead that they had to be implemented over time.

In Nigeria, with a long history of assertive women's organizations, most groups continued their concern with issues of livelihood and welfare into the 1990s, rarely questioning traditional expectations for women. During a 1993 interview, one woman lawyer observed, "When African women demand equality, we are only asking for our rights not to be tampered with, and the removal of laws that oppress and dehumanize women. We are not asking for equality with our husbands. We accept them as the bosses and heads of the family."[15] Nonetheless, a direct challenge to such attitudes had occurred in 1983, with the launch of WIN (Women in Nigeria). Critical of state domination of women's organizations, WIN adopted a socialist, feminist ideology (reminiscent of Funmilayo Ransome-Kuti), explaining women's subordination as a product of both class and gender oppression. Active mainly in research and documentation and the dissemination of information and policy recommendations, WIN transformed the debate on gender subordination in Nigeria by taking on issues of reproductive choice and rights, sexual harassment, and violence against women. Although the group changed the discourse on women's subordination, like elite organizations in Namibia, it was unable to broaden its membership base to include the poorer women and men whom it sought to represent. After 1999, when democratic elections were reinstated following a long period of military rule, women remained underrepresented in the political process at all levels and continued to

[14] "Wangari Maathai – Nobel Lecture." *Nobelprize.org.* Oslo, December 10, 2014. www.nobelprize.org/nobel_prizes/peace/laureates/2004/maathai-lecture.html.

[15] Hussaina J. Abdullah, "Wifeism and Activism: The Nigerian Women's Movement," in *Challenge of Local Feminisms*, ed. Basu, 212.

be marginalized outsiders in political parties, the ultimate gatekeepers in determining who would run for office.

Thus, despite Nigeria's long history of women's activism, by the end of the decade and into the twenty-first century women were unable to escape state cooptation of women's issues and to effect even minor change in political institutions, although as in Namibia, the situation varied from one region to the next. In the oil-rich Ogoni area of southeastern Nigeria, for example, women believed that a decade of violent conflict with the central government had enhanced respect for women, reduced gender discrimination, and increased their confidence in dealing with community issues.

Genital cutting, women's activism, and sexuality

Women's organizations and individual activists contributed not only to legislative and political changes that empowered women in new ways, but also to launching and sustaining campaigns that pioneered innovative approaches to women's health and sexuality. This transformation was particularly significant in efforts to end or to curb the practice of female genital cutting, linked to complications in childbirth, including maternal deaths, as well as pain, hemorrhage, infections, infertility, urinary incontinence, and sexual and psychological problems. Although international NGOs and health organizations funded many of these projects, the impetus by the end of the twentieth century came from local groups that launched new efforts to work with family and community members, health care providers, governments, and media outlets to publicize the damaging health effects for women and the human rights violations involved in subjecting young girls to the practice. Such campaigns took root across the continent, especially in areas of west Africa, Kenya, Sudan, and Somalia where excision remained widespread. Although opposition remained strong, these efforts contributed to changing behavior in significant ways. By the first decade of the twenty-first century, a significant drop in cutting among young women aged 15–19 in many countries as compared to those aged 35–39 indicated that these campaigns were effective in changing cultural attitudes.

Women involved in these efforts expressed a variety of motivations for their work. Asma El Dareer, whose 1983 book *Woman, Why Do You Weep?* inspired action both internationally and locally, explained,

"I was circumcised in 1960, at the age of 11 years. I remember every detail of that operation, and that the worst part was when the wound became infected and I had to be given five injections of penicillin by the operator, a qualified nurse. From that time, I began to think, to wonder why girls are circumcised and to learn more about it."[16] Also emphasizing women's well-being, Mansata, a former female circumciser in the Gambia explained, "If you do not understand your health, you cannot appreciate the problems of female genital cutting, and if you do not continue to educate people they will not understand. All we are seeking is knowledge. Knowledge will change people's attitudes."[17] Like El Dareer, Sudanese feminist Amna Mahgoub Osman, who convinced numerous relatives to abandon the practice, emphasized the pain and risks of genital cutting. One of her family members recounted a critical conversation with Osman:

> Amna convinced me that circumcision is a harmful practice and reminded me about the suffering of my two elder daughters. She said to me 'Khadjia: are you going to be happy if one of your daughters dies in the surgery? You should instill good values in your daughters and help them be strong young women. Circumcision is not going to inculcate good values, only life-long injuries.'[18]

These programs to eradicate FGC and their levels of success varied from country to country. In Kenya, long a site of controversy over circumcision, the established women's group Maendeleo Ya Wanawake Organization (MYWO), in partnership with PATH (Program for Appropriate Technology in Health), an international nonprofit health agency, took an innovative approach to their campaign, which became a priority in 1991. Recognizing that excision was only one aspect of coming-of-age ceremonies, the Alternative Rites of Passage program sought to end cutting while preserving the celebratory nature of the ritual and the transmission of knowledge associated with this important stage of life. Instruction from older women covered topics such as sexuality and reproduction, birth control, HIV/AIDS, marriage and family life, and responsible decision making. In one area, where

[16] Asma El Dareer, *Woman, Why Do You Weep? Circumcision and its Consequences* (London: Zed Books, 1983), iii.

[17] Rogaia Mustafa Abusharaf, "Introduction: The Custom in Question," in *Female Circumcision: Multicultural Perspectives, ed. Rogaia Mustafa Abusharaf* (Philadelphia: University of Pennsylvania Press, 2006), 1.

[18] Abusharaf, "Introduction," 15.

festivities were called Ntanira Na Mugambo, "Circumcision with Words," girls prepared songs, drama, and poetry to celebrate their new status and received certificates of "community wisdom." In combination with other approaches, this project succeeded in lowering the rate of circumcision in four targeted districts from 78 to 56 percent.

In the Maasai area of Kenya, a program called Safe Kenya, which began in 2008, engaged all members of the community in developing safe alternatives to cutting. Writing in 2014, the group's project manager explained the task not only of developing an alternative ceremony in partnership with members of the community, but of engaging men to accept their work. She explained: "As part of the project, some of the men who used to be warriors teach the new warriors about the dangers of female genital cutting for girls, and encourage them to say publicly that they would marry uncut girls. This is important because one of the main reasons parents have their girls circumcised is to make sure they can find a husband."[19]

Similar efforts occurred in Senegal, Burkina Faso, and Mali, where rates of excision were much higher – almost universal in Mali and in particular areas of Senegal. The most successful strategies occurred in Mali, where the Village Empowerment Program, also known as the Tostan program after the local NGO that developed it, took a broader approach than elsewhere. The project sought to advance understanding of reproductive health and basic human rights in part through raising literacy rates and empowering women to be more active in community development. In addition, village committees were mobilized to discuss not only genital cutting, but related controversial issues such as early marriage and family planning. As in Kenya, these programs also sought to persuade traditional specialists to stop the practice and to act as agents of change in their communities.

Campaigns also were initiated in Sudan and Somali, where the most severe form of cutting – infibulation – prevailed. These efforts were inspired in part by the WHO (World Health Organization) seminar on "Traditional Practices Affecting the Health of Women and Children" held in Khartoum in 1979. In Sudan, the National Committee on the Eradication of Harmful Traditional Practices Affecting the Health of Women and Children carried out a wide range of programs including mass media campaigns, training sessions, and the distribution of informational materials to health care providers and grassroots groups.

[19] Sarah Tenoi, "An Alternative to Female Genital Mutilation That Prevents Girls Suffering," *Guardian*, February 6, 2014.

Another leading force was the Babiker Badri Scientific Association for Women's Studies operating under the auspices of Ahfad University for Women in Khartoum. As elsewhere, these efforts were most successful in changing attitudes in the cities and among younger and more educated women. Somali women launched similar campaigns beginning in the 1980s. Among other strategies, these women challenged the connections of infibulation with purity, cleanliness, and religious observance and, as in Sudan, either refused to have their daughters cut or opted for the less extreme "sunna" circumcision, the removal of all or part of the clitoris rather than also excising the inner and outer labia, leaving only a tiny opening for urinating and menstruation.

Not surprisingly, a key source of resistance to all of these initiatives came from the women who performed the procedure, many of whom lacked an alternative source of income. Furthermore, in many areas, campaigners' stress on negative health consequences led not to ending genital cutting, but to its increasing medicalization, offering low-paid health care providers an important supplement to their salaries. Reacting to this situation, medical circumcisions were outlawed in Kenya and the Ministry of Health in Mali banned the practice by MOH employees in its facilities. But in another of the unintended consequences of the campaigns, in Sudan, although the incidence of cutting decreased significantly both among participants in the program and among daughters of village women who did not take part, many other people began having girls excised at a younger age, before they were old enough to resist.

The words of an Imam in central Sudan illustrated the complex politics surrounding the effort to eradicate FGC. After taking part in a training workshop, he became convinced that circumcision was harmful and violated the Islamic principle that "No harm should be exerted on an individual from a presumably Islamic practice."[20] He explained his efforts, at first unsuccessful, to convince his wife of his viewpoint:

> I told my wife not to circumcise my daughter Amal who was then 9 years old ... My wife refused, and was even surprised that such remarks came from me because I never objected about any of the older girls. Moreover, it is not part of our tradition or of any people we know

[20] Hamid El Bashir, "The Sudanese National Committee on the Eradication of Harmful Traditional Practices and the Campaign Against Female Genital Mutilation," in *Female Circumcision*, ed. Abusharaf, 157.

> not to circumcise girls. Circumcision of girls is taken for granted as something Islamic and appreciated by the culture ... When my wife insisted, I told her that if she did so she had to leave the house, which effectively means she is divorced. Then she complied with my point, although without being convinced. Gradually I reflected to her what we learned in the workshop, and now she is convinced.[21]

Campaigns against genital cutting also drew attention to African sexuality as did the more open discussion of gay rights during the 1990s. During this period, South Africa – with a longer history of homosexual advocacy than any other African country (in earlier decades primarily among white men) – became the leading proponent of greater equality on the grounds of sexual orientation. Under pressure from increasingly outspoken gay activists, in 1992 the African National Congress manifesto included "sexual orientation" among proposed constitutionally protected categories. The provision was included in the country's new constitution adopted in 1996. After this victory, the National Coalition for Gay and Lesbian Equality (NCGLE) waged a successful struggle through the ANC to expand their rights and benefits. This pressure led the Constitutional Court to rule in 2002 that same-sex couples could legally adopt children, and a year later that they should receive the same benefits as married heterosexual couples. In 2006, South Africa became the fifth country in the world and the first in Africa to legalize same-sex marriages.

Elsewhere, however, strong anti-gay sentiment persisted into the new century, with prohibitions in former British colonies dating back to colonial laws. Sudan and Mauretania, with the direst penalties, punished homosexuality by death, while in most other countries penalties ranged from fines to corporal punishment or imprisonment. In only fifteen nations, homosexuality was not legally banned. Although public sentiment in most countries remained strongly opposed to gay and lesbian rights, activists challenging these punitive laws, inspired by events in South Africa and international struggles for equality, became more active and vocal beginning in the 1990s. In 2011, Chi Mgbako, Clinical Professor of Law at Fordham University Law School expressed "cautious hope" that the climate was improving. She wrote: "African NGOs and community groups championing the rights of Africa's sexual minorities are publicly condemning institutionalized

[21] El Bashir, "Sudanese National Committee," 157.

homophobia, filing lawsuits arguing for the recognition of LGBT rights, and taking their grievances directly to government officials."[22] African feminist scholars such as Sylvia Tamale were vocal in these debates. Arguing against repressive laws from women's perspective, she wrote:

> Ugandan women's sexuality is often reduced to their conventional mothering role, and conflated with their reproductive capacities ... What is therefore particularly threatening to patriarchy is the idea of intimate same-sex relationships where a dominating male is absent, and where women's sexuality can be defined without reference to reproduction. The main factor in the patriarchal equation is missing; that is, power along sex lines, and thus the preservation of the gender hierarchy.[23]

Conclusion

In relation to women's rights and to human rights more generally, the twentieth century ended on a contradictory note. The expansion of multiparty governments and women's push for inclusion gave them and their organizations greater voice in government as women began to conceptualize their demands in new ways. No longer satisfied with acting as subsidiaries of male-dominated political parties, women's organizations pushed the boundaries of politics to include gender quotas in national and local legislatures and campaigns opposing violence against women, sexual harassment, male domination of political and economic life, and an end to customary ceremonies that threatened women's health. These changes represented a significant transformation of women's politics from the immediate postindependence years.

Alongside this push for new rights, however, continuing conflicts continued to threaten women's safety and to subject them and their families to horrific violence. As the new century dawned, some of the most shocking of these wars either had ended, or were coming to an end, often leading to postconflict political reorganization that offered women a new political voice. Nonetheless, continuing political clashes, along with poverty and dislocation, global economic pressures, and

[22] Chi Mgbako, "Africa's LGBT Rights Movement," 7/3/2011, www.twitter.com/@chiadanna.

[23] Sylvia Tamale, "Out of the Closet: Unveiling Sexuality Discourses in Uganda," *Feminist Africa* 2 (2003), www.feministafrica.org.

the threat of HIV/AIDS persisted, endangering women's lives and their sense of security.

In South Africa, President Thabo Mbeki's obtuse response to the AIDS epidemic illustrates the challenges that confronted the new generation of politically successful women. Questioning whether the HIV virus caused the illness, Mbeki refused to allow the government to provide medication to HIV-positive pregnant women. His insistence on denying the scientific consensus on the causes of AIDS led to Parliament's loss of a long-time women's advocate. In 2002, ANC MP Pregs Govender resigned her seat in anger and frustration after government officials tried repeatedly to silence her and to thwart her demands for action. Reflecting on the crisis in her memoir, she wrote:

> What did it mean to be a loyal party member when mothers, fathers, daughters, sons, brothers and sisters, husbands and wives, were dying of HIV/Aids? Over and over again the same thing was repeated: "The president is a very intelligent man." ... until I wanted to scream out, "Yes, but he's not infallible. He needs to look at what's actually happening." ... In the ANC caucus and in parliament I looked at Thabo Mbeki, ... and wanted him to open his eyes to what was happening to women who have HIV/Aids, and use his power for their lives.[24]

Govender's career trajectory, from playing a prominent role in antiapartheid, trade union, and women's struggles to an influential government position, revealed both women's achievements and their frustrations with public life. These tensions unfolded not only in politics, but also in end-of-century social, economic, and religious transformations that reflected – and reinforced – a growing gap between privileged women and those who were increasingly marginalized in a new economic order.

[24] Pregs Govender, *Love and Courage: A Story of Insubordination* (Johannesburg: Jacana Media, 2007), 224.

8

Empowerment and inequality in a new global age

Dramatic increases in the number of women educated through secondary school and university provided the backdrop for women's political advances in the late twentieth century. Their education notwithstanding, these women still confronted the pressures that Tsitsi Dangarembga explored in her novel *Nervous Conditions*, set in colonial Zimbabwe. Prompted by her uncle's questioning about how much schooling she should have before she thought about marrying "a decent man" and setting up "a decent home," the main character, Tambudzai, reflected,

> Marriage. I had nothing against it in principle. In an abstract way I thought it was a very good idea. But it was irritating the way it always cropped up in one form or another, stretching its tentacles back to bind me before I had even begun to think about it seriously, threatening to disrupt my life before I could even call it my own.[1]

Educating girls and women

Across postcolonial Africa, girls continued to confront similar pressures of balancing their desire for education with social pressures to marry, often at an early age. Nonetheless, by the 1990s, revolutionary changes in education had swept across the continent. Between 1970

[1] Tsitsi Dangarembga, *Nervous Conditions* (Seattle: Seal Press, 1988), 180.

and 2009, sub-Saharan Africa was one of the two world regions with the most dramatic gains in girls' education at the primary level, with gender parity reached in ten countries in east and southern Africa. On the secondary level, boys continued to outnumber girls, although the difference was not substantial. Overall, as of 2006, 21 percent of girls attended secondary school, as compared with 26 percent of boys. Nonetheless, on the worldwide list of ten countries with the strongest gender imbalance, nine were African. Matching global trends, African women were the main beneficiaries of a dramatic expansion in tertiary education. Enrollment figures for 2006 were twenty-four times higher than in 1970, with women outnumbering men in Namibia, Botswana, and Lesotho.

These transformative increases in schooling also helped to fuel the contradictions of the 1990s, which extended not only to the contrast between catastrophic wars and dramatic political transformations, but also to the growing gap between rich and poor. At a time when intensive global contacts and the increased number of educated women helped to fuel the growth of a larger middle class, more and more women sunk into poverty. In urban shantytowns and rural villages, these impoverished women struggled to provide their families with food, clothing, housing, and sanitation. They lined up daily to pump water from standpipes, trudged miles to streams where they fetched water in five-gallon jugs or calabashes, sold tiny quantities of food at market stalls, and eked out maize or cassava from small plots of barren land that they rarely owned. The scourge of HIV/AIDS, which devastated some communities in South Africa, exacerbated the pain of impoverishment and thrived in its midst. The Christian religious revivals of the period, sometimes path breaking in empowering individual women as preachers and prophets, framed their appeals according to the poverty or prosperity of their audience. Also reflecting growing economic disparities, new Muslim revivals expanded some religious opportunities for wealthy women, while reviving discourses of women's immorality as a cause of economic distress.

Yet many hurdles to improving girls' schooling remained: constraints on educational spending as a result of austerity programs, poor households preferring to educate boys, and the cost of school fees and uniforms. Also working against girls were long distances to travel and schools' inadequate water and sanitation facilities. These dynamics differed from one country to the next. In Kenya, for example, with schools and adult education programs concentrated in the Central Highlands and Lake Victoria areas, regional disparities in educational levels were pronounced. Girls also benefitted from class advantages when urban professional women helped to fund the education of their younger sisters and their siblings' daughters. Furthermore, whereas families in many rural communities tended to view educated girls as a financial liability because they required larger bridewealth gifts, city dwellers often made the opposite case – since many educated women rejected the practice as outdated. In addition, despite a general preference for sending boys to school, some mothers believed that educated daughters would be more likely than sons to care for them in old age.

Overcoming obstacles to girls' education often required policies specifically designed to increase their enrollment. In Benin, for example, in the decade following the 1995 Beijing Conference, the gender gap narrowed from 32 to 22 percent when the government coupled a media campaign encouraging girls' enrollment with reduced fees for girls in rural primary schools. When Mauritania hired more female teachers and built separate latrines for girls, the gender gap in primary schools was erased. Similarly, in the early 1990s, the government of Guinea launched a program to build latrines, aid pregnant students, distribute free textbooks, and increase the number of female teachers – policies that more than doubled the number of girls in school and increased boys' attendance by 80 percent. Although effective, such campaigns did not necessarily overcome longstanding attitudes. A decade later, Guinea remained among the countries worldwide with the greatest discrepancy between male and female students.

Even the most highly educated women faced obstacles and suspicion when they attempted to enter male-dominated workplaces. In Nigeria, Igbo women were disproportionately represented among girls and women at both the secondary and university levels. But gaining powerful, high-status positions did not exempt these women from widespread sexual harassment or from family and societal expectations that they marry and bear children, preferably sons. Furthermore, women were suspected of succeeding through "bottom power," using their sexuality to gain access to opportunities. Based on interviews in the early 1990s, many high-achieving women, while acutely aware of the stigma of being single, strongly resisted polygyny and family pressure to accept a suitor they had not chosen. They were less critical, however, of "outside wife" arrangements (informal relationships with married men) as an option for unmarried women.

Given these suspicions of accomplished women and a scarcity of jobs, many women also accepted the need for bribery and having the support of a "godfather," an older, highly placed family member or sponsor. Nnenna, a legal manager in a commercial bank, explained: "Officially, they will advertise the positions, but it is those who know people that will be considered. The result is that merit rarely comes in."[2] None of the women interviewed admitted to exchanging sexual favors for jobs or promotion; but most defended women who did – viewing "bottom power" as one more weapon in a workplace in which women, especially those without "godfathers" were greatly disadvantaged.

Mamphela Ramphele, one of South Africa's most highly educated black women, attributed her accomplishments to her willingness to rebel against her country's constraints on both blacks and women under apartheid. As a political activist and a medical doctor who survived banishment to a remote rural area following the Soweto student uprising in 1976, her personal achievements were substantial. While serving her sentence, she opened a medical clinic, earned additional degrees in commerce and public health by distance learning, and upon release a PhD in anthropology from the University of Cape Town. Ramphele's thesis, published in 1993 as *A Bed Called Home*, explored the ways that both male and female migrants struggled to create "homes" for their families in an environment where each bed was shared by 2.8 people.

These achievements notwithstanding, she continued to fight public portrayals of her not as a political figure in her own right, but as the lover of Steve Biko, murdered by the police after the student revolt. "One way in which people attempt to deal with the transgression [of black women executives]," she wrote in her autobiography, "is to find a male connection with whom to identify the successful woman … Her own discomforting agency is thus denied."[3] Reflecting further on these experiences, she explained, "The double jeopardy of being black and female in a racist and sexist society may well make one less afraid of the sanctions against success. A non-subservient

[2] Philomena E. Okeke, "Negotiating Social Independence: The Challenges of Career Pursuits for Igbo Women in Postcolonial Nigeria," in *"Wicked" Women and the Reconfiguration of Gender in Africa*, eds Dorothy L. Hodgson and Sheryl McCurdy (Portsmouth, NH: Heinmann, 2001), 243.

[3] Mamphela Ramphele, *Across Boundaries: The Journey of a South African Woman Leader* (New York: The Feminist Press, 1999), 178.

black woman is by definition a transgressive – she is the ultimate outsider."[4]

Despite persistent gender disparities, by the end of the twentieth century, the vastly increased numbers of educated women had created new professional opportunities in politics, government, education, business, and intellectual life in many African countries. For most women in both the cities and the countryside, however, survival remained a challenge.

Economic change and women's work

In an era of dramatic political and social change, the poorest women, in both cities and rural areas, continued to bear the brunt of globalization, austerity programs, and supporting and raising children, often on their own. Even married women or those with partners generally shouldered the burden of paying for their families' food, clothing, and school fees. According to United Nations figures, poverty for women increased by 60 percent between 1970 (when the continent's economic woes intensified) and the 1990s, compared to a 30 percent increase for men. In the countryside larger numbers of women were growing cash crops than earlier in the century, but the income they earned varied substantially from one area to the next and was often threatened by drought and price fluctuations for the goods they produced. Even while farming, most women engaged in small-scale trade to supplement other sources of income. Although many women traders struggled to survive, others were able to earn an independent living, and sometimes to thrive and become relatively prosperous entrepreneurs. In addition, factory jobs, mainly producing textiles and clothing, continued to expand in a few areas, particularly in Lesotho, Botswana, and new rural settings in South Africa (Figure 7).

Successful efforts to improve women's economic position illustrate the complex family dynamics that could occur when women's success destabilized the balance of power between them and their husbands. In the Gambia, for example, a boom in women's vegetable farming that grew out of Women in Development and UN Decade for Women initiatives during the 1970s and 1980s transformed relations between

[4] Mamphela Ramphele, *Across Boundaries*, 181.

FIGURE 7 Sudanese women from Rahad, an irrigated agriculture project 175 miles southeast of Khartoum, carrying water to their homes in 20 liter containers. In some parts of Africa, women and children walk for miles each day to collect water for their families. According to a UN estimate in 2014, women and girls in sub-Saharan Africa spent forty billion hours each year collecting water. Source: Tor Eigeland/Alamy.

wives and husbands in sometimes unsettling ways. By the 1990s, these projects were so profitable that, in some parts of the country, women's communal market gardening surpassed men's return from growing peanuts as the main source of family income. The consequences were so significant that men began to refer to women's gardens as their "husbands," rhetorically suggesting that women were neglecting their conjugal responsibilities for their fields. In response to these charges, women replied that they might as well be married to their gardens since financial crises had so undermined men's incomes that their farming often provided the only means of family support. One husband explained: "A wife is brought home to fulfill her obligations to her husband … When women are away from home almost the whole day gardening, they do not perform what is required of them."[5]

[5] Richard A. Schroeder, "'Gone to Their Second Husbands': Marital Metaphors and Conjugal Contracts in The Gambia's Female Garden Sector," in *Wicked Women*, eds Hodgson and McCurdy, 88.

In women's eyes, however, "Women are doing what men *should* be doing."[6]

By the early '90s, these Gambian women were using their income to pay for most household expenses, including rice, home furnishings, school expenses, clothes for themselves and their children, and even the animals required for religious sacrifices. As a result, marital struggles centered on how men might get their hands on their wives' income. As men turned to asking their wives for gifts, or for loans that they promised to repay, women began to experiment with strategies to protect their financial resources – hiding their income from their husbands and giving money to older relatives or trusted neighbors for safekeeping. When other tactics failed, they might resort to spending their money as quickly as possible. In the words of one woman: "... when we go to market [with our produce], we simply spend all our money on things that we need, and come home with no money at all, to avoid the loan requests altogether."[7]

In Mozambique, the 1992 Peace Accord that ended the postindependence civil war led to an increase in commercial activity and to general economic improvement. Yet most women continued to suffer from poverty. As a woman named Akima explained, "We need money but we don't know where to get it."[8] In rural areas, where both women and men were engaged in agricultural work, men were more likely than women to seek supplementary sources of income. But they generally reserved these earnings for themselves, leaving women to cover household expenses. The women who started small businesses to supplement their agricultural income, brewing beer and selling other alcoholic beverages, fish, or vegetables, generally earned only two-thirds of what men did. Poverty was particularly acute in southern Mozambique where large numbers of men migrated from rural regions, leaving behind desperately poor female-headed households. Some women in the region worked alongside men on corporate-owned cotton farms, but at lower paid, seasonal jobs such as weeding the fields; they also continued to produce manioc, maize, and beans on their small plots of land.

Women fared better in Makua areas of northern Mozambique where matrilineal practices persisted. Here men and women worked

[6] Schroeder, "Second Husbands," 90.

[7] Schroeder, "Second Husbands," 100.

[8] Quoted in Kathleen E. Sheldon, *Pounders of Grain: A History of Women, Work, and Politics in Mozambique* (Portsmouth, NH: Heinemann, 2002), 254.

together to grow cotton for the market and women worked alongside their husbands in the fields. Even more important to women's economic well-being, most men showed their wives the money they earned from selling cotton and in three-quarters of families interviewed, women kept the money themselves. Although some women described this arrangement as traditional, others explained that men were unable to handle money, or spent it on beer. Women also supervised the food supply to be sure that it would last until the next harvest. Also in contrast to other regions of the country, families went shopping in the market together, sharing decisions about expenses. Women's importance in this matrilineal system was tied to their control over the allocation of land, which was passed down through the woman's family. In another Makua area, where women handled nearly all the agricultural work in addition to preparing food, fetching water, and collecting firewood, even those who wished for more assistance from their husbands shared the view expressed by Luisa: "We come to the conclusion that it is best to leave things as they are, not try to change things. Because, you know, we might lose our husbands."[9] Her remark expressed a widespread fear that men might not stay with a woman who refused to perform these expected responsibilities.

Women also continued to earn an income by leading initiation rituals (which in some areas involved both instruction in the responsibilities of womanhood and elongating the labia of girls approaching womanhood) and as *nyamusoros* (spiritual leaders and healers) who instructed new initiates in the esoteric knowledge of the ancestral spirits. These positions, often hereditary, continued to be prestigious. Women who were possessed by a spirit during an illness apprenticed to an experienced healer, paying her a fee and working in her fields during the training period. Some of these women were quite successful, counseling people about the conflicts in their lives and also administering medicine.

A new one-party state in Uganda brought a measure of peace and security to the country in 1986, after fifteen years of dictatorship and civil war. As the formal economy took off once again, both Kampala – the country's largest city – and smaller towns expanded, opening new opportunities for women. Although the majority of women continued to work within the family or to be self-employed, from this period on,

[9] Quoted in Sheldon, *Pounders of Grain*, 254.

they also began to dominate market trade, generally selling food and drink, textiles and clothing, or handicrafts. Women also reached the upper levels of business and the professions in much greater numbers than in the past. Even in lower-paying jobs, most women in formal employment explained their decision for economic reasons. One young woman said, "I took a job as a housegirl in Kampala because rural life was so hard and we were so poor."[10] The benefits of formal work included not simply a greater ability to pay for food, clothing, housing, and school fees but also more freedom from their husbands' control. A nurse outside Kampala explained: "Life is better today, for we can get our own money, we can afford to make decisions. In earlier days our mums could only depend on the man."[11]

With economic expansion, the range of jobs for women opened up in all areas. Professional women continued to work mainly as teachers and nurses, although more men were also entering nursing programs, aspiring to become administrators in clinics or hospitals. Entering jobs previously reserved for men, small numbers of women were selling fuel at petrol stations, repairing cars, painting houses, or making furniture; others were becoming more entrepreneurial, opening drug stores, setting up private schools, or investing in land and real estate. As in west Africa, these women often experimented with different businesses until one became successful and provided a launching pad for other enterprises. Margaret Birungi, a successful businesswoman in the early 2000s, had sold maize, wheat, and produce across the Kenya border with mixed success until, at the age of thirty, she founded her own company making and selling juice. After consulting with government chemists to learn about preservatives, she turned it into a profitable business.

Despite these successes for some women, implementation of the structural reforms demanded by international financial institutions threatened the financial security of many others. With particularly negative consequences for women, these mandates included reducing government spending and cutting back funding for social services. By the late 1990s, after a decade under Uganda's new regime, at least one-third of all women lived in absolute poverty, unable to meet their basic needs. Interviews confirmed women's awareness of

[10] Grace Bantebya Kyomuhendo and Marjorie Keniston McIntosh, *Women, Work & Domestic Virtue in Uganda, 1900–2003* (Oxford: James Currey, 2006), 219.

[11] Kyomuhendo and McIntosh, *Women, Work & Domestic Virtue*, 220.

the increasing gap between rich and poor. Commenting on this disparity, a secretary in Mpigi explained: "People who have, have a lot, and those who don't have nothing at all."[12] In the words of a domestic worker in Arua, "Everything is available in the market if you have the money. You have to have brains and to work very hard to get things and survive."[13]

In this environment, poverty became a main focus of Ugandan women's organizations, which worked together with government programs to run workshops to improve women's economic circumstances, often by setting up small-scale enterprises and cooperatives. Most projects failed quickly, however, because of their members' low literacy levels and lack of management experience. Microfinance loans to groups of poor women also blossomed during the 1990s, although the high interest rates and short duration of these loans (usually no more than three months), meant that they rarely moved borrowers out of poverty.

Women traders in the Kumasi Central Market in Ghana's second largest city also emphasized the challenges of survival for women without substantial resources. They explained the critical importance of having at least one family member overseas, a trend of international migration that dated back to the military regimes of the 1970s and continued in response to the economic hardships of the following decade. While school fees, clothes, and medical expenses threatened to drain women's resources, women perceived well-educated, healthy, and loyal children as the best source of long-term economic security. In the words of Amma Pokuaa, who grew up selling yams because that was what her mother sold: "Today, the only [yam trader who is prosperous] is the one whose brother has traveled and brought her money. Only if her child has traveled, then she can build property and maybe her living conditions will be good ... But of those of us who stayed on like this without any help, some are even staying home now."[14] She continued: "Right now in Ghana here, if you have money to do business, money is here. There is money here. But if you don't have money to do business, that is it. You will have so much trouble. If God hasn't helped you, you can only die. Nobody will help you."[15]

[12] Kyomuhendo and McIntosh, *Women, Work & Domestic Virtue*, 190.

[13] Kyomuhendo and McIntosh, *Women, Work & Domestic Virtue*, 189.

[14] Gracia Clark, *African Market Women: Seven Life Stories from Ghana* (Bloomington: Indiana University Press, 2010), 126.

[15] Clark, *African Market Women*, 128.

Even successful women emphasized the difficulties confronting most women traders. Auntie Afriyie was one of the few to move from retailing into food processing. With a palm oil press made locally, she began a thriving business producing palm oil, attributing her success to the "house wisdom" she learned from her mother. "Her wisdom that she used to live in Ghana, that is what I studied. So right away, I grew up and had not gone to school, so the trading that my mother did, I observed and learned it."[16] She continued: "If you have that wisdom, living in Ghana here, everything of yours will make you get ahead. But if you don't know this wisdom, if you live here today, you will say that Ghana is hard."[17]

In this difficult climate, in addition to striving to send a family member abroad, women also found solidarity by relying on each other as "family," referring to their colleagues with the English word "sisters," to adult subordinates as children, and to their group leader as a mother looking after her children. Christian groups that preached the second coming of Christ provided women traders with a shared explanation of their troubles.

Living with AIDS

The most critical health issue of the 1990s, HIV/AIDS, had devastating consequences for women, particularly young women – and was inseparable from the desperate poverty in many areas of the continent. Sbongile, a twenty-four-year-old South African woman, explained the connection:

> In my family nobody is working so when I go out with a man, I must at least come with something, you see. I just can't come back in the morning and go for the bread meant for the children ... They all expect that I come with something at home ... even R10 to buy bread and milk at least.[18]

Unlike the United States, in Africa heterosexual women were more likely than elsewhere to be infected with the virus. Building on

[16] Clark, *African Market Women*, 136.

[17] Clark, *African Market Women*, 139.

[18] Nthabiseng Motsemme, "'Loving in a Time of Hopelessness': On Township Women's Subjectivities in a Time of HIV/AIDS," in *Basus'iimbokodo, bawel'imilambo/They Remove Boulders and Cross Rivers: Women in South African History*, ed. Nomboniso Gaso (Cape Town: HSRC Press, 2007), 391.

the observation of Stephen Lewis, Special Envoy for the Secretary General of the UN in Africa, that "this pandemic increasingly has a woman's face," South African scholar Nthabiseng Motsemme countered he forgot to add that it has "a young African woman's face."[19] By 2005 about 57 percent of Africans living with HIV were women, the highest proportion anywhere in the world. Following its outbreak in east and central Africa during the mid 1980s, by the later years of the decade the disease spread southward, with its most virulent impact during the 1990s in South Africa, then opening up to the rest of the continent as apartheid ended. The country's extensive labor mobility, densely packed and impoverished urban townships, and high levels of sexually transmitted diseases provided ideal conditions for the outbreak of an epidemic.

Throughout the continent, HIV/AIDS intensified gender inequalities, creating high levels of fear and distrust in marriage systems that continued to accept both polygyny and double standards for women and men. Although marriage might have seemed to offer women greater security than casual sexual relationships, husbands were responsible for the virus in somewhere between 50 and 80 percent of women. Despite these dangers, many women remained with their husbands, concerned primarily about the fate of their children. One woman explained:

> When he first learned he has HIV, he asked me to stay with him, to stay by him.
>
> And because God gave me a soft heart, I stayed…
>
> We don't sleep together, because he won't use condoms. I told him, "My body is my body, please don't abuse it." …
>
> My children are all I think about. They are what I live for.[20]

By 2003 with over five million people living with HIV/AIDS, South Africa had the largest infected population in the world, many of whom were young women from the informal settlements that skirted the country's major cities. During the late 1990s, the country became the site of intense conflict over whether the government should provide pregnant women with the antiretroviral drug that could dramatically reduce transmission of the virus from mother to child, the controversy

[19] Motsemme, "'Loving in a Time of Hopelessness,'" 373.

[20] Quoted in John Iliffe, *The African AIDS Epidemic: A History* (Athens, OH: Ohio University Press, 2006), 86.

that Pregs Govender highlighted in her resignation from Parliament. Only in 2003, facing a lawsuit by the grassroots Treatment Action Campaign (TAC), did President Thabo Mbeki's government agree to provide medication to HIV-positive pregnant women. Under the leadership of pioneering gay rights activist Zackie Achmat, the TAC coupled legal action with marches and civil disobedience to persuade the government to distribute free medicine to millions infected with the virus and to establish a comprehensive program of AIDS education and prevention.

Interviews from KwaZulu-Natal, the province worst hit by the illness, illustrate the impact of this scourge for women. As in many of the country's provinces and townships, HIV/AIDS could not be separated from South Africa's history of poverty, staggeringly high unemployment rates, ethnic bloodshed, and other chronic violence, including high levels of rape and sexual assault. During the 1980s, death became embedded in everyday life through the frequent mass political funerals for young men murdered by the state and vigilante groups, while parental authority collapsed as angry young people accused their parents of accommodating too easily to the apartheid government. Victims of state persecution were celebrated as heroes of the liberation struggle, however, while HIV/AIDS deaths were hidden as shameful. The persistent violence of everyday life shaped women's (and men's) perceptions of "safe" and "risky" behavior, leading one researcher to ask the question: "What is it like to try to love in a time of hopelessness?"[21]

These desperate circumstances were inseparable from the way both women and men responded to AIDS education that focused on condom use. However rational these messages might appear, in a time of despair many young women saw childbearing as a means of affirming life and perpetuating themselves in the face of possible death. Furthermore, giving birth to a healthy baby was public evidence that neither they nor the child's father carried the stigma of AIDS. In addition, many married women feared that urging their husbands to use condoms might be interpreted as jeopardizing the expectation that their partners would be faithful. And, perhaps most critical, was the frequency of *ukuphanta*, "getting by," through informal survival strategies, including women's relationships with men, especially older men.

[21] Motsemme, "'Loving in a Time of Hopelessness,'" 373.

Despite the risk of contracting HIV infections, these men provided money, gifts, groceries, and consumption goods such as cell phones in exchange for sex.

Poverty and massive unemployment in KwaZulu-Natal cast a strong shadow over sexuality and marriage. With male unemployment exceptionally high, by the late twentieth century many men were unable to marry and support stable families. These dire economic conditions led marriage rates to plummet and made "transactional sex," men giving gifts to poorer girlfriends, a common practice. By 2001, less than 30 percent of African men and women over the age of fifteen were married, down from 56 percent in 1951. More and more couples with children were consigned to one-roomed shacks in informal settlements.

If in the past, men had expressed their love by supporting a wife and family, by the early twenty-first century they did so by giving gifts to girlfriends, for whom disposable income and consumer goods formed a vital part of romantic relationships. Many women were forced to accept such gifts as a sign of love, and often to have relationships with more than one partner in order to survive. And despite the prevalence of multiple partners for both men and women, many of these relationships lasted for long periods of time. According to one young woman, "If you really love the number one boyfriend truly, there is nothing that can change that because you love the others for their money only."[22]

Attitudes toward these changes were complex. When surveyed on the topic of bridewealth (*lobolo*), many young women supported *lobolo* as a way to test a man's character and commitment to "true love." With modern forms of birth control widespread in South Africa by the late 1990s, some women justified their right to multiple partners as a sign of the emerging equality between women and men. Women could also be pragmatic in explaining the benefits of particular attachments, calling a boyfriend who provided gifts the minister of finance and one with a car the minister of transport.

Women's activism during the 1990s, coupled with intense support from international sources, led to a proliferation of national and continent-wide organizations offering preventive education for sex

[22] Mark Hunter, "Providing Love: Sex and Exchange in Twentieth-Century South Africa," in *Love in Africa*, eds Jennifer Cole and Lynn M. Thomas (Chicago: University of Chicago Press, 2009), 147.

workers and general support for women living with AIDS. Tasintha, a Zambian group formed in 1992, ran community education programs in the schools, encouraged sex workers to protect themselves by using condoms and seeking treatment for sexually transmitted diseases, and offered training programs to instruct them in alternative means of earning a living. By 2000, 5,005 sex workers had learned new skills including textile work, tailoring and sewing, and bookkeeping. In Uganda, after testing positive for AIDS, Beatrice Were created the National Community of Women Living with AIDS (NACWOLA). Founded in 1991, by 1999, 46,000 members in eighteen branches ran support groups and training programs as well as advocating for women's rights. With a continent-wide focus, the women who attended the Stockholm AIDS Conference in 1988 launched the Society for Women and AIDS (SWAA). Under the group's auspices Dr Eka Esu-Williams initiated programs to assist Nigerian sex workers, while Dr Nkandu Luo (later Zambia's Health Minister), created a network of thirty national AIDS advocacy groups, including Tasintha. Elsewhere national and local affiliates began a variety of programs, developing microcredit facilities and projects to assist AIDS orphans, training caregivers, and offering counseling services.

Contradictions of religious revivals

A decade of both hope and despair provided fertile terrain to sustain women's active involvement in the religious lives of their communities and to open them to messianic trends in both Christianity and Islam. While new Pentecostal Christian churches found enthusiastic adherents throughout Africa, Muslim revival movements sought to rejuvenate and transform cultures not perceived as sufficiently orthodox. Although these renewal movements opened new opportunities for women, their consequences also could be confining, contradictory, or even devastating. Furthermore, as the economic divide on the continent deepened, religious movements reflected this growing chasm. While countries such as Nigeria, Kenya, and Ghana with a growing middle class provided fertile terrain for evangelical groups that emphasized individual achievement and success for women as well as for men, in countries with deep pockets of poverty Pentecostal movements mirrored the dispossession and despair of their followers.

By the late twentieth century, women in the Maasai region of northern Tanzania thrived as members of the Congregation of the Holy Spirit (Spiritans). The Catholic missionaries who founded the church had spent more than fifty years trying with limited success to convert Maasai men. But despite the restrictions on women's religious education and their exclusion from formal leadership positions, women still made up the majority of church members. Women seemed to ignore, or simply put up with their presumed authority, however, while often mocking or gossiping about them in private.

For these women, churches provided alternative female social spaces, including opportunities for conversation, singing, and prayer before and after classes and services, especially in their *jumuiya*, small Christian communities. In the words of one elderly woman: "[Our *jumuiya*] discusses all the good words of Eng'ai [God] that were talked about in church ... When we meet we have a service. Often we take a collection to help sick people or the family of someone who has died, or we go to help work on the farm of someone who is sick or the family of someone who has died."[23] Another woman, Mwalimu Lea, who was widowed very young, was at first drawn to the Catholic Church because she and others believed that it had helped two barren women to have children; she also appreciated what she had learned about the rights of widows. Believing that God would help her if she were in need confirmed her belief that remarrying was unnecessary. Unconcerned with men's formal power in the church, she expressed her interest in becoming a catechist to help her friends, and teach them how to pray.

Among Christians, however, the main transformational energy in the late twentieth century came not from established groups such as the Spiritans, but from the new Pentecostal churches that swept across the continent. Although some of these churches had roots in the 1970s and 1980s, their popularity soared from the 1990s onward. In Malawi, for example, by 2000, 20 percent of people belonged to Pentecostal churches, a dramatic increase from 1 percent in 1960. These groups emphasized the protective powers of the "Holy Spirit" as communicated through speaking in tongues, divine healing, and prophesying and, unlike many other Christian churches, banned any engagement with traditional religious practices. While in the past most

[23] Dorothy L. Hodgson, *The Church of Women: Gendered Encounters between Maasai and Missionaries* (Bloomington: Indiana University Press, 2005), 186.

African Instituted (or Independent) Churches (AICs) had trained only men to become evangelists, confining women to their customary roles as healers and prophetesses, Pentecostal groups were more open to women leaders, some of whom went on to found separate religious communities.

Following conventional narratives of religious innovation, the women who established separate churches claimed divine inspiration, often a spur to overcoming challenges earlier in their lives. Transnational encounters with evangelical leaders outside their countries of origin also helped to launch their careers. Margaret Wangare, whose dreams and visions began when she was a high school student in Kenya, became an itinerant revival evangelist and faith healer in the 1980s. After receiving theological training at the All Nations Bible School in Benin City, Nigeria, she presided as bishop over her own congregation, the Church of the Lord. In Malawi, Bishop Mercy Yami was "born again" in 1976 and, choosing evangelism over marriage, began to preach to the most deprived people in the country, on the streets, in prison, and among the blind and destitute. In 1995 she set up the Love of God Church after an earlier congregation failed because her male cofounder was uncomfortable with female leadership.

During the 1990s, a few of these evangelical women became famous celebrities. Margaret Wanjiru, who initiated the Jesus Is Alive Ministry in Nairobi, came to evangelism after a difficult childhood and time spent in what she later described as "satanic cults." During a crusade by Emmanuel Eni, a famous Nigerian evangelist, she confessed her "seamy" past, renounced her possessions, and joined an evangelical group. In 1993 she opened the Jesus Is Alive Ministry in Nairobi. After the terrorist bombing near her church in 1998, Wanjiru became famous for ministering to victims; as her reputation soared, thousands of people began flocking to her Sunday morning services. Her renown allowed her to build an ultramodern church, to launch the magazine *Faith Digest* and the television program *Healing the Nation* to publicize her ministry, and eventually to become a Member of Parliament.

With women making up the majority of their followers, Pentecostal churches established single-sex groups focused on prayer, childbearing, and promoting women's achievement and self-confidence. The Action Chapel International in Ghana featured a women's wing called Women in Action, as well as "Fruit of the Womb," a prayer and deliverance meeting for childless women; a Post-Marital Department; and the Pastors' Wives Association. Based in Accra, Ghana, Christie Doe

Tetteh's Solid Rock Chapel hosted a women's convention called "The Excellent Woman," designed to foster women's self-esteem. Evangelical churches also assisted women in coping with their daily hardships. One Ghanaian woman explained, "I might have gone crazy by now if I had not resorted to seeking divine intervention in solving my problems."[24]

The example of Doe Tetteh, who used her magazine *Solid Rock* and the prayer band Striking Force to attract thousands of worshipers to her services, raises questions about the extent to which these charismatic churches, which challenged traditional barriers to women's leadership and formal authority, also empowered ordinary women. By contrast with Ghana's older churches, charismatic congregations embraced the idea of women's leadership as pastors. Church leaders also proclaimed the spiritual equality of believers and preached that in terms of worldly success and prosperity, there was no difference between women and men. Yet, with regard to marriage, the group espoused a philosophy of gender complementarity rather than equality. Believing that because of their inherent differences, women and men played distinct roles in society, they preached that women had a duty to be submissive to their husbands.

Gender differences notwithstanding, many church leaders, male and female, challenged women to confront the status quo, to assert themselves in both religion and society, and to strive for personal achievement by building their self-esteem. Women were also encouraged to insist on intimate and satisfying sexual relationships with their husbands. Furthermore, the rhetoric of these churches was new and inspiring. At one national women's convention, Christie Doe Tetteh encouraged women:

> You have looked down on yourselves for too long. You know that you have been caged. You have to come out of that cage before you can break barriers. We are afraid of so many things: the barrier of religion, the barrier of tradition, the barrier of family, the barrier of class. We are breaking it! Anything that made you afraid, I have come to tell you, go for the gold![25]

[24] Paul Gifford, *Ghana's New Christianity: Pentecostalism in a Globalizing African Economy* (Bloomington: Indiana University Press, 2004), 184.

[25] Jane E. Soothill, "The Problem with 'Women's Empowerment': Female Religiosity in Ghana's Charismatic Churches," *Studies in World Christianity* (2010), 86. euppublishing.com.

Echoing such sentiments, a famous male pastor in Ghana, Mensa Otabil, admonished women in one of his sermons, "Most of you women have great potential but you will die pathetic creatures ... A woman's lot is not to depend on a man. Have your own house, car ... I'm looking for purpose-driven, achievement-orientated women."[26]

Whereas Pentecostalism in west Africa promoted what scholars have termed "prosperity theology," in many other parts of the continent, the popularity of these churches rested more on the insecurity and conflict within households caused by economic restructuring and the growing gap between rich and poor than on an appeal to a rising middle class. In Mozambique, for example, men benefited from new wage-paying jobs, cash-cropping schemes, and access to land whereas women lost the safety net that had provided health care, food subsidies, and other social services. With new market forces unleashed, women's cooperatives were disbanded, produce was no longer sold at guaranteed rates, and the cost of food skyrocketed. The explosion of sex work in the 1990s clearly signaled women's economic vulnerability. In one set of interviews in the city of Chimoio, 60 percent of women had earned no cash income in the previous month, by contrast with 10 percent of men.

Here and in shantytowns across southern Africa, with deepening conflicts between women and men over resources, Pentecostalism exploded during the 1980s and 1990s. As men came increasingly to earn and control most domestic income, the new churches provided poor women with social and spiritual protection, especially for child and reproductive health problems. They also appealed to women by emphasizing men's responsibility to live sober lives and to support their families. One member of the Graça de Deus (Church of God's Grace) explained her conversion in relation to conflicts with her neighbors and her husband, and her children's repeated illnesses: "So I heard that there was this church ... It helps you but without having to pay, ... so I came here. My daughter also gave birth to two children that died, but now it's okay."[27] Churches, which some women described as new families, provided mutual aid, social support, and refuge from a perilous world in which they were vulnerable to spousal abuse and

[26] Gifford, *Ghana's New Christianity*, 184.

[27] Quoted in James Pfeiffer, Kenneth Gimble-Sherr, and Orvalho Joaquim Augusto, "The Holy Spirit in the Household: Pentecostalism, Gender, and Neoliberalism in Mozambique," *American Anthropologist* 109, 4 (2007), 695.

charges of infidelity and prostitution. Not surprisingly, membership also mushroomed in areas with the highest rates of HIV infection.

The rise of Pentecostalism also had a darker side, however, precipitating a rise in accusations of witchcraft, especially against the most vulnerable members of society – children and older women. In communities where an overwhelming majority of people believed in witchcraft, Pentecostal pastors promoted the belief in the satanic powers of witches, positioning themselves aggressively as the guardians against the practice. In Malawi, leading Catholic priests were pressured to confirm the existence of witchcraft to keep their converts from leaving the church to join Pentecostal movements. With accusations particularly targeting the powerless, children accused of witchcraft were stigmatized for life, and in west Africa, where traffickers deliberately manipulated witchcraft beliefs, accused children might be forced into involuntary labor on cocoa farms. Accused witches expelled from their communities often ended up living on the streets, vulnerable to trafficking, prostitution, and even death. At the same time, the pastors who fomented these fears earned substantial fees from performing exorcisms and selling anti-witchcraft goods and services.

The negative consequences of Pentecostalism continued to reverberate into the twenty-first century, targeting both witchcraft and homosexuality. In Malawi, for example, older women found themselves behind bars for their alleged crimes as witches. Although the country's legal code did not recognize the reality of witchcraft, in 2010 authorities jailed eighty-six people, mainly elderly women, for this crime. Despite their pleas of not guilty, all received sentences of four to six years. Religious revival in Uganda also produced harsh laws against gays and lesbians. Spurred on by evangelical missionaries from the United States, in December 2013, the Ugandan Parliament passed a bill that made "aggravated homosexuality" punishable by life in prison. Although the law was overturned in July 2014, the technical grounds of the decision – that the bill had been passed without a proper quorum – meant that the law might be revived at a later date. With public opinion inflamed during the course of the debate, David Kato, one of the country's most outspoken gay rights campaigners, was beaten to death with a hammer. But even after this brutal murder, other activists continued to speak out.

In Muslim communities, Islamic revival movements paralleled the rise of Pentecostal Christian churches during the 1990s. The town of Dogondoutchi in Niger experienced two competing waves of religious renewal, one in the early 1990s and the second beginning later in the decade and continuing into the early 2000s. Both movements presented new visions of Islamic moral order, responding to and helping to sustain the belief that the country's economic problems were rooted in immorality – often explained as a failure to curb female sexuality – and that only widespread moral reforms could reverse the devastating effects of poverty and underdevelopment.

A major source of this Islamic resurgence came from a group known as Izala (whose acronym meant Movement for Suppressing Innovations and Restoring the Sunna), which by the early 1990s had spread into Niger from neighboring northern Nigeria. Its followers advocated a return to a "pure" form of Islam and adherence to conservative moral standards. In the heated atmosphere produced, as reformists and their religious opponents competed for public attention via loudspeakers and cassette recorders, ordinary people became increasingly aware that their choices of dress, marriage partners, and other aspects of daily life influenced how they would be perceived as Muslims. In addition to monitoring other social and cultural choices, reformers condemned women's *bori* spirit possession ceremonies, strongly denouncing them as superstition.

In urban areas of Niger, such as the capital Niamey, the influence of Izala was complex. New schools were built for female students and more women were appointed as teachers. These improvements in girls' education reflected reformers' belief (similar to that of nineteenth-century Nigerian jihadists) that women should receive an education to further their sacred task of educating children and caring for the household. Yet critics worried about the repercussions for women of other aspects of Islamic renewal, including the prospect of *sharia* law being imposed and the results of new dress codes. They expressed alarm that young girls and women whose dress was deemed skimpy had been beaten and had their clothes ripped off. These attacks reflected Izala's insistence that women wear the *hijabi*, a veil covering much of their bodies, and live in total or partial seclusion. In the past, by contrast, only elite wives or the pious and wealthy were secluded and women had many opportunities to visit neighbors, family members, and friends.

The heated debates over Muslim reform intensified after 1997 when a new Islamic teacher Mahamane Awal arrived in Niamey. Denouncing Izala, Awal preached his own brand of revival that included promoting women's education, frugality in bridewealth gifts, and opposition to a national Family Code designed to protect women's rights. Like his Azala opponents, he condemned what he viewed as female permissiveness. Even after Awal was discredited by 2005, the reformist concern persisted and most people continued to see seclusion and veiling as remedies against immorality. These movements to purify Islamic practice also brought renewed condemnations of *bori* spirit possession ceremonies, which attracted more strident disapproval for creating a forum in which beautifully dressed, sometimes scantily clad women (those possessed by older, indigenous spirits) were able to perform sensuous dances before crowds of people.

Although women across the continent continued to be excluded from most orthodox Islamic ceremonies, small numbers of women with sufficient resources were able to perform the *hajj*, the annual pilgrimage to Mecca, in the latter years of the twentieth century. In Niger, government subsidies and air travel allowed more women to carry out this important pillar of their faith and earn the prestigious title of "Hajiya" given to those who had gone on the pilgrimage. In Maradi, aristocratic women or to those old enough to have accumulated capital from trade were most likely to travel to Mecca; but all successful women traders made saving money for the pilgrimage a priority. By the end of the twentieth century, a new class of prominent female merchants, the Hajiyoyi (the plural form of Hajiya), had emerged. Women and men who performed the pilgrimage returned not only with an enhanced sense of themselves as Muslims, which they broadcast through performing songs about their travel. Signaling a combination of modernity and piety, they also came back bearing prestigious, expensive gifts such as VCRs, video cameras, and brocaded wall hangings of the Great Mosque. In an added benefit, the association of pilgrimage with age supported women's sometimes fictitious claims that they were postmenopausal and thus no longer subject to the constraints on younger women.

Conclusion

By the end of the twentieth century African women faced new opportunities and new crises, the culmination of a tumultuous period that transformed women's lives in innumerable ways, yet left many of their expectations – and their hopes and dreams for themselves and their children – difficult to fulfill. Overshadowing the lives of both women and men, the economic liberalization demanded by international agencies intensified a growing gap between rich and poor, offering new opportunities to educated middle-class women. At the same time, the poverty of many women deepened, particularly in rural areas, in the shantytowns surrounding most of Africa's major cities, and in countries devastated by war. In some cases such as the eastern Congo, southern Sudan, Somalia, and the Central African Republic, violence had persisted for decades.

Responding to these challenges, women seized the opportunities presented by a more open political climate to organize in new ways. They pressed for gender equity and women's full representation in national legislative bodies and for expanded educational opportunities for girls and women. They also redefined the goals of women's organizations to confront men's domination in both private and public life and to design innovative approaches to health and healing. In doing so, they took full advantage of new technologies to sustain vital international contacts both within the continent and with international and national women's groups in other areas of the world.

Contradictions and challenges

In her play *A New Earth*, inspired by local ritual, Cameroonian writer Werewere Liking dramatically portrays women's contradictory feelings of power and oppression. So, the female protagonist, expresses these ambivalent views of her life in the opening scene:

> "This is where I live out my life. Static, but coiled, ready to overflow from the calabash enclosed in a much too small container...
>
> This is where I live out my life, bubbling with energy which gushes from me like lava from a crater, like resin from the pores in the barks of the trees, hollow and unnoticed...
>
> Oh yes! I, slave-girl, wife of Ntep [...]
>
> This is where I drown my life in a torrent of unexploited juice, under the weight of stifled talents. Ah, why could resin not be active energy, and my blood be combustible oil?"[1]

During a century of dramatic and sometimes explosive transformation, women's lives retained this tension between strength and vulnerability. They continued to carry the weight of a continent on their backs, while resisting men's efforts to curb their independence, confidence, and sexuality.

With the steep population decline that accompanied the early years of European conquest, women became the focus of conflicting

[1] Quoted in Nalova Lyonga, "African Women and Feminist Theory," *Defining New Idioms and Alternative Forms of Expression* (Amsterdam: Rodopi, 1996), 157.

strategies for restoring African societies. Perpetually short of labor and anxious to transform personal life in line with European notions of "civilization," colonial powers often blamed the demographic crisis on local coming-of-age and birthing practices, which they depicted as "immoral." In condemning women's behavior, missionaries and colonial officials were joined by African men, who favored strengthening customary law to maintain control over young women. African women forged their own strategies for renewal, however. Healers founded new religious movements and transformed older ones. Women also creatively adapted their economic lives to the new cash crop and migrant labor economy, tested the boundaries of both colonial and customary law, and staged collective protests against policies that threatened their ability to care for their families.

As educational opportunities expanded for both girls and boys in the years following the Second World War, increasing numbers of women began to embrace new identities. Eager to shed earlier condemnations of their "immorality," many women learned skills in cooking, home decorating, and child care associated with being "modern" and "respectable." They also turned their collective power to organizing separate women's protests. More often, however, they backed the efforts of male-dominated political parties that were fighting for independence from colonial rule. Although women's strong connections with grassroots political and social groups lent a populist edge to many of these anticolonial political movements, women only rarely challenged male domination of their societies. Rather they tended to rely on the hope that freedom would automatically bring a better life for women as well as for men.

Despite the Africanization of political power that came with independence from colonial rule, during the period from the late 1950s through the 1980s many aspects of women's lives changed little. Women's branches of nationalist political parties continued to dominate their public activities. Seldom challenging men's power in politics or the family, these groups favored projects that stressed small-scale farming, crafts, and skills in home life and childcare. This domestic emphasis mirrored the era's larger-scale economic development projects that focused on strengthening men's skills and economic position, while disregarding women's key roles as farmers and traders. Adding to their disempowerment, women had little voice in either the one-party states or the military governments that dominated the postindependence political landscape. Indeed, many African rulers echoed colonial critiques of independent women by waging campaigns against those whose mini-skirts were judged to be "un-African."

At the same time, tensions over customary practices remained high. Many young people were drawn to films and magazines that openly portrayed romantic love and sexual relationships; they also continued to resist arranged marriages and other efforts to limit their freedom. The governments that attempted to end such deeply rooted practices as polygyny were no more successful than their colonial predecessors in implementing cultural change from above.

In the postindependence era, however, new forces were emerging that would upend the gender balance of power. By the 1980s, the austerity policies imposed on debt-ridden governments forced many women to make new economic demands on their husbands to contribute to clothing, food, and school fees for their families. In addition, the growing involvement of African women in transnational women's movements and in the armed struggles for independence in southern Africa and the Portuguese colonies began to undercut men's power in numerous ways.

New challenges confronted the male-dominated status quo during the 1990s. While prolonged civil wars and genocide were still tearing some countries apart, in others dictatorships were yielding to pressures for democratization. Supported by new international norms declaring that women's rights are human rights and greater openness to feminism in the global South, women began to push for their own empowerment when postconflict constitutions were being drafted. Focusing on quotas for women in legislative bodies, women activists succeeded in transforming African politics in significant ways. They pressed for gender equity and women's full representation in national legislatures and for expanded educational opportunities for girls and women. They also redefined the goals of women's organizations to challenge men's domination in both private and public life.

As the twentieth century came to a close, African women faced new opportunities and new obstacles. Overshadowing the lives of both women and men, the free-market economic reforms demanded by the World Bank and the International Monetary Fund intensified a growing gap between rich and poor. These policies offered new opportunities to women in the expanding educated middle class. At the same time, the poverty of many women deepened, particularly in rural areas, in the shantytowns surrounding most of Africa's major cities, and in countries devastated by war, sexual violence, and HIV/AIDS.

Despite the upheavals of the colonial and postcolonial periods, important continuities in attitudes and institutions persisted, sometimes with contradictory consequences. Strong families remained vital to African communities, offering women both a source of strength and a source of conflict. Often disregarding pressure from local and international advocates of family planning, both women and men continued to value large families and to equate women's fertility with the health and welfare of their communities. Although birth rates fell in some countries during the late twentieth century, by 2000 African states overall had the highest birth rates in the world. In a survey of forty-seven nations for the period 1995–2000, the total fertility rate in western, middle (central), and eastern Africa was at least six children per woman. A significant drop (to 3.3) occurred only in the southern region. Given the weakness and instability of many postcolonial states, large families provided a form of insurance, helping to distribute resources, care for family members, and provide continuity in times of crisis. Perhaps more importantly, sub-Saharan African countries also had the world's highest rates of child mortality. In 2010, despite significant improvement from the 1990s, one in eight children died before the age of five, many in the first few months of life. These statistics helped to explain not only the widespread resistance to birth control, but women's continuing quest for new forms of healing and therapy.

However highly valued, African families faced numerous challenges. Following a trend that dated to the nineteenth and early twentieth centuries, young people increasingly struggled to pave their own paths in life, in part by choosing their spouses and sexual partners rather than deferring to family preferences. More often than in the past, widowed women refused to marry men from their husbands' families. The persistence of polygyny and bridewealth (often in cash rather than precolonial forms of exchange) and the prevalence of informal sexual relationships continued to provoke debate and conflict. These persistent anxieties over family and sexuality helped to fuel a major source of backlash against women.

A less ambiguous basis of continuity with the past was the long history of women's solidarity. Rooted in a precolonial legacy of religious rituals, dance societies, political systems that gave women control of their own affairs, sex-segregated age grades, and cooperative farming groups, this collective tradition formed the basis of women's activism throughout the twentieth century, enhancing their ability to challenge policies that disrupted the well-being of their families and communities. During the 1990s women's organizations were critical to re-empowering women and giving them a new political voice. Although the struggle for gender equity was ongoing and women often bore the brunt of social and political turbulence, by the end of the century they were better able to advocate for women in governing bodies and to promote and support efforts to insure women that "their time will come."

Political transformation continued into the twenty-first century, placing many African countries among the top-ranked in the world in terms of women's representation. Rwandan women held 64 percent of legislative seats in 2012 and in seven other countries women's representation surpassed 35 percent. In 2012 Joyce Banda was elected President of Malawi, a position she held for two years. Challenging stereotypes that women were consistently oppressed under Islam, many predominantly Muslim nations established quotas to increase the number of women in national legislatures. These changes were implemented in all countries in the Maghreb as well as in Tanzania, Mauritania, Senegal, Eritrea, Sudan, Niger, and Somalia. Women also became prominent as prime ministers, judges, and cabinet members. Defying gender stereotypes, their positions often demanded expertise in such areas as defense, finance, and foreign affairs.

A Liberian women's leader, describing this new political environment, emphasized the changes in her country following the end of the civil war:

> During the war we got to know our value because we were forced to find food for the children; men could not go out. When Ellen [Johnson Sirleaf] took over things changed for women ... Women can speak anywhere [in public] now. In the past, women were in the back and were silent ... Women did not read and write. Women stayed at the back too long, and now we have decided to speak for ourselves.[2]

Assessing women's power in 2004, feminist scholar Amina Mama, then the Director of the Africa Gender Institute at the University of Cape Town, emphasized stark contrasts between countries with elaborate national policies on gender equity and those that had rejected

[2] Aili Tripp, "Women and Politics in Africa Today," adaptation of 2012 African Studies Association Presidential Address, *Democracy in Africa* (December 9, 2013), www.democracyinafrica.org/women-politics-africa-today.

even rudimentary measures to empower women. But, in Mama's view, even in the most favorable circumstances, "Affirmative action strategies have so far been too easily appropriated and manipulated by male political actors, the majority of whom remain deeply resistant to gender equality."[3]

Opposition to equality came not only in the egregious examples of massive rape and violence in areas such as the eastern Congo and Darfur, but also in backlash from churches, political parties, traditional leaders, and rural officials. This response was particularly forceful in countries where women had made the greatest strides. Writing in the *New York Times* early in 2015, South African journalist Sisonke Msimang decried public harassment of mini-skirted women in Nairobi and Harare; "decency bills" introduced in Uganda's Parliament that defined revealing clothing as "anti-African"; and a bill drafted by the Congress of Traditional Leaders in South Africa that would have returned all women in rural areas to the status of legal minors. Fortunately, she reported, "loud" and "organized" women's movements successfully weakened or resisted many of these efforts. While acknowledging the difficulties women confronted, she concluded optimistically, "[Women's] protests have been daring and their collective message has been clear: The walk from the streets to the halls of power may be long, but the goal is well within reach."[4]

[3] Amina Mama, "Editorial," *Feminist Africa* 3 (2004), "National Politricks." agi.ac.za/journal/feminist-africa-issue 3-2004-national politricks.

[4] *New York Times*, January 11, 2015, "Sunday Review" 4.

References and further reading

1– Colonizing African families

For a broad historical synthesis of African women's history, see Catherine Coquery-Vidrovitch, *African Women: A Modern History* (Boulder, CO: Westview Press, 1997); Iris Berger and E. Frances White, *Women in Sub-Saharan Africa: Restoring Women to History* (Bloomington: Indiana University Press, 1999); Toyin Falola and Nana Akua Amponsah, *Women's Roles in Sub-Saharan Africa* (Santa Barbara, CA: ABC-CLIO, 2012); and Patricia W. Romero, *African Women: A Historical Panorama* (Princeton: Markus Weiner, 2014). Many of the edited collections that cover the twentieth century will be cited below. But important additions to this list include Toyin Falola and Nana Akua Amponsah, eds, *Women, Gender, and Sexualities in Africa* (Durham, NC: Carolina Academic Press, 2013) and Jan Bender Shetler, ed., *Gendering Ethnicity in African Women's Lives* (Madison: University of Wisconsin Press, 2015). An excellent reference is Kathleen Sheldon, *Historical Dictionary of Women in Sub-Saharan Africa* (Methuen, NJ: Scarecrow Press, 2005). The four regional collections of *Women Writing Africa*, a pioneering series published by the Feminist Press, include two centuries of women's texts (from songs, poems, and folk tales to diaries, court cases, and political speeches) selected by a distinguished panel of local women scholars. For an introduction to writing by African women, see Juliana Makuchi Nfah-Abbenyi, *Gender in African Women's Writing: Identity, Sexuality and Difference* (Bloomington: Indiana University Press, 1997) and Chikwenye Okonjo Ogunyemi and Tuzyline Jita Allan, *The Twelve Best Books by African Women: Critical Readings* (Athens, OH: Ohio University Press, 2009).

The Joys of Motherhood (New York: George Braziller, 1979) is the best known of Buchi Emecheta's many novels that vividly portray the struggles of African women on the continent and as immigrants in Britain. Studies of women's work in Africa were influenced by Ester Boserup's influential book, *Woman's Role in Economic Development* (New York: St Martin's Press, 1970). Among the most important for colonial period are Majorie Keniston McIntosh, *Yoruba Women, Work, and Social Change* (Bloomington: Indiana University Press, 2009); Grace Bantebya Kyomuhendo and Marjorie Keniston McIntosh, *Women, Work & Domestic Virtue in Uganda, 1900–2003* (Oxford: James Currey, 2006); Claire C. Robertson, *Sharing the Same Bowl: A Socioeconomic History of Women and Class in Accra, Ghana* (Bloomington: Indiana University Press, 1984) and *Trouble Showed the Way: Women, Men, and Trade in the Nairobi Area, 1890–1990* (Bloomington: Indiana University Press, 1997); Elizabeth Schmidt, *Peasants, Traders and Wives: Shona Women in the History of Zimbabwe, 1870–1939* (Portsmouth, NH: Heinemann, 1992); Iris Berger, *Threads of Solidarity: Women in South African Industry, 1900–1980* (Bloomington: Indiana University Press, 1992); Kathleen E. Sheldon, *Pounders of Grain: A History of Women, Work, and Politics in Mozambique* (Portsmouth, NH: Heinemann, 2002); and Luise White, *The Comforts of Home: Prostitution in Colonial Nairobi* (Chicago: University of Chicago Press, 1990). Also discussed is Margaret Jean Hay, "Luo Women and Economic Change During the Colonial Period," in *Women in Africa: Studies in Social and Economic Change*, edited by Nancy Hafkin and Edna Bay (Stanford: Stanford University Press, 1976).

Case studies of marriage come from Jean Allman and Victoria Tashjian, *"I Will Not Eat Stone": A Women's History of Colonial Asante* (Portsmouth, NH: Heinemann, 2000); Judith Byfield, "Women, Marriage, Divorce and the Emerging Colonial State in Abeokuta (Nigeria) 1892–1904," in *"Wicked" Women and the Reconfiguration of Gender in Africa*, edited by Dorothy L. Hodgson and Sheryl A. McCurdy (Portsmouth, NH: Heinemann, 2001); Barbara Cooper, *Marriage in Maradi: Gender and Culture in a Hausa Society in Niger, 1900–1989* (Portsmouth, NH: Heinemann, 1997); Heidi Gengenbach, "'What My Heart Wanted': Gendered Stories of Early Colonial Encounters in Southern Mozambique," in *Women in Colonial African Histories*, edited by Jean Allman, Susan Geiger, and Nakanyike Musisi (Bloomington: Indiana University Press, 2001); and Rachel Jean-Baptiste, *Conjugal Rights: Marriage, Sexuality and Urban Life in Colonial Gabon* (Athens, OH: Ohio University Press, 2014). Emily S. Burrill traces the history of marriage in Mali in *States of Marriage: Gender, Justice, and Rights in Colonial Mali* (Athens: Ohio University Press, 2015). See also Brett L. Shadle, *"Girl Cases": Marriage and Colonialism in Gusiiland, Kenya, 1890–1970* (Portsmouth, NH: Heinemann, 2006) and the excellent collection of essays on family violence edited by Emily S. Burrill, Richard L. Roberts, and Elizabeth Thornberry, *Domestic Violence and the Law in Colonial and Postcolonial Africa* (Athens, OH: Ohio University Press, 2010).

On coming-of-age controversies in colonial Kenya, see Jean Davison, *Voices from Mutira: Changes in the Lives of Rural Kikuyu Women, 1910–1995* (Boulder, CO: Lynne Rienner, 1996); Tabitha Kanogo, *African Womanhood in Colonial Kenya, 1900–1950* (Athens, OH: Ohio University Press, 2005); Lynn M. Thomas, *Politics of the Womb: Women, Reproduction and the State in Kenya* (Berkeley: University of California Press, 2003). Important discussions of childbirth, demography, and sexuality include Nancy Rose Hunt, *A Colonial Lexicon: Of Birth Ritual, Medicalization, and Mobility in the Congo* (Durham, NC: Duke University Press, 1999); Jane Turrittin, "Colonial Midwives and Modernizing Childbirth in French West Africa," in *Women in Colonial African Histories*, edited by Jean Allman, Susan Geiger, and Nakanyike Musisi (Bloomington: Indiana University Press, 2001); Sheryl A. McCurdy, "Urban Threats: Manyema Women, Low Fertility, and Venereal Diseases in Tanganyika, 1926–1936," in *"Wicked" Women and the Reconfiguration of Gender in Africa*, edited by Dorothy L. Hodgson and Sheryl A. McCurdy (Portsmouth, NH: Heinemann, 2001); and Lynette Jackson, "'When in the White Man's Town': Zimbabwean Women Remember *Chibeura*," in *Women in Colonial African Histories*, edited by Jean Allman, Susan Geiger, and Nakanyiki Musisi (Bloomington: Indiana University Press, 2001). Diana Jeater's important book, *Marriage, Perversion, and Power: The Construction of Moral Discourse in Southern Rhodesia, 1894–1930*

(Oxford: Clarendon Press, 1993) was among the first to explore how colonialism transformed women's sexuality. Nakanyike Musisi, "Gender and Sexuality in African History: A Personal Reflection," *Journal of African History* 55, 3 (2014), 317–30 provides an insightful overview of relevant research.

2– Confrontation and adaptation

The literature on religious innovation and adaptation in colonial Africa is extensive. Important sources for this chapter include Robert R. Edgar and Hilary Sapire, *African Apocalypse: The Story of Nontetha Nkwenkwe, a Twentieth-Century South African Prophet* (Athens: Ohio University Press, 1999); Paul Landau, *The Realm of the Word: Language, Gender, and Christianity in a Southern African Kingdom* (Portsmouth, NH: Heinemann, 1995); Catherine Robins, "Conversion, Life Crises, and Stability among Women in the East African Revival," in *The New Religions of Africa*, edited by Bennetta Jules-Rosette (Norwood, NJ: Ablex Publishing Corp., 1979); and Leroy Vail and Landeg White, *Power and the Praise Poem: Southern African Voices in History* (Charlottesville: University of Virginia Press, 1991). In *The Gender of Piety: Family, Faith, and Colonial Rule in Matabeleland, Zimbabwe* (Athens, OH: Ohio University Press, 2015), Wendy Urban-Mead traces the lives of women and men in a mission church over the course of the twentieth century. Iris Berger, "Women's Movements in Twentieth-Century Africa: A Hidden History," *African Studies Review* 57, 3 (December, 2014), 1–19 explores the idiom of "public healing" in a wide range of women's groups.

On women and Islam, an early life history is Mary F. Smith, *Baba of Karo: A Woman of the Muslim Hausa* (New Haven, CT: Yale University Press, 1954); for a later period, see Sarah Mirza and Margaret Strobel, eds, *Three Swahili Women: Life Histories from Mombasa, Kenya* (Bloomington: Indiana University Press, 1989). Other local analysis comes from Barbara Cooper, "Gender and Religion in Hausaland: Variations in Islamic Practice in Niger and Nigeria," in *Women in Muslim Societies*, edited by Herbert L. Bodman and Nayereh Tohidi (Boulder, CO: Lynne Rienner, 1998); Margaret Strobel, *Muslim Women in Mombasa, 1890–1975* (New Haven, CT: Yale University Press, 1979); and Margaret Strobel, "Women in Religion and in Secular Ideology," in *African Women: South of the Sahara*, edited by Margaret Jean Hay and Sharon Stichter (London: Longman, 1995, 2nd edn).

Writing on women, politics, and resistance in the early colonial period is also extensive. This chapter draws on Cynthia Brantley, "Mekatalili and the Role of Women in Giriama Resistance," in *Banditry, Rebellion, and Social Protest in Africa*, edited by Donald Crummey (London: Heinemann, 1986); Thaddeus Sunseri, "Famine and Wild Pigs: Gender Struggles and the Outbreak of the Maji Maji War in Uzaramo (Tanzania)," *Journal of African History* 38, 2 (1997), 235–59; Marc Matera, Misty L. Bastian, and Susan Kingsley Kent, *The Women's War of 1929: Gender and Violence in Colonial Nigeria* (New York: Palgrave Macmillan, 2011); Judith Van Allen, "'Aba Riots' or Igbo 'Women's War?' Ideology, Stratification, and the Invisibility of Women," in *Women in Africa: Studies in Social and Economic Change*, edited by Nancy Hafkin and Edna Bay (Stanford: Stanford University Press, 1976); and Julia C. Wells, *We Now Demand! The History of Women's Resistance to Pass Laws in South Africa* (Johannesburg: Witwatersrand University Press, 1993). Nwando Achebe's books, *Farmers, Traders, Warriors, and Kings: Female Power and Authority in Northern Igboland, 1900–1960* (Portsmouth, NH: Heinemann, 2005) and *The Female King of Colonial Nigeria: Ahebi Ugbabe* (Bloomington: Indiana University Press, 2011) are particularly important in illustrating how powerful women were able to turn flexible concepts of gender to their advantage in the early colonial period.

The articles in Jean Allman's edited collection, *Fashioning Africa: Power and the Politics of Dress* (Bloomington: Indiana University Press, 2004), explore the politics of clothing and identity. This chapter includes references to Margaret Jean Hay, "Changes in Clothing and Struggles over Identity in Colonial Kenya," in *Fashioning Africa: Power and the Politics of Dress*, edited by Jean Allman (Bloomington: Indiana University Press, 2004); Laura Fair, "Remaking Fashion in the Paris of the Indian Ocean: Dress, Performance, and the Cultural Construction of a Cosmopolitan Zanzibari Identity," in *Fashioning Africa: Power and the Politics of Dress*, edited by Jean Allman (Bloomington: Indiana University Press, 2004); and Judith Byfield, "Dress and Politics in Post-World War II Abeokuta (Western Nigeria)," in *Fashioning Africa: Power and the Politics of Dress*, edited by Jean Allman (Bloomington: Indiana University Press, 2004). Lynn M. Thomas addresses related issues in "The Modern Girl and Racial

Respectability in 1930s South Africa," *Journal of African History* 47, 3 (November 2006), 461–90. In *Veiling in Africa* (Bloomington: Indiana University Press, 2013), Elisha P. Renne's edited collection takes another approach to dress and fashion.

3– Domesticity and modernization

Many works address the relationship between domesticity and modernization. An important overview is Karen Tranberg Hansen, ed., *African Encounters with Domesticity* (New Brunswick, NJ: Rutgers University Press, 1992). This chapter also draws on Teresa A. Barnes, *"We Women Worked So Hard": Gender, Urbanization, and Social Reproduction in Colonial Harare, Zimbabwe, 1930–1956* (Portsmouth, NH: Heinemann, 1999) and Iris Berger, "An African American 'Mother of the Nation': Madie Hall Xuma in South Africa, 1940–1963," *Journal of Southern African Studies* 27, 3 (September 2001), 547–66.

Carol Summers's article, "'If You Can Educate the Native Woman…': Debates over the Schooling and Education of Girls and Women in Southern Rhodesia, 1900–1934," *History of Education Quarterly* 36, 4 (Winter, 1996), 449–71 provides background for this chapter. Works discussed also include: Gertrude Mianda, "Colonialism, Education, and Gender Relations in the Belgian Congo: The Évolué Case," in *Women in Colonial African Histories*, edited by Jean Allman, Susan Geiger, and Nakanyike Musisi (Bloomington: Indiana University Press, 2002); Kathleen Sheldon, "'I Studied with the Nuns, Learning to Make Blouses': Gender Ideology and Colonial Education in Mozambique," *International Journal of African Historical Studies* 31, 3 (1998), 595–625; Margaret Strobel, *Muslim Women in Mombasa, 1890–1975* (New Haven, CT: Yale University Press, 1979); Corrie Decker, "Reading, Writing, and Respectability: How Schoolgirls Developed Modern Literacies in Colonial Zanzibar," *International Journal of African Historical Studies* 43, 1 (2010), 89–114. She also covers these issues in her book, *Mobilizing Zanzibari Women: The Struggle for Respectability and Self-Reliance in Colonial East Africa* (New York: Palgrave Macmillan, 2014). See also Abosede A. George, *A History of Girlhood, Labor, and Social Development in Colonial Lagos* (Athens, OH: Ohio University Press, 2014).

Sources on the tensions and debates generated by modernization are varied. They include I.S. Manoin, "The Black Press,

1945–1963: The Growth of the Black Mass Media and Their Role as Ideological Disseminators," M.A. thesis, Witwatersrand University, 1983; Lynn Thomas, "'*Ngaitana* (I will circumcise myself)': The Gender and Generational Politics of the 1956 Ban on Clitoridectomy in Meru, Kenya," *Gender and History* 8, 3 (1996), 338–63; and Kenda Mutongi, *Worries of the Heart: Widows, Family, and Community in Kenya* (Chicago: University of Chicago Press, 2007). For fictional and first-hand accounts of these conflicts see Tsitsi Dangarembga, *Nervous Conditions: A Novel* (Seattle: Seal Press, 1988) and Shula Marks, ed., *Not Either an Experimental Doll: The Separate Worlds of Three South African Women* (London: The Women's Press, 1987). Timothy Burke explores cultural change and consumption patterns in *Lifebuoy Men, Lux Women: Commodification, Consumption, and Cleanliness in Modern Zimbabwe* (Durham, NC: Duke University Press, 1996).

African independent, or African-initiated, churches have generated significant research from scholars in many disciplines. An excellent book on women that covers this period is Cynthia Hoehler-Fatton, *Women of Fire & Spirit: History, Faith, and Gender in Roho Religion in Western Kenya* (New York: Oxford University Press, 1996). On the Deima Church, see Sheila S. Walker, "Women in the Harrist Movement," in *The New Religions of Africa*, edited by Bennetta Jules-Rosette (Norwood, NJ: Ablex Publishing Corp., 1979). Paul Breidenbach discusses Grace Tani's church in "The Woman on the Beach and the Man in the Bush: Leadership and Adepthood in the Twelve Apostles Movement of Ghana," in *The New Religions of Africa*, edited by Bennetta Jules-Rosette (Norwood, NJ: Ablex Publishing Corp., 1979). Because of its political implications, there is extensive writing on the Lumpa Church. Most informative for the roles of women are Hugo Hinfelaar, "Women's Revolt: The Lumpa Church of Lenshina Mulenga in the 1950s," *Journal of Religion in Africa* 21, 2 (1991), 99–129 and David M. Gordon, *Invisible Agents: Spirits in a Central African History* (Athens, OH: Ohio University Press, 2012).

4– Mothers of nationalism

For an excellent historical overview of African women in politics, see Aili Marie Tripp, Isabel Casimiro, Joy Kwesiga, and Alice Mungwa, *African Women's Movements: Changing Political Landscapes* (Cambridge: Cambridge University Press, 2009). See also Jean

O'Barr, "African Women in Politics," in *African Women: South of the Sahara*, edited by Margaret Jean Hay and Sharon Stichter (London: Longman, 1984). Susan Geiger's innovative research based on women's life histories was published as *TANU Women: Gender and Culture in the Making of Tanganyikan Nationalism, 1955–1965* (Portsmouth, NH: Heinemann, 1997).

Selected writing on nationalism and grassroots women's actions includes a number of works on Cameroon: Eugenia Shanklin, "ANLU Remembered: The Kom Women's Rebellion of 1958–61," *Dialectical Anthropology* 15, 2–3 (1990), 159–81; Susan Diduk, "Women's Agricultural Production and Political Action in the Cameroon Grassfields," *Africa* 59, 3 (1989), 338–55; Henry Kam Kah, "Women's Resistance in Cameroon's Western Grassfields: The Power of Symbols, Organization, and Leadership, 1957–1961," *African Studies Quarterly* 12, 3 (Summer 2011), 67–91; and Meredith Terretta, *Petitioning for Our Rights, Fighting for Our Nation: The History of the Democratic Union of Cameroonian Women, 1949–1960* (Bamenda, Cameroon: Langaa Research & Publishing, 2013). On other protests, see Tom Lodge, *Black Politics in South Africa since 1945* (London: Longman, 1983); Sondra Hale, *Gender Politics in Sudan: Islamism, Socialism, and the State* (Boulder, CO: Westview Press, 1997); and Nina Emma Mba, *Nigerian Women Mobilized: Women's Political Activity in Southern Nigeria, 1900–1965* (Berkeley: Institute of International Studies, University of California, 1982).

Sources for the case studies on nationalist movements include: Cheryl Johnson-Odim and Nina Emma Mba, *For Women and the Nation: Funmilayo Ransome-Kuti of Nigeria* (Urbana-Champaign, University of Illinois Press, 1997); Iris Berger, *Threads of Solidarity: Women in South African Industry, 1900–1980* (Bloomington: Indiana University Press, 1992); Julia C. Wells, *We Now Demand! The History of Women's Resistance to Pass Laws in South Africa* (Johannesburg: Witwatersrand University Press, 1993); and Frances Baard and Barbie Schreiner, *My Spirit is Not Banned* (Harare: Zimbabwe Publishing House, 1986). *The ANC Women's League: Sex, Gender and Politics* (Athens, OH: Ohio University Press, 2015) by Shireen Hassim covers the long history of South African's most important women's organization. Anne Kelk Mager, *Gender and the Making of a South African Bantustan: A Social History of the Ciskei, 1945–1958* (Portsmouth, HN: Heinemann, 1999) analyzes the impact of apartheid in one key rural area of South Africa. The main sources on Kenya are Wambui Waiyaki Otieno, ed., with an introduction by Cora Ann Presley, *Mau Mau's Daughter: A Life History* (Boulder, CO: Lynne Rienner, 1998); Cora Ann Presley, *Kikuyu Women, the Mau Mau Rebellion, and Social Change in Kenya* (Boulder, CO: Westview Press, 1992); and Luise White, "Separating the Men from the Boys: Constructions of Gender, Sexuality, and Terrorism in Central Kenya, 1939–1959," *International Journal of African Historical Studies* 23, 1 (1990), 1–25. On Guinea, see Elizabeth Schmidt, *Mobilizing the Masses: Gender, Ethnicity and Class in the Nationalist Movement in Guinea, 1939–1958* (Portsmouth, NH: Heinemann, 2005) and on Cameroon, Meredith Terretta, "A Miscarriage of Revolution: Cameroonian Women and Nationalism," *Stichproben. Wiener Zeitschrift für kritische Afrikastudien Nr.* (12/2007, 7), 61–90.

5– The struggle continues

Wangari Maathai relates her life history in *Unbowed: A Memoir* (New York: Anchor Books, 2007). Women and development projects are analyzed in Jennie Dey, "Gambian Women: Unequal Partners in Rice Development Projects?" *Journal of Development Studies* 17, 3 (1981), 109–22; Dolores Koenig, "Women's Roles in Settlement and Resettlement in Mali," in *African Feminism: The Politics of Survival in Sub-Saharan Africa*, edited by Gwendolyn Mikell (Philadelphia: University of Pennsylvania Press, 1997); and Monica L. Munachonga, "Women and the State: Zambia's Development Policies and Their Impact on Women," in *Women and the State in Africa*, edited by Jane L. Parpart and Kathleen A. Staudt (Boulder, CO: Lynne Rienner, 1990). Kathleen Sheldon's edited collection, *Courtyards, Markets, City Streets: Urban Women in Africa* (Boulder, CO: Westview Press, 1996) is another important source for this period. See in particular, Catherine M. Coles, "Three Generations of Hausa Women in Kaduna, Nigeria, 1925–1985," in *Courtyards, Markets, City Streets: Urban Women in Africa*, edited by Kathleen Sheldon (Boulder, CO: Westview Press, 1996); Mary Johnson Osirim, "Beyond Simple Survival: Women Microentrepreneurs in Harare and Bulawayo, Zimbabwe," in *Courtyards, Markets, City Streets: Urban Women in Africa*, edited by Kathleen Sheldon (Boulder, CO: Westview Press, 1996); and Paulette Beat-Songue (Laura Mitchell, trans.), "Prostitution, a *Petit-métier* During Economic Crisis: A Road to Women's Liberation?

The Case of Cameroon," in *Courtyards, Markets, City Streets: Urban Women in Africa*, edited by Kathleen Sheldon (Boulder, CO: Westview Press, 1996). Sources on southern Africa include Martha Mueller, "Women and Men, Power and Powerlessness in Lesotho," *Signs* 3, 1 (Autumn 1977), 154–66; Carolyn Baylies and Caroline Wright, "Female Labour in the Textile and Clothing Industry of Lesotho," *African Affairs* 92 (October 1993), 577–91; and Iris Berger, *Threads of Solidarity: Women in South African Industry, 1900–1980* (Bloomington: Indiana University Press, 1992). Women's education is covered in Claire Robertson, "Women's Education and Class Formation in Africa, 1950–1980," in *Women and Class in Africa*, edited by Claire Robertson and Iris Berger (New York: Holmes & Meier, 1986).

Aili Marie Tripp, Isabel Casimiro, Joy Kwesiga, and Alice Mungwa, *African Women's Movements: Transforming Political Landscapes* (Cambridge: Cambridge University Press, 2008) is among the best sources on postcolonial politics. Also see Maria N. Nzomo, "Kenyan Women in Politics and Public Decision Making," in *African Feminism: The Politics of Survival in Sub-Saharan Africa*, edited by Gwendolyn Mikell (Philadelphia: University of Pennsylvania Press, 1997); Wilhelmina Oduol and Wanjiku Mukabi Kabira, "The Mother of Warriors and Her Daughters: The Women's Movement in Kenya," in *The Challenge of Local Feminisms: Women's Movements in Global Perspective*, edited by Amrita C. Basu, with the assistance of Elizabeth McGrory (Boulder, CO: Westview Press, 1995); Catharine Newbury and Brooke Grundfest Schoef, "State, Peasantry, and Agrarian Crisis in Zaire: Does Gender Make a Difference?" in *Women and the State in Africa*, edited by Jane L. Parpart and Kathleen Staudt (Boulder, CO: Lynne Rienner, 1988); and "Kaba and Khaki: Women and the Militarized State in Nigeria," in *Women and the State*, edited by Jane L. Parpart and Kathleen Staudt (Boulder, CO: Lynne Rienner, 1988). Other writing on Nigeria includes Hussaina Abdullah, "Wifeism and Activism: The Nigerian Women's Movement," in *The Challenge of Local Feminisms; Women's Movements in Global Perspective*, edited by Amrita C. Basu, with the assistance of Elizabeth McGrory (Boulder, CO: Westview Press, 1995); Carolyne Dennis, "Women and the State of Nigeria: The Case of the Federal Military Government, 1984–85," in *Women, Work and Ideology in the Third World*, edited by Haleh Afshar (London: Tavistock, 1985); and Kamene Okonjo, "Sex Roles in Nigerian Politics," in *Female and Male in West Africa*, edited by Christine Oppong (London: George Allen and Unwin, 1983). Alicia

C. Decker explores Ugandan politics in *Idi Amin's Shadow: Women, Gender, and Militarism in Uganda* (Athens, OH: Ohio University Press, 2014). Ernest Harsch, *Thomas Sankara* (Athens, OH: Ohio University Press, 2014) and Thomas Sankara, *Women's Liberation and the African Freedom Struggle* (New York: Pathfinder Press, 2007) are key sources on Burkina Faso.

Writing on women in liberation wars is wide-ranging, including both analytical and first-hand accounts. Selected sources on Eritrea include Nicole Cowan, "Women in Eritrea: An Eyewitness Account," *Review of African Political Economy* 27–28 (1983), 143–52 and Amrit Wilson, *The Challenge Road: Women and the Eritrean Revolution* (London: Earthscan, 1991). For Zimbabwe, see Irene Staunton, *Mothers of the Revolution: The War Experiences of Thirty Zimbabwean Women* (Bloomington: Indiana University Press, 1990); A.P. Cheater and R.B. Gaidzanwa, "Citizenship in Neo-Patrilineal States: Gender and Mobility in Southern Africa," *Journal of Southern African Studies* 22, 2 (1996), 189–200; Josephine Nhongo-Simbanegavi, *For Better or Worse? Women and ZANLA in Zimbabwe's Liberation Struggle* (Harare: Weaver Press, 2000); Tanya Lyons, *Guns and Guerrilla Girls: Women in the Zimbabwe Liberation Struggle* (Trenton, NJ: Africa World Press, 2003); and Gay W. Seidman, "Women in Zimbabwe: Post-Independence Struggles," *Feminist Studies* 10, 3 (1984), 419–40.

Mozambique is covered in Stephanie Urdang, *And Still They Dance: Women and the Struggle for Change in Mozambique* (New York: Monthly Review Press, 1989); Kathleen Sheldon, "Women and Revolution in Mozambique: *A Luta Continua*," in *Women and Revolution in Africa, Asia, and the New World*, edited by Mary Ann Tétrault (Columbia SC: University of South Carolina Press, 1994); Namibia in Teckla Shikola, "We Left Our Shoes Behind," in *What Women Do in Wartime: Gender and Conflict in Africa*, edited by Meredith Turshen and Clotilde Twagiramariya (London: Zed Press, 1998); and Dianne Hubbard and Colette Solomon, "The Many Faces of Feminism in Namibia," in *The Challenge of Local Feminisms; Women's Movements in Global Perspective*, edited by Amrita C. Basu, with the assistance of Elizabeth McGrory (Boulder, CO: Westview Press, 1995). The extensive writing on South Africa includes Shireen Hassim, *Women's Organizations and Democracy in South Africa: Contesting Authority* (Madison: University of Wisconsin Press, 2006); Gay W. Seidman, "'No Freedom without the Women': Mobilization and Gender in

South Africa, 1970–1992," *Signs* 18, 2 (1991), 291–320; and Raymond Suttner, "Women in the ANC-led Underground," in *Basus'iimbokodo, bawel'imilambo (They remove boulders and cross rivers): Women in South African History*, edited by Nomboniso Gasa (Cape Town: HSRC Press, 2007). In *491 Days: Prisoner Number 1323/69* (Athens, OH: Ohio University Press, 2014), Winnie Madikizela-Mandela documents her maltreatment while imprisoned for sixteen months.

The most detailed source on international women's movements is Margaret C. Snyder and Mary Tadesse, *African Women in Development: A History* (London: Zed Books, 1995). For a longer-term history, see Iris Berger, "Decolonizing Women's Activism: Africa in the Transformation of International Women's Movements," in *Women and Social Movements, International*, edited by Tom Dublin and Katherine Kish Sklar (Alexandria, VA: Alexander Street Press, 2012). Mandana Hendessi, "Fourteen Thousand Women Meet: Report from Nairobi, July 1985," *Feminist Review* 23 (June 1986), 147–56 and Nilüfer Çağatay, Caren Grown, and Aida Santiago, "The Nairobi Women's Conference: Toward a Global Feminism?" *Feminist Studies* 12, 2 (Summer 1986), 401–12 review the UN Conference in Nairobi.

6– "Messengers of a new design": marriage, family, and sexuality

So Long a Letter (Harlow, Essex: Heinemann, 2008) by Mariama Bâ received the first prestigious Noma Prize for Publishing in Africa in 1981; her only other novel *Scarlet Song* came out after her death, in 1986. Writing on the politics of the family includes: Barbara Cooper, *Marriage in Maradi: Gender and Culture in a Hausa Society in Niger, 1900–1989* (Portsmouth, NH: Heinemann, 1997); Philippe Antoine and Jeanne Nanitelamio, trans. Laura Mitchell, "Can Polygyny Be Avoided in Dakar?" in *Courtyards, Markets, City Streets: Urban Women in Africa*, edited by Kathleen Sheldon (Boulder, CO: Westview Press, 1996); Jeanne Maddox Toungara, "Changing the Meaning of Marriage: Women and Family Law in Côte d'Ivoire," in *African Feminism: The Politics of Survival in Sub-Saharan Africa*, edited by Gwendolyn Mikell (Philadelphia: University of Pennsylvania Press, 1997). Gwendolyn Mikell, "Pleas for Domestic Relief: Akan Women and Family Courts," in *African Feminism: The Politics of Survival in Sub-Saharan Africa*, edited by Gwendolyn Mikell

(Philadelphia: University of Pennsylvania Press, 1997); Karen Tranberg Hansen, "Washing Dirty Laundry in Public: Local Courts, Custom, and Gender Relations in Postcolonial Lusaka," in *Courtyards, Markets, City Streets: Urban Women in Africa*, edited by Kathleen Sheldon (Boulder, CO: Westview Press, 1996); and Dorothy L. Hodgson, "'My Daughter … Belongs to the Government Now': Marriage, Maasai, and the Tanzanian State," in *"Wicked" Women and the Reconfiguration of Gender in Africa*, edited by Dorothy L. Hodgson and Sheryl A. McCurdy (Portsmouth, NH: Heinemann, 2001) analyze cases brought to local courts.

The section on love comes from the pioneering collection, Jennifer Cole and Lynn M. Thomas, eds, *Love in Africa* (Chicago: University of Chicago Press, 2009). The articles discussed include: Kenda Mutongi "'Dear Dolly's' Advice: Representations of Youth, Courtship, and Sexualities in Africa, 1960–1980," in *Love in Africa*, edited by Jennifer Cole and Lynn M. Thomas (Chicago: University of Chicago Press, 2009); Laura Fair, "Making Love in the Indian Ocean: Hindi Films, Zanzibari Audiences, and the Construction of Romance in the 1950s and 1960s," in *Love in Africa*, edited by Jennifer Cole and Lynn M. Thomas (Chicago and London: University of Chicago Press, 2009); and Daniel Jordan Smith, "Managing Men, Marriage, and Modern Love: Women's Perspectives on Intimacy and Male Infidelity in Southeastern Nigeria," in *Love in Africa*, edited by Jennifer Cole and Lynn M. Thomas (Chicago and London: University of Chicago Press, 2009). For a fascinating in-depth analysis of Somali love songs, consult Lidwien Kapteijns, with Maryan Omar Ali, *Women's Voices in a Man's World: Women and the Pastoral Tradition in Northern Somali Orature, c. 1899–1980* (Portsmouth, NH: Heinemann, 1999).

Sources on girls' rites of passage include Jean Davison, *Voices from Mutira: Changes in the Lives of Rural Kikuyu Women, 1910–1995* (Boulder, CO: Lynne Rienner, 1996); Asma El Dareer, *Woman, Why Do you Weep?* (London: Zed Books, 1983); Elizabeth Heger Boyle, *Female Genital Cutting: Cultural Conflict in the Global Community* (Baltimore: The Johns Hopkins University Press, 2002); and Nawal el Saadawi, *The Hidden Face of Eve* (London: Zed Press, 1980), among the most influential of her numerous books. Widowhood is discussed from an anthropological perspective in Betty Potash, ed., *Widows in Africa: Choices and Constraints* (Stanford: Stanford University Press, 1986). Kenda Mutongi, *Worries of the Heart: Widows, Family and*

Community in Kenya (Chicago: University of Chicago Press, 2007) is a pioneering historical analysis of the topic. Patricia Stamp, "Burying Otieno: The Politics of Gender and Ethnicity in Kenya," *Signs* 16, 4 (Summer 1991), 808–45 and David W. Cohen and Atieno Odhiambo, *Burying SM: The Politics of Knowledge and the Sociology of Power in Africa* (Portsmouth, NH: Heinemann, 1992) discuss the contested burial of S.M. Otieno.

John Iliffe, *Africans: The History of a Continent* (New York: Cambridge University Press, 2007) provides a cogent overview of demography and family planning. See also Karl Ittmann, Dennis D. Cordell, and Gregory H. Maddox, eds, *The Demographics of Empire* (Athens, OH: Ohio University Press, 2010). More specific case studies include Amy Kaler, *Running After Pills: Politics, Gender, and Contraception in Colonial Zimbabwe* (Portsmouth, NH: Heinemann, 2003) and Caroline H. Bledsoe, Allan G. Hill, Umberto D'Allesandro, and Patricia Langerock, "Constructing Natural Fertility: The Use of Western Contraceptive Technologies in Rural Gambia," *Population and Development Review* 20, 1 (March 1994), 81–113. Iliffe's book *The African AIDS Epidemic: A History* (Athens, OH: Ohio University Press, 2006) is an excellent introduction to the topic. Also see Carolyn Baylies, "Perspectives on gender and AIDS in Africa," in *AIDS, Sexuality and Gender in Africa: Collective Strategies and Struggles in Tanzania and Zambia*, edited by Carolyn Baylies and Janet Bujra with the Gender and AIDS Group (London: Routledge, 2000).

For discussions of religion and healing, sources include Cynthia Hoehler-Fatton, *Women of Fire & Spirit: History, Faith, and Gender in Roho Religion in Western Kenya* (New York: Oxford University Press, 1996); Bennetta Jules-Rosette, "Women as Ceremonial Leaders in an African Church: The Apostles of John Maranke," in *The New Religions of Africa*, edited by Bennetta Jules-Rosette (Norwood, NJ: Ablex Publishing Corp., 1979; and Lucy Quimby, "Islam, Sex Roles, and Modernization in Bobo-Dioulasso," in *The New Religions of Africa*, edited by Bennetta Jules-Rosette (Norwood, NJ: Ablex Publishing Corp., 1979). Important monographs that cover postcolonial religion include Phyllis M. Martin, *Catholic Women of Congo-Brazzaville: Mothers and Sisters in Troubled Times* and Adeline Masquelier, *Women and Islamic Revival in a West African Town*, both published by Indiana University Press in 2009.

7– Women's rights: the second decolonization?

Numerous sources address postapartheid politics in South Africa. They include Hannah E. Britton, *Women in the South African Parliament: From Resistance to Governance* (Urbana: University of Illinois Press, 2005) and Glenda Fick, Sheila Meintjes, and Mary Simons, eds, *One Woman, One Vote: The Gender Politics of South African Elections* (Johannesburg: Electoral Institute of Southern Africa, 2002). On the political and intellectual climate in the 1990s, see Aili Marie Tripp, Isabel Casimiro, Joy Kwesiga, and Alice Mungwa, *African Women's Movements: Changing Political Landscapes* (Cambridge: Cambridge University Press, 2009); Charlotte Bunch, "Women's Rights as Human Rights: Towards a Re-Vision of Human Rights," *Human Rights Quarterly* 12, 4 (November 1990), 486–98; and Gwendolyn Mikell, "Introduction," in *African Feminism: The Politics of Survival in Sub-Saharan Africa*, edited by Gwendolyn Mikell (Philadelphia: University of Pennsylvania Press, 1997). Two path-breaking books, Ife Amadiume, *Male Daughters, Female Husbands: Gender and Sex in an African Society* (London: Zed Press, 1987) and Oyèrónkẹ́ Oyěwùmí, *The Invention of Women: Making an African Sense of Western Gender Discourses* (Minneapolis: University of Minnesota Press, 1997), helped to define and to launch African gender studies. On the development of women's studies, see Amina Mama, *Women's Studies and Studies of Women in Africa During the 1990s* (Dakar: CODESRIA, 1996). Nalova Lyonga outlines a literary interpretation of African feminism in "African Women and Feminist Theory," in *Defining New Idioms and Alternative Forms of Expression* (Amsterdam: Rodopi, 1996). See also Ruth Meena, ed., *Gender in Southern Africa: Conceptual and Theoretical Issues* (Harare: SAPES, 1992) and Oyèrónkẹ́ Oyěwùmí, ed., *African Gender Studies: A Reader* (New York: Palgrave Macmillan, 2005). Among the new journals sparked by this era of women's politics were two with a specifically feminist focus, *Agenda*, launched in Durban in 1987, and *Feminist Africa*, a project of the African Gender Institute at the University of Cape Town, in 2002. JENdA, first published in 2001, was initiated by African women to redefine the space of African women's studies.

African womanism defined itself both in relation to feminism and to novelist Alice Walker's concept of womanism. Key sources include Chikwenye Okonjo Ogunyemi, "Womanism: The Dynamics of the Contemporary Black Female Novel in English," *Signs* 11, 1 (1985), 63–80; Mary E. Modupe Kolawole, *Womanism and African Consciousness* (Trenton, NJ: African World Press, 1997); and relevant articles in Molara Ogundipe-Leslie, ed., *Re-Creating Ourselves: African Women and Critical Transformations* (Trenton, NJ: African World Press, 1994).

Numerous works cover the gendered aspects of civil conflicts during the 1990s. David Newbury's cogent overview article on Rwanda, "Understanding Genocide," *African Studies Review* 41, 1 (April 1998), 73–97, has a section on gender. Other important works include Jennie Burnet, *Genocide Lives in Us: Women, Memory, and Silence in Rwanda* (Madison: University of Wisconsin Press, 2012); Christopher C. Taylor, "A Gendered Genocide: Tutsi Women and Hutu Extremists in the 1994 Rwandan Genocide," *PoLAR* 22, 1 (May 1999), 42–54; and the first-hand account by Marie Béatrice Umtesi, *Surviving the Slaughter: The Ordeal of a Rwandan Refugee in Zaire* (Madison: University of Wisconsin Press, 2004). Sources on Sierra Leone include Megan Mackenzie, *Female Soldiers in Sierra Leone: Sex, Security, and Post-Conflict Development* (New York: NYU Press, 2012); Chris Coulter, "Female Fighters in the Sierra Leone War: Challenging the Assumptions?" *Feminist Review* 88 (2008), 54–73; and Dara Kay Cohen, "Female Combatants and the Perpetuation of Rape in the Sierra Leone Civil War," *World Politics* 65, 3 (July 2013), 383–415. For Liberia, see Berkley Center for Religion, Peace and World Affairs, "Ending Liberia's Second Civil War: Religious Women as Peacemakers" (Washington, DC: Berkley Center, Georgetown University, 2013); Leymah Gbowee and Carol Mithers, *Mighty Be Our Powers: How Sisterhood, Prayers and Sex Changed a Nation* (Philadelphia: Beast Books, 2013); and the documentary film directed by Gini Reticker, *Pray the Devil Back to Hell* (New York: Fork Films LLC, 2008).

The essays in Sheila Meintjes, Anu Pillay and Meredeth Turshen, eds, *The Aftermath: Women in Post–Conflict Transformations* (London: Zed Books, 2001), provide the best analysis of women and postconflict politics. They include: Sheila Meintjes, "War and Post-War Shifts in Gender Relations," in *The Aftermath: Women in Post-Conflict Transformations*, edited by Sheila Meintjes, Anu Pillay, and Meredeth Turshen (London: Zed Books, 2001); Codou Bop, "Women in Conflicts, Their Gains and Losses," in *The Aftermath: Women in Post-Conflict Transformations*, edited by

Sheila Meintjes, Anu Pillay, and Meredeth Turshen (London: Zed Books, 2001); Sondra Hale, "Liberated, But Not Free: Women in Post-War Eritrea," in *The Aftermath: Women in Post-Conflict Transformations*, edited by Sheila Meintjes, Anu Pillay, and Meredeth Turshen (London: Zed Books, 2001); and Okechukwu Ibeanu, "Healing and Changing: The Changing Identity of Women in the Aftermath of the Ogoni Crisis in Nigeria," in *The Aftermath: Women in Post-Conflict Transformations*, edited by Sheila Meintjes, Anu Pillay, and Meredeth Turshen (London: Zed Books, 2001). See also Meredeth Turshen and Clotilde Twagiramariya, eds, *What Women Do in Wartime* (London: Zed Press, 1998). Sources on violence include United Nations, *Report of the United Nations High Commissioner for Refugees, 1999*, General Assembly Official Records, Fifty-fifth Session, Supplement No. 12 (A55/12) (New York: UN, 2000) and Ros Hirschowitz, Seble Worku, and Mark Orkin, *Quantitative Research Findings on RAPE in South Africa* (Pretoria: Statistics South Africa, 2000). Jacklyn Cock's book *Colonels & Cadres: War and Gender in South Africa (Contemporary South African Debates)* (Cape Town: Oxford University Press, 1994) explores broader issues of gender and militarism.

African Women's Movements: Transforming Political Landscapes (Cambridge: Cambridge University Press, 2008) by Aili Marie Tripp, Isabel Casimiro, Joy Kwesiga, and Alice Mungwa provides the best overview of political transformation during the 1990s. For specific countries see the important articles in Amrita Basu, ed., with the assistance of Elizabeth McGrory, *The Challenge of Local Feminisms: Women's Movements in Global Perspective* (Boulder, CO: Westview Press, 1995). They include: Heike Becker, "'We Want Women to Be Given an Equal Chance': Post Independence Rural Politics in Northern Namibia," in *The Challenge of Local Feminisms: Women's Movements in Global Perspective*, edited by Amrita Basu, with the assistance of Elizabeth McGrory (Boulder, CO: Westview Press, 1995); Hussaina Abdullah, "Wifeism and Activism: The Nigerian Women's Movement," in *The Challenge of Local Feminisms: Women's Movements in Global Perspective*, edited by Amrita Basu, with the assistance of Elizabeth McGrory (Boulder, CO: Westview Press, 1995); and Wilhelmina Oduol and Wanjiku Mukabi Kabira, "The Mother of Warriors and Her Daughters: The Women's Movement in Kenya," in *The Challenge of Local Feminisms: Women's Movements in Global Perspective*, edited by Amrita Basu, with the assistance of Elizabeth McGrory (Boulder,

CO: Westview Press, 1995). The essays in Gretchen Bauer and Hannah E. Britton, eds, *Women in African Parliaments* (Boulder, CO: Lynne Rienner, 2006) cover a wide range of cases. Judith van Allen discusses Botswana in "Women's Rights Movements as a Measure of Social Democracy," *Journal of African and Asian Studies* 36, 1 (2001), 39–63.

Writing on female genital cutting is extensive. For a cogent set of articles on the topic, see Rogaia Mustafa Abusharaf, ed., *Female Circumcision: Multicultural Perspectives* (Philadelphia: University of Pennsylvania Press, 2006). Particularly relevant to this discussion are: Asha Mohamud, Samson Radeny, and Karin Ringheim, "Community-Based Efforts to End Female Genital Mutilation in Kenya: Raising Awareness and Organizing Alternative Rites of Passage," in *Female Circumcision: Multicultural Perspectives*, edited by Rogaia Mustafa Abusharaf (Philadelphia: University of Pennsylvania Press, 2006); Nafissatou J. Diop and Ian Askew, "Strategies for Encouraging the Abandonment of Female Genital Cutting: Experiences from Senegal, Burkina Faso, and Mali," in *Female Circumcision: Multicultural Perspectives*, edited by Rogaia Mustafa Abusharaf (Philadelphia: University of Pennsylvania Press, 2006); Hamid El Bashir, "The Sudanese National Committee on the Eradication of Harmful Traditional Practices and the Campaign Against Female Genital Mutilation," in *Female Circumcision: Multicultural Perspectives*, edited by Rogaia Mustafa Abusharaf (Philadelphia: University of Pennsylvania Press, 2006); Shahira Ahmed, "The Babiker Badri Scientific Association for Women's Studies and the Eradication of Female Circumcision in the Sudan," in *Female Circumcision: Multicultural Perspectives*, edited by Rogaia Mustafa Abusharaf (Philadelphia: University of Pennsylvania Press, 2006); and Raqiya D. Abdalla, "'My Grandmother Called It the Three Feminine Sorrows': T. Struggle Against Female Circumcision in Somalia," in *Female Circumcision: Multicultural Perspectives*, edited by Rogaia Mustafa Abusharaf (Philadelphia: University of Pennsylvania Press, 2006). Statistics on the practice come from Population Reference Bureau, *Female Genital Mutilation/ Cutting: Data and Trends, Update 2010*, www.ncbi.nim.nih.gov/pmc/ articles/PMC3349920 and UNICEF, *Female Genital Mutilation/ Cutting: A Statistical Overview and Exploration of the Dynamics of Change* (Paris, UNICEF, July 2013). Two important collections that critically engage Western attitudes toward excision include: Obioma Nnaemeka, ed., *Female Circumcision and the Politics of Knowledge* (Westport, CT: Praeger, 2005) and Stanlie M. James and Claire C. Robertson, eds, *Genital Cutting and Transnational Sisterhood: Disputing U.S. Polemics* (Urbana-Champaign: University of Illinois Press, 2002).

Marc Epprecht, *Hungochani: The History of a Dissident Sexuality in Southern Africa* (Montreal: McGill-Queen's University Press, 2004) provides a pioneering analysis of homosexuality. See also relevant essays in Signe Arnfred, *Re-thinking Sexualities in Africa* (Stockholm: Nordiska Afrikainstitutet, 2006); Sylvia Tamale, ed., *African Sexualities: A Reader* (Cape Town: Pambazuka Press, 2011); and Toyin Falola and Nana Akua Amponsah, eds, *Women, Gender, and Sexualities in Africa* (Durham, NC: Carolina Academic Press, 2013).

8– Empowerment and inequality in a new global age

International organizations provide the best material on girls' education. For this period, they include: *World Atlas of Gender Equality in Education* (Paris: UNESCO, 2012); *Global Education Digest 2010: Comparing Educational Statistics Across the World* (Montreal: UNESCO Institute for Statistics, 2010); and Codou Diaw, "Quality and Gender Equality in Education: What Have We Learned from FAWE's 15 Years of Experience," in *Girls' Education in the 21st Century: Gender Equality, Empowerment, and Economic Growth*, edited by Mercy Tembon and Lucia Fort (Washington, DC: The World Bank, 2008). See also Gumisai Mutume, "African Women Battle for Equality," *African Renewal* (July, 2005) www.un.org/africarenewal/magazine/july-2005/african-women-battle-equality and Philomena E. Okeke, "Negotiating Social Independence: The Challenges of Career Pursuits for Igbo Women in Postcolonial Nigeria," in *"Wicked" Women and the Reconfiguration of Gender in Africa*, edited by Dorothy L. Hodgson and Sheryl McCurdy (Portsmouth, NH: Heinemann, 2001).

Writing on economic change and women's work is extensive. This chapter draws on Wilma Wentholt, Annlies Zoomers, and Loes Jansen, "A Critical Review of Structural Adjustment and Increasing Women's Economic Participation," in *Advancing Women's Status: Women and Men Together?*, edited by M. de Bruyn (Amsterdam: Royal Tropical Institute, 1995); Richard A. Schroeder, "'Gone to Their Second Husbands': Marital Metaphors and Conjugal Contracts in The

Gambia's Female Garden Sector," in *"Wicked" Women and the Reconfiguration of Gender in Africa*, edited by Dorothy L. Hodgson and Sheryl A. McCurdy (Portsmouth, NH: Heinemann, 2001); Kathleen E. Sheldon, *Pounders of Grain: A History of Women, Work, and Politics in Mozambique* (Portsmouth, NH: Heinemann, 2002); Grace Bantebya Kyomuhendo and Marjorie Keniston McIntosh, *Women, Work & Domestic Virtue in Uganda, 1900–2003* (Oxford: James Currey, 2006); and Gracia Clark, *African Market Women: Seven Life Stories from Ghana* (Bloomington: Indiana University Press, 2010).

Research on HIV/AIDS is also voluminous. For the 1980s, John Iliffe, *The African AIDS Epidemic: A History* (Athens, OH: Ohio University Press, 2006) is an important source as is Carolyn Baylies and Janet Bujra, eds, with the Gender and AIDS Group, *AIDS, Sexuality and Gender in Africa: Collective Strategies and Struggles in Tanzania and Zambia* (London: Routledge, 2000). For insights on gender and AIDS in South Africa, see Nthabiseng Motsemme, "'Loving in a Time of Hopelessness': On Township Women's Subjectivities in a Time of HIV/AIDS," in *Basus'iimbokodo, bawel'imilambo/They Remove Boulders and Cross Rivers: Women in South African History*, edited by Nomboniso Gasa (Cape Town: HSRC Press, 2007) and Mark Hunter, *Love in the Time of AIDS: Inequality, Gender, and Rights in South Africa* (Bloomington: Indiana University Press, 2010). A remarkable Canadian-South Africa project is recounted in Mary Chazan, *The Grandmothers' Movement: Solidarity and Survival in the Time of AIDS* (Montreal: McGill-Queens University Press, 2015).

Many sources cover gender and Christianity at the end of the twentieth century. In *The Church of Women: Gendered Encounters between Maasai and Missionaries* (Bloomington: Indiana University Press, 2005), Dorothy L. Hodgson discusses Catholicism in one Tanzanian community. Two important general studies of Pentecostalism, Ogbu Kalu, *African Pentecostalism: An Introduction* (Oxford: Oxford University Press, 2008) and Paul Gifford, *Ghana's New Christianity: Pentecostalism in a Globalizing African Economy* (Bloomington: Indiana University Press, 2004) include discussions of women-led churches. Jane E. Soothill, "The Problem with 'Women's Empowerment': Female Religiosity in Ghana's Charismatic Churches," *Studies in World Christianity* 16, 1 (2010), 82–99, euppublishing.com raises critical questions, as do James Pfeiffer, Kenneth Gimble-Sherr, and Orvalho Joaquim Augusto in "The Holy Spirit in the Household: Pentecostalism, Gender, and Neoliberalism in

Mozambique," *American Anthropologist* 109, 4 (2007), 688–700. Selected writing on the underside of Pentecostalism includes, "The Modern Magic in Africa's Witchcraft Industry," thinkafricapress.com/society/Africa-witchcraft; "Angels and Demons," *FP* (December 20, 2013), foreignpolicy.com/articles; and the documentary film, "The Witches of Gambaga," co-produced by Yaba Badoe and Amina Mama (Accra: Fadoa Films, 2010).

Key writing on end-of-century Islam includes Adeline Masquelier, *Women and Islamic Revival in a West African Town* (Bloomington: Indiana University Press, 2009) and Barbara M. Cooper, "The Strength in the Song: Muslim Personhood, Audible Capital, and Hausa Women's Performance of the Hajj," in *Gendered Modernities: Ethnographic Perspectives*, edited by Dorothy Hodgson (New York: Palgrave, 2001).

Contradictions and challenges

Werewere Liking, born in Cameroon and now living in Côte d'Ivoire, is a prolific writer of plays, novels, and poetry who has dedicated her life to the rebirth of African culture. The original source of the quote is Werewere Liking, *African Ritual Theatre*, translated by Jeanne N. Dingome (Bethesda, MD: International Scholars Publications, 1997). Aili Tripp summarizes the gains in women's political participation in "Women and Politics in Africa Today," *Democracy in Africa* (December 9, 2013), adaptation of 2012 African Studies Association Presidential Address, www.democracyinafrica.org/women-politics-africa-today. The extensive research and publication program of CODESRIA (Council for the Development of Social Science Research in Africa), based in Dakar, illustrates some of the current research in African gender studies on the continent. Key CODESRIA publications include Felicia Oyekanmi, ed., *Men, Women and Violence* (Dakar: CODESRIA, 2000); Olutoyin Mejiuni, ed., *Women and Power: Education, Religion and Identity* (Dakar, CODESRIA, 2013); and Laroussi Amri and Ramola Ramtohul, eds, *Gender and Citizenship in a Global Age* (Dakar: CODESRIA, 2014).

Index

CPSIA information can be obtained
at www.ICGtesting.com
Printed in the USA
LVHW09s1943221018
594381LV00012B/28/P

9 780521 741217